For Steve Fineberg

As a reminder
of friendship.

John Mc Call

June 30, 1993

Chaucer among the Gods

CHAUCER
AMONG THE GODS
The Poetics of Classical Myth

John P. McCall

The Pennsylvania State University Press
University Park and London

For Mary-Berenice

Library of Congress Cataloging in Publication Data

McCall, John P
  Chaucer among the Gods.

  Includes bibliographical references and index.
    1. Chaucer, Geoffrey, d. 1400—Knowledge—Folk-
lore, mythology. 2. Mythology in literature.
3. Mythology, Classical. I. Title.
PR1933.M96M3   821'.1   78-50003
ISBN 0-271-00201-8

Preface

This work began several years ago as an effort to explain Chaucer's uses of classical myth in *Troilus and Criseyde*. At that time I assumed that one could elucidate "the meanings" of Chaucer's allusions to ancient deities and fable through a comprehensive understanding of classical and medieval glosses, dictionaries, and commentaries on mythical allusions by authors ranging from Servius, Macrobius, and Fulgentius, for example, to Boccaccio, Bersuire, and other contemporaries or near-contemporaries of Chaucer. That background study was interesting in its own right and to the extent that it succeeded I have tried to incorporate its results in these pages. It also raised some serious dissatisfactions, however. It read too much like a dictionary, and one friendly critic (whose advice I have tried to follow) suggested a reorganization that would focus at least partly on Chaucer's different modes of handling myth. Another reader repeated the advice of Horace—to put the text aside for a few years. That was a dear counsel which I have satisfied several times over, perhaps because of my own haunting awareness that the *Troilus* does not stand alone; that Chaucer's uses of classical myth extend from his first works to his last, and that a broad consideration might create a context for analyzing something more than "meanings." It might lead to a greater sensitivity to the style, the tone, and the poetics of Chaucer's classical mythology.

The text presented here does not purport to do everything that one would like, but it may serve as a useful introduction to Chaucer's attitude toward classical materials and, more important, to his various ways of handling them. The opening chapter seeks to establish an intellectual setting somewhat in the style of Seznec, Panofsky, or D.W. Robertson, Jr. It differs from their approaches, however, in the emphasis which I give to the literal, historical, and natural/moral interpretations of myth as distinguished from those which might more properly be labeled allegorical. The second chapter focuses on some of the brief allusions in the *Book of the Duchess* and the *Troilus* to describe how myth amplifies and comments on character and action; ultimately to describe how clusters or patterns of allusions help to reinforce certain dominant and primarily tragic themes. Chapter 3 is an exploration or "essay" into the thorny problem of myth and allegory. It is not meant to be a definitive discussion, but I hope it will say some persuasive things about allegorized mythology in the *House of Fame*, the *Parliament of Fowls*, and particularly the *Knight's Tale*. The *Knight's Tale*, in fact, is central to the whole book because it incorporates so much of what Chaucer found valuable in classical myth: resources for building character, theme, language, structure—all of a literary work. In dealing with classical places in Chapter 4 (Scythia, Thebes, Athens, Troy, and Rome), I have tried to show that Chaucer follows a familiar ancient and medieval practice of linking setting with the history of behavior in certain locales—with conventional ideas about what happened in a place rather than with its physical details. This will further suggest that classical or natural time, such as one finds in the *Legend of Good Women*, has an important impact on what we think and feel about Chaucer's antique world. Finally, Chapter 5 examines some of the things that happen to classical myth when it is put to comic use: when it is debased, mocked, contorted, or dismissed for naught.

It would have been practically impossible to engage in this project without the prior source work by scholars such as Wise, Shannon, Root, Lowes, Meech, Hoffman, and many more. But the aim of these pages is consciously different: to show some of Chaucer's various ways of adapting his classical materials; to show how he understood myth, based on the dominant conventions of his day, and then how he manipulated myth to suit his own purposes.

I owe thanks to many people who have indirectly encouraged this work by their kind words or example. In particular I am indebted to William F. Lynch, S.J., Morton Bloomfield, David Fowler, Robert Jordan, Charles Muscatine, and Robert W. Frank, Jr. The trustees of the Taft Foundation and the Research Council of the University of Cincinnati provided support at an early stage, and a fellowship from the John Simon Guggenheim Foundation gave me the uninterrupted time needed to organize and revise the text in its final form. Evelyn Schott and Roberta Gausmann handled the typing chores cheerfully and patiently, and Pat Overbeck and Robert Correale read the complete text and helped save me from a number of errors.

I also wish to express my appreciation to the editors of *ELH: A Journal of English Literary History* for permission to use the materials on the Trojan setting in *Troilus and Criseyde* which originally appeared in their publication. Finally, I should like to say a special word of thanks to William Ringler and Jesse Reese for the help they gave this work many years ago, and to D.W. Robertson, Jr., who directed my first research on this subject and who has been its interested friend since that time.

Contents

1 The Backgrounds

Had Geoffrey Chaucer been as naive and casual as he liked to picture himself, he surely could not have been a comic poet. And if he wore his learning lightly, as part of a role he played, we should be forewarned that this was a sign of his confidence, and of that underlying studiousness which sent him hurrying home from office duties to read "another book" (*HF* 657) in quiet, scholarly isolation.[1] Chaucer was devoted to learning and, more than that, to the spread of learning among English men and women of his day. He reworked the great stories of classical literature: the *Aeneid*, the *Thebaid*, the epic of Troy, and more tales "of loveris up and doun" than ever Ovid "made of mencioun" (*MLT* 53–54). He translated, though we do not know how much, the most influential vernacular poem of the Middle Ages, the *Roman de la Rose*, and the most significant ascetic treatise of the times, Innocent III's *De Contemptu Mundi*. He rendered what was for a thousand years the most important moral tract in western Christendom, Boethius's *De Consolatione;* and he prepared English versions of the *Liber Consolationis et Consilii* (*Livre de Melibée*), and a popular compilation of pastoral theology on penance and the seven deadly sins.

Like Pierre Bersuire and Nicole Oresme in fourteenth-century France, Chaucer popularized in English courts some of the great literature and lore of classical antiquity and the Latin Middle Ages. In their own language he brought to English men and women the contemporary literatures of France and Italy so that his audience became aware—sometimes by name, sometimes not—of Graunson, Dante and Petrarch, de Lorris, de Meun, Machaut, Deschamps, Froissart, and Boccaccio. For one youngster he also produced the first extensive scientific tract in English. In an easy-seeming way, then, Chaucer made himself the first humanist of English literature.

Although self-effacing, he could, like Dante, see himself and his work as part of a great literary heritage: following in the steps of "Virgile, Ovide, Omer, Lucan, and Stace" (*Tr.* 5. 1792), "glenyng here and there" (*LGW* F75) the harvest left for him. Indeed, if Chaucer had a great love it was with books, "thurgh whiche that olde thinges ben in mynde," and his love found its vocation in keeping alive the memory of those "olde appreved stories" and the "doctrine of these olde wyse" (*LGW* F17 ff.).

Once we accept the notion that Chaucer was a learned author interested in the survival of learning,[2] we must also assume that any approach to his work (classical myth being only a part) is sure to be complicated by the poet's penchant for variety, ambiguity, and uncertainty. Chaucer never did anything simple. The difficulties that readers have in their own minds, or with each other, over such matters as the characterization of the Prioress or the Wife of Bath, or over the tonal and stylistic contrasts within the *Knight's Tale*, or between that tale and the *Miller's Tale;* or in grasping for a satisfying central theme in the *Parliament of Fowls* or the *Book of the Duchess*—all these and more are ample testimony to a conscious search for complexity. Our difficulties arise, then, not so much from a failure to fathom "medieval traditions" (although that does present its problems) as from an insistent intricacy in Chaucer's own vision and imagination. For one not ready to accept the indefinite, the eschewal of decisive judgments, and the creation of multiple effects, much of what Chaucer wrote is lost.

Thus, classical myth was not simply part of a great tradition which Chaucer handed on to his generation; it was the stuff of art, to be used and manipulated, twisted and pulled about to suit his complicated purposes. It is reassuring to recall that classical myth has always survived and flourished when artists look back and draw upon traditional or "historical" sources of reference and, at the same time, freely adapt those materials to their own peculiar aims. Geoffrey Chaucer knew both these faces of myth, its past and its present: one looking to antiquity from the Middle Ages and the other viewing fourteenth-century England from the vantage of poetic memory.

It is not an easy matter, however, for a student of Chaucer and of medieval literature to feel entirely at home with the traditions of classical mythology in the Christian Middle Ages. Apart from the question of what constitutes ancient mythology—the deities, the

great heroes, the ancient legends and history—there is the problem
of evaluating "the meanings" that were sometimes attached to
pagan myth. What, in short, were the traditions? If we are to believe
some of what has been written, we should conclude that mythology
in classical times was clear-cut, idealized, naturalistic, and relatively
easy to comprehend—which it was not; that with the rise of
Christianity in the West, pagan myth was adapted to a new culture,
subjected to allegorization, and so Christianized—when, for the
most part, it was not; and that with the dawn of the Renaissance
"medieval allegorization" declined in importance, to be replaced by
a new, more valid, historical appreciation of pagan survivals—which
is only partly true.[3]

All of this calls for some explanation and qualification. To begin,
it does not make sense to assume that classical myth (or the classical
tradition generally) should reflect either a fresh and unself-con-
scious naturalism, or a humane rationalism in Greek and Roman
culture.[4] The well-known deities, Egyptian-born if we could believe
Herodotus, certainly embodied different ideas at different times for
different people, so that at every significant stage and with practically every major writer of antiquity, myth was somehow altered
to serve the purposes of poet and playwright, or to suit a philosophical stance or a political position. Again if we follow Herodotus,[5] we
can take Homer and Hesiod as the writers who "established" the
deities—but clearly their approaches were not the same. At times in
the *Iliad* Zeus is portrayed as all-powerful, standing apart from and
above the other gods; at other times he is a patient, persuasive father
trying to solve the problems which vex the heavenly household.
Most often, as Whitman has observed,[6] the deities of the *Iliad* are
"symbolic predicates of action, character, and circumstance." They
do not "represent" universal forces—divine law, victory, strife, or
the like—but are concrete images of "the force and consequence" of
particular human actions, raised beyond the limit and restrictions
of time. In short, they are literary and anthropomorphic. Yet in
Hesiod the deities become part of a mythic philosophy of history;
they are personifications of powers in nature which live above the
world of human action.

In subsequent Greek literature myth was treated in a variety of
ways. Brooks Otis describes one change broadly when he observes
how, after Homer and Hesiod, myth "ceased to be taken as a simple
reflection of life or actuality" and became *exemplum*, "a kind of

paradigm of the values upheld by a particular poet," the expression "of quite contemporary feelings and ideas."[7] In the *Oresteia*, for example, Zeus expresses an evolving new concept of justice (fifth century B.C., Athenian variety); in Orphicism he is "that which lives"; in Stoicism he is the *aether*, the First Principle; to the skeptical Euhemerist he is a historical king who has been glorified in fable; and to the Epicurean—we are not sure what he is.

As meanings varied, so did attitudes. Callimachus treated the gods as though they were "bourgeois Alexandrines," and he colored their lives with realistic and sentimental details. But to others the gods and ancient heroes "were not only remote, but actually irrational, unbelievable or unreal."[8] And in Plato's view, of course, the poets and mythologers knew nothing of the real gods: their fables were improbable lies which led only to the corruption of society so that such writers (including their allegorizers) were to be turned out of the ideal state. Plato would surely have agreed with the character in Euripides who remarked that "if the gods do anything base, they are no gods" (*Frag* 292), and with Hercule Poirot in our own century: "These gods and goddesses—they seemed to have as many different *aliases* as a modern criminal. Indeed they seemed to be definite criminal types. Drink, debauchery, incest, rape, loot, homicide and chicanery. . . . No decent family life. No order, no method."[9]

Whether divine or indecent, the deities as treated by Euripides may remind us that they could become representations of moral concepts—even in antiquity. How else can we think of Aphrodite in the *Hippolytus* when she is clearly not "a goddess" so much as a figure for the power of human passion—a figure, as it were, from a classical morality play? Or how else is one to read the famous story of Hercules' choice, which Socrates reported from Prodicus, but as a moral fable—almost in a dream vision form?[10] The moral uses of myth, as well as the naturalistic, the philosophical, and historical, appear of course in Ovid (as in the stories of Niobe's pride and Narcissus's self-love). So, when Fulgentius, in the fifth or sixth century A.D., gave his influential interpretation of the Judgment of Paris—as a choice between a life of pleasure (Venus), of worldly success (Juno), or of wisdom (Minerva)—he was looking back to an ancient tradition of moralized myth. He was neither inventing something new nor Christianizing a pagan legend. Similarly, the practice of disclosing the nature of the gods by analyzing the etymologies of their names was not a Christian invention by Fulgentius or Isidore of Seville, but an old practice dating back through pagan antiquity to such works as Cicero's *De Natura Deorum* and Plato's *Cratylus*. [11]

In general, the treatment of myth by the Roman poets was largely a continuation of various Greek traditions, modified and characterized by a strong subjective focus. Virgil, for example, adapted one version of the Dido legend so as to arouse feelings for the way his heroine thought and felt. He makes us see many things at once: her regal dignity, her rash affections, her fear, her shame, her doom. She is disclosed from within in self-conflict and also from without against the broad temporal backgrounds of the past, present, and future. If Virgil interiorized and complicated myth, his mythic figures nevertheless grow into representations of broad concepts. "His gods and, in large degree, his heroes," Brooks Otis observes, "stand for very serious ideas—for supreme fate (Jupiter), for the *furor* that resists it (Juno), for hellish conflict (Allecto), for baneful rumour (Fama), for the *pietas* and *violentia* on whose workings the epic depends." [12]

Like Virgil, Ovid adapted mythology to his particular concerns: to focus on the moral psychology of character, the pathos of human suffering, and the comedy inherent in the dilemmas of men and "gods." With wit and rhetorical flourish he creates pity for Phaeton's adolescent rashness, horror at the crimes of Tereus, Procne, and Philomela, and sentimental comedy from the passions of Apollo for Daphne and of the Cyclops for Galatea. There is little dignity in the world of Ovid's mythology, but there is an abundance of what the poet had—cleverness, irony, and humanity.

In sum, the classical myth of antiquity encompassed a broad, variegated tradition which included extremes ranging all the way from a seriously moral mythology in Plato, to the semicomical treatment of deity and hero in Euripides' *Alcestes*, to the slapstick and bawdy of Aristophanes. It included naturalistic, scientific interpretations and an astrologized mythology which survived—to greater and lesser degrees—in the Middle Ages and after. [13] What is important, however, is not the particulars so much as the overall complexity of the subject. The Middle Ages did not inherit one clear tradition, to be shunned by ascetics or adapted by wily allegorizers, but a hodgepodge of traditions. And the reactions to those traditions would be as various among medieval writers as they were among the ancients themselves.

Certainly Christianity had an effect, and the world of the old mythology took on a new look in the Middle Ages; but it is difficult to define that change. Saint Augustine and some of the other early Christian apologists made the pantheon an object of theological scorn—of a derision which would often be repeated in later times.

> Why then did [Romulus] clog the Romans with such a load of gods, Janus, Jove, Mars, Picus, Faunus, Tiberinus, Hercules, and all the rest? And what did Tatius, bringing in Saturn, Ops, Sol, Luna, Vulcan, Lux, and to crown all, sweet Cloacina [deity of the sewerage system], leaving Felicity in the dust? And what was in Numa's mind, that he should gather such a host of he-gods and she-gods, and leave [Felicity] out? Could he not find her for the multitude?   (*City of God* IV. 23)

The deities became that great "rabble of false gods," "those innumerable demons"—or what Chaucer was later to call "swich rascaille" (*Tr* 5. 1853). Yet even this language was not entirely new. There was a long tradition among ancient writers themselves for doubting or denouncing the credibility of myth and denying its relevance to a true theology. Plato and Euhemerus were only two examples; but, as Augustine reminds his readers, there were many others, including Varro, whom he cites frequently with respect. These pagans found the fables of the gods "fraught with fictions most disgraceful to the deities"; and what the poets wrote was made only worse in the cruel and obscene civil ceremonies to the gods, ceremonies which Seneca freely denounced.[14] In short, a Christian apologist could find ample classical authority when he came to reprehend the indecencies of mythology.

At the same time, early Christian writers often allowed a degree of credit to the old philosophical and naturalistic views of myth. Augustine passed on a good deal of information on these aspects of the deities (using Varro's now-lost *Antiquitates*), because he wished to emphasize that pagan mythology had to do with nature rather than divinity. But even naturalized mythology, as Augustine saw it, was often contradictory and foolish: at best it represented the pitiful effort of good men to make something reasonable out of "vain fables."[15]

The Christian castigation of the old mythology did not, then, annihilate the gods of ancient story. What it did was to take them out of the heavens—if such deities had ever really been there—and set them firmly on the earth. They were either legendary men and women, "corporal, temporal, mutable, and mortal" (*City of God* VII. 19), historically alive and well in the tradition of Euhemerism, or they had to do with the elements of nature—the sky (Jove), the air (Juno), the sea (Neptune), and the nether earth (Pluto). Through etymology they could also serve as signs for human characteristics and behavior: Cupid for desire, Venus for sensual pleasure, Jove for power, or justice, or the natural generation of things. And their adventures in fable could point to certain facts of nature or to general lessons in human conduct (and misconduct) which might benefit those who wished to learn and to live well. Thus the survival of classical mythology depended upon certain learned Christians who adopted a variety of ancient traditions. There was no *new* allegorization as such. The dressing of Christian conceptions in mythological ornament, as in Augustine's allusions to God (by way of Virgil) as "deus omnipotens" or "pater ille deum . . . [sic altus Apollo]"—these were no more than metaphorical expressions which assumed that pagan deities are false, while the one God is true. Such transferred language was based not simply on equivalence, but on difference and distance.[16]

Contrary to what some scholars have said or implied, pagan mythology, legend, and literature were not Christianized to any significant degree in the early Middle Ages. Augustine could, it is true, imagine that a Christian writer might adapt pagan fable to a Christian work;[17] and Boethius could practice that prescription in the *De Consolatione*. But this is far from reading the *Aeneid* or the *Metamorphoses* as though either one contained hidden or sustained doctrinal meanings. Indeed, the prevailing view in the West runs consistently counter to Christianized interpretations.[18] The influential *Mitologie* of Fulgentius is illustrative. Its explanations of deities and fables are strictly etymological, naturalistic, and moral in the ancient philological and philosophical styles. Apollo, for example, is the sun; the Python is credulity ("pithos enim Grece credulitas dicitur"); and so the fable tells how the light (of truth or wisdom) slays the serpent of false credulity. Or, again, Venus stands for the life of pleasure; and her ancient name, "Aphrodite, comes from the Greek *afros* (meaning foam) because, like foam, sensual desire rises momentarily and comes to nothing; or because the surge of semen is itself filled with foam."[19]

Interpretations such as these (sometimes including *picturae*[20] or lists of accompanying details) became the commonplaces of the Middle Ages. The reputation of the *Mitologie* saw to that. But in addition, *all* the major "classical" sources of information used the same authoritative methods—for example, the glosses of Servius and Lactantius and the chapter on the pagan gods in Isidore's *Etymologiae:* the etymological, moral, and physical modes of interpretation.[21]

> The Latins call this god "Cupid" because he makes love ("*amorem*"). But here [Virgil] imitated the Greeks who signify both Cupid and Amor under one name. . . . For, since desire (cupiditas) for shameful behavior is foolish, Cupid is pictured as a boy. . . . And again because his discourse in things of love is imperfect, as in a boy. . . . Moreover he is winged because nothing is lighter than love, nothing more fickle . . . as is proved by Dido herself. . . .   (Servius on the *Aeneid* I. 663)

> And what is the pleasure of Venus but unadulterated madness? And so Venus is called fire, as the consort of Vulcan and Mars, that is of fire [Vulcan] and of furor [Mars].   (Lactantius on the *Thebaid* V. 66)

> They say that Mars is the god of war, and that he is called Mars because men do the fighting, and Mars is male (*mas*). . . . Again he is called Mars as if to say he brings about death (*effectorem mortium*). For by Mars death is named (*a Marte mors nuncupatur*). . . . However among the Thracians Mars is called Gradivus because those who fight take a stand in battle (*in bello "gradum" inferant*) or because they march briskly (*inpigre gradiantur*).   (Isidore, *Etymologiae* VIII. xi. 50–52)

Thus, in both pagan and early medieval sources, the discussions of the deities are about the same. The *Mitologie* was simply the most influential, organized interpretative compendium to survive; and there is nothing peculiarly Christian about it apart from some scattered Biblical allusions which serve to elaborate or comment on a familiar interpretation.

> The nine Muses are also assigned to Apollo, and he himself is added as the tenth Muse because there are ten modulations of the human voice. And so Apollo is pictured with a ten-stringed cither. The divine law also says that the psalter is ten-stringed [Psalm 32.2]. (*Mitologie* I. 15)

There is no Christian allegorizing here or, for that matter, elsewhere in the *Mitologie*.

Nor can any such allegorization be found in Fulgentius's commentary on the *Aeneid*.[22] There, again, the very brief glossing is etymological, philosophical, and moral—in the tradition of Donatus, Servius, and Macrobius. Aeneas is seen as Everyman on his passage through life. The storm which is instigated by Juno ("dea partus") is associated with the dangers of childbirth; Dido and Carthage with the allurements and turmoil of a love that is abandoned on the advice of Mercury ("deus ingenii"). The golden bough is the study of science and letters which Aeneas must grasp before his descent into hell—into the obscure and secret mysteries of wisdom ("sapientiae obscura secretaque misteria"); and although Fulgentius compares this to Christian precept concerning a contrite and humble heart, he specifically distinguishes Virgil's meaning from Christian teaching ("nostra . . . preceptio"). Finally Aeneas seeks the help of Evander ("Grece bonus vir dicitur") and engages in battle with Turnus ("furibundus sensus") in order to wed himself to a path of sorrows (Lavinia: "laborum viam").

By the time of the Carolingian Renaissance, Fulgentius's name was equivalent to "classical mythology" in the West, and the major compilation of the time, the *Second Vatican Mythography*, illustrates that very little change has taken place in the approach to gods and heroes. There are some additional details, more myths, more interpretations, but the basic methods are the same; and there is no Christianizing of either deities or fables. The gods and goddesses are men and women who had been honored locally by their people and by poets in song. Moreover, the mythical stories assume (we are told) that there is only "one god and one goddess, equal in power, who by reason of their offices and activities are called by different

names. The god is sometimes called Sol, sometimes Liber, some-
times Apollo. And similarly the goddess is sometimes Luna, some-
times Diana, sometimes Ceres, sometimes Juno, and sometimes
Proserpina. But because they are incorporeal, the Numina seem to
be of either sex."[23] So goes the nonspiritualized Proem of the *Second
Vatican Mythography*, and what follows from that introduction is
largely a conflation of familiar sources: Hyginus, Servius, Lactantius, Fulgentius, and Isidore.

Even in the twelfth century, in the very important *Third Vatican
Mythography*, although there is much more amplification and
complication and a more sophisticated ordering of materials, the
traditions of mythological interpretation remain constant. The
author of the *Third Mythography* learnedly specifies the standard
authorities by name: Servius, Lactantius, and Fulgentius. He cites
others whom he may have consulted: Cicero, Macrobius, Martianus
Capella, and Remigius the glossator. Still others he names as sources
of facts and interpretations, or to illustrate his comments: Homer,
Thucydides, Plato, Terence, Lucretius, Virgil, Horace, Juvenal, Persius, Livy, Lucan, Statius, Pliny, Petronius, and Varro. As has been
noted elsewhere, "morality and physics play important roles," and
"Euhemeristic and Stoic interpretations abound."[24]

Again the insistent conclusion is that the author of this widely
circulated encyclopedia of myth (who was perhaps an Englishman)
showed no inclination to Christianize his interpretations. He
complicates matters by offering more information and more various
explanations and sources; he introduces "long discussions on the
origin of evil, types of wickedness and manifestations of it, methods
of knowledge, and the nature of the soul, the capabilities of the
human mind, and the like";[25] yet etymology, the most literalistic of
methods, dominates his commentary; and his self-conscious allusions, quotations, and name-dropping have the effect of firmly
setting his discussions on a foundation of pagan authority and
pagan poetic practice. For example:

> They consider Pallas the greatest daughter of Jove. As Ovid
> says in his *Fasti*, they consider her the goddess—now of war,
> now of wisdom, and now of all the arts. They also attribute
> different names to her for, though one and the same goddess,
> she is called Pallas, Minerva, Tritonia and (among the Greeks)
> *Athena*. She is called Pallas either from the Greek *pallein*, that

is from the *shaking* of the spear, which the goddess did, or. . . .

According to Remigius she is named Tritonia from *Tritonoia,* that is the three kinds of knowledge ("*terna notitia*"). . . . Nevertheless, Fulgentius feels otherwise about this name. He claims that Triton, as we said earlier, comes from *tetrimenon* or in Latin, grieved ("*Contritum*"). And so he says that Tritonia is called the goddess of wisdom because all *contritio* makes one wise. According to Servius Tritonia is interpreted *trein,* to fear (timere); so, as he says, she is named Tritonia as if to say *terribilis.* . . . The poet [Lucan] writes that "She called herself Tritonia after the lake (Triton) which she loved" [*Pharsalia* IX. 3547]. (*MV* 3, 10, 1)

Although the *Third Mythography* is elaborately traditional, something new does begin to happen about the time it was written. There are signs that some learned men had begun to impose pious and specifically Christian meanings on the ancient myths. Thus Arnolph of Orleans, who provided annotations on Lucan in the manner of his predecessors, suggests something bordering on Biblical exegesis in his commentary on Ovid. He omits anagogy, as from the familiar four levels of theological exegesis, but he claims that his exposition on Ovid's *Metamorphoses* is "sometimes allegorical, sometimes moral, and sometimes historical."[26] For example, his discussion of Niobe's story includes interpretations of Apollo as wisdom, and Latona as religion or piety ("religio") and then as *charity.* Bernard Silvester's commentary on the first six books of the *Aeneid* is clearer still. Although it follows generally the tradition of Fulgentius's interpretation, it goes beyond its predecessor from time to time: Apollo may stand for the sun, for human wisdom, or for *divine* wisdom; Jupiter is fire, or the planet, or the creator himself—the highest God.[27] And in the interpretation of legend, Bernard links Venus with worldly harmony ("mundana musica"), her offspring Aeneas with the human spirit, and Anchises with the Creator!

There is a significant change between Fulgentius and Bernard. Although he is a Christian writing for Christians, the sixth-century writer has disclosed meanings from pagan natural philosophy and Stoic moralizing—lessons that related to the good and virtuous man in his natural condition. But the twelfth-century author has begun to cross the bridge between the natural and supernatural. His contemporary, John of Salisbury, recognized this when he condensed Bernard's commentary.[28] On one hand he confines his redaction to the natural morality in Bernard's analysis: "The first book of the *Aeneid* then, under the figure of a shipwreck, sets forth the manifest tribulations of childhood. . . ." But then he also observes that he himself cannot "follow in the footsteps of Virgil or the heathen to such a degree as to believe that anyone can obtain [supernatural] knowledge and virtue by the strength of his own will." In the final analysis John is uncertain or ambiguous about whether Virgil had some hint of divine wisdom; for "although ignorant of the truth and walking in the darkness of the heathen" he may have perceived that Aeneas could not be "admitted to the Elysian Fields of the blessed until instructed by the Sibyl (the word Sibyl . . . meaning counsel of Jove or wisdom of God). . . ."

There is, of course, an old tradition behind the idea that a pagan writer might have had shadowy hints of divine truth, but a link between this concept and later Christian interpretations of pagan myth is not always firm or clear. When Arnolph of Orleans verges on doctrinal interpretation, and Bernard Silvester too, they are treading an uncertain path historically, doctrinally, and literarily. My own view, rather changed from a position I took some years ago, is that a number of different and not necessarily related things happened to classical myth simultaneously during the later Middle Ages. First, some assumed that a pagan writer could have a glimpse of divine truth which he could express through myth. But this is not a certain matter; the assumption could, in fact, be doctrinally dangerous or (in Jerome's words) simply puerile. John of Salisbury's reservations have been noted, and they are reiterated by Boccaccio in the course of his defense of the notion that ancient poets were often considered *natural* theologians: but, "of course, if any one were to call them sacred, the veriest fool would detect the falsehood."[29] The mystery of faith was no easy thing to be given away, even to good pagans. Second, there were the standard etymological, natural, and ethical interpretations which—given their antiquity—became practically the equivalent of literal renderings. For example, by the thirteenth or fourteenth century Venus is not an "allegorical figure" for love or sensual pleasure, or scarcely even a metaphor: she is a cliché for love or sensual pleasure.[30] Third, there was the possibility that a Christian writer might *use* classical material in a transferred sense, as Augustine and Dante did when they referred to

God as "high Jove," and Christ as "the true Apollo," or as when an ancient fable was made the subject of a Christian work, as in Lactantius's *De Ave Phenice* or in the story of Perseus described anagogically by Boccaccio in the *Genealogia Deorum*. And finally, there were pious Christian interpretations that were consciously *imposed upon* classical myth for the purpose of edification or for providing elaborately learned examples to illustrate Christian conduct or doctrine.

This last phenomenon did not really flourish until the fourteenth century and after—in the *Ovide Moralisé*, in Pierre Bersuire's *Ovidius Moralizatus*, in Christine de Pisan's *Epistle of Othea*, and in John Ridewall's *Fulgentius Metaforalis*. Bersuire is forthright about his procedure. "Since I see that Scripture uses fables to describe some truth, sometimes natural and sometimes historical, it seems appropriate to me—according to the manner of moralizing the natural properties of things—to apply the same kind of moralizing to the fables of the ancient poets so that through these human fictions we might confirm the mysteries of the life of Faith."[31] Bersuire was a learned man with a sense of history; he does not say that Christian meanings exist in classical myth, but rather that he will *apply* to myth a special kind of "moralizing" method which will show how myth can be made to confirm Christian doctrine. He uses and then goes beyond the literal, historical, natural, and moral traditions in order to create spiritual interpretations that are specifically religious. Saturn, for example, was the first of the gods (*literaliter*); he stands for "time" (*naturaliter*) and was a king of Crete (*historaliter*). Moreover, *in malo* he stands for some evil religious superior or aged prelate, old in his evil ways, and *in bono* he signifies a pious and just prelate. Or, as Ridewall wrote, Saturn signifies not only the virtue of prudence in a traditional interpretation, but also the vice of gluttony.[32]

Although these last interpretations may seem strained and capricious, they are based on old traditions, and even in their pious elaborations they have an inner consistency which is understandable. They begin with the explanations of Fulgentius and others, and then (through free association and analogy) become subject to familiar religious-symbolic modes of interpretations from Biblical exegesis. In the Cephalus and Procris legend, for example, the javelin and the hound of the pagan myth are simply read as standard exegetical symbols: the javelin stands for the word of God and the

hound for a priest.[33] Interpretations like these are consciously
pietistic and consciously unhistorical. They are related neither to a
syncretism which joins Christian and pagan theologies, as in
Clement of Alexandria's *Stromata*, nor to the position that pagan
myths might be used by Christian writers with Christian meanings,
as in Lactantius's *De Ave Phenice*, nor to the Neoplatonism in
Bernard Silvester's commentary on the *Aeneid*. Their real kin is the
exemplum or fable of late medieval homiletics in which moral or
spiritual lessons were freely and ingeniously developed without any
real concern for the obvious meaning of a story or text.[34]

It would be a mistake, then, to think of the religious, *mystical*, or
anagogical interpretations of the *Ovide Moralisé*, of Bersuire, and
of Ridewall as having behind them the same value or weight of
tradition that their literal renderings or familiar glosses had. What
these authors did is not the same as interpreting a literary text, or
using a classical story as moral *exemplum*.[35] And when such
readings were mocked by Rabelais and condemned by both Luther
and the Council of Trent they were encountering the last reactions
from an overriding tradition, of both medieval and Renaissance
humanism, which dated back to Boccaccio, John of Salisbury, and
St. Jerome. That reaction was not against the old etymological,
naturalistic, philosophical, or moral interpretations of Fulgentius or
the *Third Vatican Mythography*, or of a work like the *De Archana
Deorum* by Chaucer's contemporary, Thomas of Walsingham; it
was against a playful, decorous, well-intentioned pietism that was
ultimately judged to be "un-Christian" or foolish because it was
unhistorical.[36]

Our assessment of Chaucer's poetry is helped by an understanding of the development of classical myth in the Middle Ages
because that development says something about the range of his
options, his actions and reactions as a writer. Certain broad, long-
lived traditions were familiar to him, but his choices were various.
Chaucer could and did parody tradition as well as follow it; and he
also could and did depend on original sources without recourse to
commentaries. Working strictly from original material, for example,
he twisted the legend of Ceyx and Alcyone, which is a sentimental
commedia in Ovid and a straightforward *exemplum* in his French
source, so that it became a pathetic tragedy in the *Book of the*

Duchess. His approach in this case is entirely his own. Then, too, he might be imitative. Scholars have assured us for a long time that Chaucer first drew his knowledge of classical deities and legends from his reading of the ancients—especially Ovid, Virgil, and Statius. That is a simple fact which should not be forgotten for the sake of glosses and encyclopedias. In addition Chaucer had read medieval writers who had also used or alluded to myth. Boethius in the *De Consolatione* (with or without commentary) employed a number of legends: Orpheus and Eurydice, Ulysses and the Sirens, the labors of Hercules, and others. In each case Boethius worked with myth so as to point a moral, to indicate what the reasonable man should either do or avoid in order to live wisely. And Jean de Meun did the same kind of thing with myth—morally and comically—in the *Roman de la Rose.*[37] Here and elsewhere in his reading Chaucer found that figures from ancient legend could serve as exemplars of virtues and vices: self-love in Narcissus, pride in Niobe, greed in Midas, and fidelity in the long lists of women from Ovid's *Heroides* or Jerome's *Adversus Jovinianum.*

From books Chaucer learned, too, that certain deities were traditionally associated with specific kinds of natural human activities or moral conditions: Jupiter with governance, creation, power, and justice; Mars with wrathful and impetuous behavior, with irascibility and death; Venus with sensual delight or sexual pleasure, and Cupid with instinctive desire or concupiscence. For all practical purposes these were commonplaces—not symbols but "deities" which personified ideas—and Chaucer would have recognized them as such in the *Roman de la Rose*, in Alanus de Insulis's *De Planctu Naturae* and *Anticlaudian*, or in glosses, dictionaries, and astrological tracts. He would have known, too, that the elaborate details which might surround such deities, their paraphernalia and accompanying parts (such as those in Boccaccio's *Teseida* and its gloss) were traditional allegorical *picturae* which amplified the meaning of certain ideas ("deities") in specific ways. Cupid's blindness illustrated the unreasonableness of desire and his wings told that desire was light and fickle; Venus's birds were associated with the fervor of sexual intercourse, her roses with shame or the swift passing of sensual pleasure. To understand such things required no special knowledge.[38]

Chaucer also knew something about etymological meanings, in a sense the most literal of explanations for mythical figures. He knew that Calliope's name, for example, came from two words meaning *bona vox* or *optima vox* ("thi vois be now present" [*Tr* 3. 45]); that Polyhymnia ("id est multam memoriam faciens") was the memorial Muse (*Anel* 10–20); and that Tisiphone, etymologized as *vox* (*furiarum*), was the crying voice of the Furies ("sorwynge evere yn peyne" [*Tr* 1. 9]).[39] He was aware that the gods and goddesses were thought originally to have been historical personages ("Jupiter the likerous, / That first was fader of delicacye" [*Form Age* 56–57]), and that often the gods (like some of those in Ovid) might not be personifications at all but, like Apollo in the *Manciple's Tale* and Pluto in the *Merchant's Tale*, "real" people who were just as wise or, more likely, just as foolish as any living person.

From his acquaintance with Virgil and others he recognized that the story of Troy was a tragedy, a civic disaster caused by foolish love. He found in Statius, and perhaps was reminded by John of Salisbury in the *Policraticus*, that the tragedy of Thebes stemmed from Martian fury, strife, and discord: from battling warriors born of dragon's teeth, a son who slew his father, and brother who killed brother. And the Brooch of Thebes (*Thebaid* II. 265 ff.) he knew to be a token of tragedy, alluring and treacherous, bringing ruin to Harmonia and her daughters and to Jocasta, and finally foreshadowing doom for Argia and Eriphyle.[40]

There were, also, other possible influences on Chaucer. If he had read Saint Augustine's *City of God* in French translation or Latin original, he would have learned a good deal about the history of the gods and goddesses—the fabulous, naturalistic, and civil deities described from Varro. And if he had read Augustine with a classicizing gloss by one of the fourteenth-century English friars, he would have come away with a strong sense of Augustine's distinction between Christian and pagan (natural) theology and of the commentator's awareness of certain striking similarities between Christian and pagan peoples: between old Troy and new Troy (London), and between the ways that men and women of old (even gods and goddesses) fell in love, or prayed, or partied, or jealously defended their honor—like men and women of fourteenth-century England.[41] As far as one can tell, Chaucer was not inclined to treat pagan myths or deities as if they held hidden Christian doctrines or as if they were suitable material for pious reflection: as though Apollo (god of wisdom) stood for Christ, or Jupiter (the helping father) really meant God the Father. He seems to have been too historically oriented to adopt such a view, too much aware that the old gods came from times when men lived under the law of nature (*BD* 56), before the era of grace and redemption.[42]

Finally, it would be shortsighted not to recognize the broad historical context of Chaucer's use of classical material. As a medieval poet he was completely unconcerned with, and probably incapable of conceiving, the value of creating "a certain breath of paganism" to waft "perfumes from the old mythology"[43] through the court of Richard II. Chaucer was no cousin to Walter Pater. What he sought, and succeeded in doing, was two things. First, he saw himself as part of, and set his work in line with, the great tradition of narrative poetry which extended back to antiquity. He honored those old "approved stories," the tales of loves that were true and false, newly begun or lately won; tales of casual love or "love of stel"; tales of discord, of jealousy, of feigned repair, and trickery (*HF* 672 ff.). He knew and loved them. And second, he reworked them with a purpose which was broadly moral and from a stance of sympathetic irony toward the ways people behave on the crazily ordered pilgrimage of life.

For his audience Chaucer wanted to animate the traditions he had learned. In this he was like his contemporary, John Trevisa, whose concern is expressed in language similar to Chaucer's own in the *Legend of Good Women* (17 ff.). At one point in his translating, Trevisa observed that the Bible in Latin is "good and fair" and yet to make a Latin sermon on the Bible to men who know English, but not Latin, would be foolish for they would learn nothing.

> Then it needeth to have an English translation, *and for to keep it in mind that it be not forgotten,* it is better that such a translation be made and written than said and not written.[44]

Such was the attitude of others before Trevisa—of John the Scot who translated from Greek to Latin, and Latin to French, of King Alfred and Caedmon, and "the holy man" Bede. It was the attitude of Dante and Boccaccio when they chose the language of the living; and it seems to have been the attitude of numerous thirteenth- and fourteenth-century French writers who translated from both Italian and Latin: from such writers as Boccaccio and Ovid, Livy, Augustine, John of Salisbury, Boethius, and Aristotle.[45] It was the attitude, too, of Geoffrey Chaucer, "the great translator" (as Deschamps called him) and classicist extraordinary, England's Ovid.

2 Brief Allusions:
Character, Action, and Theme

One of the happiest features of Chaucer's writing is its variety—in mood and attitude, in theme and pace. The brief mythological allusions on which we focus are drawn primarily from the early and middle parts of his literary career—from the *Book of the Duchess* and *Troilus and Criseyde*—and they will serve, in part, to illustrate just how consciously and variously he manipulated some of the classical lore which he had learned. Chaucer was not inclined to treat mythology as a cunning device or artifice; for him it was not simply a part of narrative gimmickry or decorative opulence. At first glance the earliest materials from the *Book of the Duchess* may seem to be largely imitative of French sources and primarily aimed at heightening the style. But in fact Chaucer does two things: he simplifies and economizes on his sources and he complicates the effects of his classical material. From one point of view his rhetorical goal seems to be a "heightened style"; yet the result is often strikingly the opposite—as though Chaucer were thoroughly aware, even in his early work, that the weight of classical ornament could comically topple a literary structure or weaken a fictional creation, and so ironically undercut the normal purposes of mythical allusion.

The narrator in the *Book of the Duchess* is a curiously familiar person. Like other Chaucerian narrators he is bookish (at least he falls asleep on a book), and he has read enough to think that his subsequent dream could surely not be understood by Joseph of Egypt and scarcely at all by Macrobius, who wrote all about the dream of Scipio (*BD* 275–89). To while away his sleepless, melancholy hours the narrator reads the story of Ceyx and Alcyone, to which we will return later, and then reacts to that experience by commenting on the classical deities with a mixture of skepticism and enthusiasm.

He thinks the story of Alcyone's losing her husband and (with Juno's help) finding him in a dream would be a wonder, *if it were true:* the narrator himself has never heard of any gods who could make one sleep or wake; he knows only the one true God. But partly in game he makes a mocking prayer, a parody of Alcyone's own pathetic prayer to Juno (109–21), and he includes in it a careless comment on the deities and a luxurious bribe of bed, pillows, and so forth, for their services.

> "I wolde yive thilke Morpheus,
> Or hys goddesse, dame Juno,
> Or som wight elles, I ne roghte who,
> To make me slepe and have som reste,—
> I wil yive hym the alderbeste
> Yifte that ever he abod hys lyve."   (*BD* 242–47)

> "And thus this ylke god, Morpheus,
> May wynne of me moo feës thus
> Than ever he wan; and to Juno,
> That ys hys goddesse, I shal soo do,
> I trow that she shal holde hir payd."   (*BD* 265–69)

Reflecting on these few classical allusions, one may sense that their meaning is not nearly as significant as their tone, which is light, exaggerated, and flippant. One suggestion—that, in these passages and earlier, Juno *stands for* some idea or "meaning"[1] — appears to be unlikely. Instead, it seems that the narrator's comments on the goddess and on Morpheus, "Or som wight elles, I ne roghte who," are first used simply and mechanically to shift the narrative from book to dream; and then, more importantly, to shift the mood from tragedy to comedy and so to begin developing the thematic contrasts which dominate the poem: black and white, sorrow and joy, death and life. Thus the narrator's prayer for sleep parallels Alcyone's but, despite his sympathy for her, his is a perversion of her prayer (in "game"). Besides complicating the narrative theme by introducing lightness and life, the allusions alter our view of the narrator himself. In the opening lines he was all seriousness, filled with unnatural sorrow and despair, an insomniac verging on death but fearful of its coming. Now, however, the narrator grows more obviously complex: even though he does not want to, he can still be playful; he feels sympathy for Alcyone but he toys with the divinities that she worshiped.

The other central figure in the *Book of the Duchess* is the Black Knight, whom the narrator meets in his dream, and nearly all the mythical allusions in the poem focus on him and on his state of mind. The Knight's sorrow for loss of love cannot be cured by Ovid's remedies (of love), by Orpheus's song (of wisdom), by Daedalus's "playes slye," or by the medicines of "Ypocras, ne Galyen" (567–72). He suffers torments like Sisyphus (read: Tityus) and Tantalus (587–94, 709) and, in an admittedly vain wish, he thinks how he might have kept his beloved, his "fers" in the game of chess with Fortune, if he had only had the knowledge of "the Grek Pithagores." Questioned as to the validity of his judgment on his beloved's beauty, the Black Knight assures the narrator in no uncertain terms that he would have loved his lady no matter what—even if *he* (contrary to fact) had had the beauty of Alcibiades, the strength of Hercules, the "worthynesse" of Alexander, the riches of antiquity (of Babylon, Carthage, Macedonia, Rome, or Nineveh), the bravery of Hector, and the wisdom of Minerva (1054–74). Moreover, he will not now repent or forget his love, for that would be treachery worse than Antenor's at Troy, or Achitophel's, or Genelon's (1115–25). When his lady was alive and before he had disclosed his love to her, the knight wrote songs about his feelings of love—not so artfully as the first musician, "Lamekes sone Tubal," although the Greeks say Pythagoras came first (1155–80). Finally, when he told his lady of his love and she refused him, he suffered such woe that Cassandra who "soo / Bewayled the destruccioun / Of Troye and of Ilyoun, / Had never swich sorwe as I thoo" (1246–49).

On the face of it, all these ancient allusions may appear to "lift" the style. They seem elegantly self-conscious and, perhaps, somewhat stiff and artificial compared to what we later find in Chaucer. Most of them, too, are cast in the familiar *a fortiori* or negative phraseology of high rhetoric. Like the narrator's dream, which is so wonderful that Macrobius could scarcely fathom it, the Black Knight suffers *more* pain than Sisyphus and Tantalus; he suffers so much that the classical cures *cannot* help a bit—not the remedies of

Ovid or the music of Orpheus; and the suffering of Cassandra at the fall of Troy is no match for his suffering when he hears the "nay" of his Lady White.

From such passages one might conclude that most of the brief allusions in the *Book of the Duchess* illustrate a conventional decorousness in Chaucer's early imitative, courtly style. If this is so, then the virtue of their use lies in the clear and relatively economic ways in which they focus on two of the poem's major themes—love and sorrow. But it is also possible to think that Chaucer did more than this: that he created a cluster of allusions which, by their very weight, cast doubt on the moral, psychological stance of the Black Knight. The knight had, we may recall, "wel nygh lost hys mynde" (511) and his rhetoric may well enhance that unstable condition by amplifying an "unkynde," narrowly personal sorrow which borders on but never quite touches self-pity. In this context the allusions point up the infernal, tragic, and suicidal force of the Black Knight's sorrow. No ancient pagan (i.e., natural) good sense or skill avails against it: not the sympathy of grieving Pan, the "god of kynde" (511–13), nor the arts of Ovid and others, nor the wise example of Socrates (568–72; 717–19). The Black Knight suffers in a living hell worse than Sisyphus or Tantalus, and he travels the same road to tragic ruin (or damnation) for love as did Medea, Phyllis, Dido, and Echo (722–36). Thus he is described and describes himself, not simply in naturalistic, unregenerate pagan terms but, worse, in terms that suggest (through their extravagance) a self-indulgence which is quite unnatural.

By contrast the Black Knight portrays his Lady White as virtuous, kind, reasonable, and—ultimately—perfect. In the depths of his sorrow and devotion she ceases to be "real" at all, and by the end of his distraught account he will picture her as apotheosized.[2] For only a few short lines is she compared to classical figures—Penelope and Lucrece (1080–87)—for her goodness and truth; but she is as good or better than ("nothyng lyk") these exemplars. The Black Knight's affirmative language for his lady reminds us of the Virgin Mary— "tour of yvoyre," "soleyn fenix of Arabye," "restyng place" of "Trouthe" (946, 982, 1003–05)—and it declares in its zeal that the Lady White is *not like* the Queen of Heaven because she *is* the Queen of Heaven. Thus two languages, one of classical and the other of Marian allusion, serve as contrasting elements in a play between the Black Knight's assumptions about his own death-

dealing sorrow and then about his lady's paradisiacal goodness. The
constant which lies behind both of these is the knight's own lack of
judgment or restraint, a condition that is highlighted in turn by the
pedestrian good sense and plain style of the narrator of the dream.

Taken together, most of the brief classical and mythical allusions
in the *Book of the Duchess* have moral significance in the sense that
they elaborate a distressed condition of mind, heart, and soul; they
magnify the torments of love. In themselves they are not strictly
allegorical, however, because they serve to define character, both in
the Black Knight and the narrator. If in the end characterization
turns into idea, like white and black or joy and sorrow, then the
mythical would be subsumed in a dream allegory of ambivalence
which we have yet to understand. In addition, a few allusions are
tied to the lighter part of life, like those to Zephyrus and Flora (402)
and in the narrator's prayer to Juno and Morpheus. But the
preponderant weight of classical allusion, and with it the decorative
rhetoric of the poem, is darkly, sorrowfully tragic. In the *Book of the
Duchess*, generally, the plain style goes with comedy *(commedia)*
and with life.

Although Chaucer alters traditional forms of mythological allusion in the *Book of the Duchess* by juxtaposing simplicity with
ornament and understanding with feelings, his approach to the
classical material itself remains (as in his French sources) highly
rhetorical; and his purpose is similar to, if more complex than, that
of his sources in that they both aim at elaborating certain ideas. By
contrast, the brief mythical allusions in *Troilus and Criseyde* seem
"real" from the start. They are part of an ancient scene and,
conversely, a means of creating that scene. They are justified by
history, and they help make history live so that—aside from the
narrator's own uses—many of the mythological references appear to
be elements of everyday discourse rather than "classical allusions."
The Trojans, for example, celebrate the feast of the Palladion and its
"observaunces olde" as a matter of course: "Hire olde usage nolde
they nat letten" (*Tr* 1. 150, 160–61); the historical personages allude
to their patron deities, as when Calchas mentions "his god," Apollo
(1. 69–70) and Criseyde refers to her goddess, Pallas Athena (2. 425);
the sun is called Phoebus and the moon is Cynthia or Lucina; and a
variety of myths and legends are noted with an easy familiarity that
makes them seem at home in ancient Troy—as when Pandare cites
Oënone's love letter to Paris to prove a point, and then assumes for a
moment that Troilus has probably seen it (1. 652–56).

Such surface effects are cumulatively very important for creating what Kittredge noted as Chaucer's process for classicizing his story.[3] Sometimes the mythic name-dropping is thoroughly obvious: Phoebus the sun and Zephyrus the spring breeze (5. 8–14); "Escaphilo" the owl of ill omen (5. 319); Atropos, the Death which snips the fateful thread of life; and Penelope and Alceste as traditional figures of womanly fidelity. Moreover, in some few cases the "obvious" is not entirely clear to modern readers. There are, for example, several allusions to Mars which have little to do with warfare as such, but which are practically self-explanatory in their contexts when one is alert to Mars's traditional association with impetuous, angry behavior, and even death.[4] After Criseyde halts Pandare from presuming too much upon her recently won friendship for Troilus, Pandare quickly backtracks with an oath that aims at appeasing wrath: " 'By Mars, the god that helmed is of steel! / Now beth naught wroth, my blood, my nece dere' " (2. 593–94). When he reports to Troilus of his success with Criseyde, Troilus is first pleased, but then complains impatiently against any delay,

> "Thow maist answer, 'abid, abid,' but he
> That hangeth by the nekke, soth to seyne
> In gret disese abideth for the peyne."   (*Tr* 2. 985–87)

Having to work both sides of the street, Pandare tries to calm this rashness (and its violent image) with another oath to the rash god: " 'Al esily, now, for the love of Marte,' / Quod Pandarus, 'for every thing hath tyme' " (2. 988–89). In something of the same vein, but predictive of impetuous behavior and death, are two very brief prayers or invocations: " 'O cruel god, O dispitouse Marte' " (2. 435), and "Thow cruel Mars ek, fader to Quyryne" (4. 25). Although the context of the first of these verges on comedy, as Pandare begins his pleading to Criseyde, and the second is the narrator's totally serious introduction to Troilus's misfortune, both explicitly look forward to death:

> "But sith I se my lord mot nedes dye,
> And I with hym, here I me shryve, and seye
> That wikkedly ye don us bothe deye."   (*Tr* 2. 439–41)

> So that the losse of lyf and love yfeere
> Of Troilus be fully shewed heere.   (*Tr* 4. 27–28)

These passages assume a traditional etymology: Mars < *mors.*

Like the allusions to Mars, those to Pallas Athena or Minerva are sometimes obvious. She is invoked as the goddess of learning and wisdom when Troilus prays for her help to write a letter (2. 1062–63): " 'and thow, Minerva, the white, / Yif thow me wit my lettre to devyse' "; and late in the poem she is mentioned as the warrior goddess (5. 308) when Troilus contemplates his funeral rites.[5] But it may not be immediately clear why Pallas should be Criseyde's special protectress, unless one attends to Criseyde's widowhood, her status in life. The fact of her "estat" is, of course, emphasized from the moment she is introduced: "For bothe a widewe was she and allone / Of any frend to whom she dorste hir mone" (1. 97–98). At the feast of Pallas she is dressed, anachronistically, in a medieval "widewes habit large of samyt broun" (1. 109) and "in widewes habit blak" (1. 170).[6] Besides being garbed as a widow, she lives as one might expect a medieval widow to live: in seclusion, chastely (like a nun in Troy), and with devotion to learning and books. At home she listens to a reading of *The Siege of Thebes* (2. 80–84) and at one point she says, again anachronistically, that she would be better off praying and reading saints' lives in a cave (2. 117–18). She is concerned with wisdom and the conduct of her life in "hire estat," particularly when she consults Uncle Pandare in privacy.

> "Nay, sitteth down; by God, I have to doone
> With yow, to speke of wisdom er ye go."
> And everi wight that was aboute hem tho,
> That herde that, gan fer awey to stonde,
> Whil they two hadde al that hem liste in honde.
>
> Whan that hire tale al brought was to an ende,
> Of hire estat and of hire governaunce. . . .   (*Tr* 2. 213–19)

The notion of Christian widowhood was for centuries, and still is, tied to the ideals of wisdom and chastity.[7] What Chaucer did was to classicize that ideal and embody it in the chaste goddess of wisdom, the appropriate deity for Criseyde to address as "her Lady": " 'O lady myn, Pallas!' " she prays when Pandare counsels her to love, " 'Thow in this dredful cas for me purveye, / For so astoned am I that I deye' " (2. 425–27).[8]

The classicizing of the medieval or medievalizing of the classical (for it works both ways) is not unusual with Chaucer. It appears, for example, in one prayer that sounds like a pagan variation on the doxology—the praise of Father, Son, and Holy Spirit—whose persons were traditionally translated into the forces of Power, Wisdom, and Love. Classicized in an oath by Pandare, the three persons of the Holy Trinity become Jove, Minerva, and Venus:[9]

> "For, nece, by the goddesse Mynerve,
> And Jupiter, that maketh the thondre rynge,
> And by the blisful Venus that I serve,
> Ye ben the womman in this world lyvynge,
> Withouten paramours, to my wyttynge,
> That I best love, and lothest am to greve,
> And that ye weten wel youreself, I leve."   (Tr 2. 232–38)

The exaggerated rhetoric which characterizes Pandare on the offensive proves even funnier when one recognizes the play between one trinity and another.

We are reminded, too, by Pandare's mention of the "blisful Venus" whom he serves that each character has a deity: Calchas has "his god," "Daun Phebus or Appollo Delphicus" (1. 69–70); Criseyde her "lady," Pallas; and Troilus has Cupid, whom he scorns and then promises to serve until death (1. 908 ff.). This adoption of myth for purposes of characterization is straightforward business. Calchas works as a prophet under the tutelage of Apollo. He may be cursed or mocked for his "calkulynge" (1. 71), for his selfish treachery (1. 85–91), and later for his greed and fear of the gods (4. 1368–1414), but Calchas figures the future correctly, and when he repents his abandonment of Criseyde his tears elicit our sympathy (4. 94–133). His "character," in other words, is complex, although the mythic allusions associated with him are simple enough.

The same is true in other cases. Criseyde is devoted to Pallas and to her widowhood, but Pandare presents the allurements of security, love, and her own self-esteem in very convincing ways. As Criseyde gradually compromises her ideals she chooses the independence of widowhood ("I am myn owene womman") and the reputation ("honour") of widowhood, "as after myn estat"; but she will also be friendly, then affectionate, and then beloved to Troilus. Until the last she will maintain this ambiguous, paradoxical stance—part Pallas, part Venus, and ultimately all Fortune.[10] She will consistently desire the freedom and esteem of her status *and* the love of Troilus—or of Diomede. In truth, there is more pathos than irony in her effort to romanticize her widowhood in a prayer to the past and her erstwhile goddess.

> "But as to speke of love, ywis," she seyde,
> "I hadde a lord, to whom I wedded was,
> The whos myn herte al was, til that he deyde;
> And other love, as help me now Pallas,
> Ther in myn herte nys, ne nevere was."   (*Tr* 5. 974–78)

But neither she nor Diomede is really fooled by these haunting words.

Venus, as we have seen, is the patron of Pandare. This is to say that he is devoted to sensual pleasure, or—in the phraseology of the *Knight's Tale* (1918 ff.) and the *Parliament of Fowls* (218 ff.)—to "Plesaunce" and "alle the circumstaunces / Of love."[11] He has the "Hope" of love and its discomforts; he deceives for love ("Lesynges, Flaterye") and he thrives on the seemingly endless "Bisynesse" of love—now gentle, charming, and persuasive, and at another time (as when he delivers Troilus's letter ["Messagerye"]) bold and forceful ("Force"). He likes parties, whether at Deiphebus's or his own house, or at Sarpedoun's, which quietly suggests the traditional association between dining (Ceres), drinking (Bacchus), and the Venerian life.[12] When Pandare deceives or encourages deceit for love (Wet the letter with a few tears, please [2. 1027]), his religion is also clear. He will not discourage Troilus's love even if it be incestuous—with Helen, his brother's wife (1. 676–79); or if Troilus wants Pandare's sister, he shall have her tomorrow (1. 860–61). *Pandare:* or all for love; which is to say that he will give everything for the sensual life. So, should Criseyde not be available, there are other women in Troy (4. 401), or at Sarpedoun's (5. 447–48). But if Troilus wants Criseyde and no one else, then he should take her, by force if necessary: " 'Don as the list,' " " 'Help thiself anon,' " " 'Have mercy on thiself' " (4. 583, 590, 620).

Yet there is a twist to Pandare's devotion, a complication, because for all of his own long service to Venus he is unsuccessful in the dance of love (" 'I hoppe alwey byhynde!' " [2. 1107]). He has never served himself well (1. 622), and there are moments in the poem when his ardor on Troilus's behalf leaves one with the uneasy feeling that there is "something wrong" with Pandare. As a servant of Venus he knows all the right moves; but he is essentially incomplete or incompetent, a courtly, learned and generous version of Faulkner's Popeye. In the end, of course, it is his incompleteness that triumphs; a pathetic Placebo, he has done all he can *to please* Troilus (" 'I dide al that the leste,' " [5. 1736]), but the effort is wasted and vain.

As with the other major characters, so it is with Troilus. His devotion to Cupid seems complete and unqualified, but actually it is more complicated than his mythical epithet ("Cupides sone") suggests. The conventional significances surrounding the god of love were clichés long before Chaucer's day when the god was a figure for man's sensual instincts or concupiscible desires.[13] Cupid is blind, and so irrational; winged, and so light and fickle; boyish because he is foolishly immature, or lordly because of his power over mankind. He bears the gold-tipped arrows of keen desire (through the eyes), or he bears the torch of fiery passion; he is a metaphor for a force within man's fallen nature—the instinctive desire to have and possess whatever is attractive—a force which Petrarch says is made a god by only vain and foolish men. Troilus certainly knows how the servants of desire act and live: full of uncertain days and restless nights, stupid rituals, sorrow and suffering: " 'O veray fooles, nyce and blynde be ye!' " (1. 202). He feels the keen shot of Cupid's arrow when his eye hits its target ("Til on Criseyde it smot, and ther it stente."). He feels the embarrassment or shame of his love, the fears and first woes of it. He becomes a pathetic and somewhat comical wretch (1. 568–74), and more than that he becomes a devotee of Cupid—a humble, prayerful worshiper of his own desire (1. 932 ff.). In the process he also reflects the charms of the lover: he grows increasingly likable, agreeable, friendly, gentle, and generous (1. 1072–85). Everyone loves a lover. Then, too, he grows deceitful, suspicious, jealous, and irresponsible: "Who shal yeve a lovere any lawe?" (*KnT* 1164). Or, who can trust a lover?

Although the traditional outlines are clear, they are complicated by Chaucer's individuation of character, for Troilus fluctuates between the single-mindedness, or narrow-mindedness, of desire and some genuine concerns for the one he loves. He purposes something good, not villainous (1. 1030–36). He deceives at times, but he also weeps *real* tears (2. 1086–92), and he need *not feign* sickness at Deiphebus's (2. 1527–33), for he is really sick. He can scarcely accomplish the deceit which Pandare arranges for the night of bliss. In fact he bungles it. His goal is the consummation of love, but in his care for Criseyde there are times when that physical fact seems beyond his hope or comprehension, even his ability. In the end he has foolishly but truly (and therefore pathetically and tragically) loved Criseyde. With every reason to renege and with eyes open to the truth of her betrayal, he still loves her (5. 1695–1701). The situation is not simple or "pat" at all. If Troilus were concerned only with himself, with satisfying his cupidinous desires, he would elope or ravish Criseyde. But in fact he loves her more than he loves himself. Of such truth, consistency, and seriousness "Cupid"—light, fickle, and blind desire—knows nothing.

From an other-worldly perspective which comes with death, Troilus can distinguish his "fals felicitee" (3. 814) from the "pleyn felicite / That is in hevene above" (5. 1818–19); and he can curse the life of Cupid, and "al oure werk that foloweth so / The blynde lust, the which that may nat laste" (5. 1823–24). Assuredly he tells us how futile and frustrating is worldly love. Was it worth it? Unfortunately, unequivocally, no. Whatever one might think of Troilus's ultimate fate, this is the essential and tragic fact. We see it coming from the first lines of the poem, and when we have seen *how* it happens ("In lovynge, *how* his aventures fellen") the result is a sympathetic pathos which, again, "Cupid" knows nothing about, and which is relieved only by a hope that goes beyond man's natural condition.

Taken together, the relations between classical divinities and characterization in *Troilus and Criseyde* are, generally, simple. Myth serves to label and elaborate a "type": Calchas the prophet of truth—Apollo; Criseyde the widow—Pallas; Pandare the sensualist—Venus; and Troilus the servant of love—Cupid. But in each case the mythical label is only part of a particularized, individual mixture; it stands for only one idea in each of the fictional creations who grow more ambiguous and complex as the story proceeds.

The classical allusions we have just seen represent concepts primarily: they are static when taken by themselves, but in the surrounding contexts which Chaucer creates for them they become parts of a paradoxical mode which turns ideas into life, types into characters. As with the mythical allusions in *The Book of the*

Duchess, but now more easily handled in a more fluid narrative, these show a conscious effort to use and then alter the traditional forms. In addition to those which relate to characterization, however, there are other brief allusions which portray or predict drama rather than concepts, which provide analogies for actions. These appear to cluster around two narrative themes: sorrow for love and treachery. Tisiphone, for example, is the tragic muse of the poem (1. 6) not only because she foreshadows the torments of love which Troilus suffers in Book One, and indeed throughout the poem, but apparently because Chaucer read somewhere or learned somehow that she was the *voice* or *sound* of the woeful, "sorwynge" furies; and tragedy Chaucer knew to be a crying, a singing, or a bewailing of Fortune's turn from prosperity to ruin.[14] Thus the Fury muse of tradition supports in sorrow a sorrowful narrator and cries with him the torments of Troilus.

There are also brief parallels of the lover's condition in mythic action, like those noted above in the *Book of the Duchess:* Troilus's immobilizing sorrow is like that of Niobe who was turned to stone (1. 697–700, 757–59); his sufferings are as continuous as those of Tityus, whose "stomak" vultures continually devoured (1. 785–88), and the past tortures of his passion (escaped for a while with Criseyde) resemble the fire of the underworld river Phlegethon (3. 1600).[15] But if these woes of early love are bad, the later pains of separation and loss are worse by far: like the sufferings of blinded Oedipus, or of one in hell with Proserpina, or of Orpheus complaining eternally with Eurydice, of Myrrha weeping, and of Ixion turning with the tortuous wheel.

> "But ende I wol, as Edippe, in derknesse
> My sorwful lif, and dyen in distresse." (*Tr* 4. 300–01)

> " . . . but down with Proserpyne,
> Whan I am ded, I wol go wone in pyne,
> And ther I wol eternaly compleyne
> My wo, and how that twynned be we tweyne." (*Tr* 4. 473–76)

> [Criseyde, more optimistic than Troilus]
> "Myn herte and ek the woful goost therinne
> Byquethe I, with youre spirit to compleyne
> Eternaly, for they shal nevere twynne.

> For though in erthe ytwynned be we tweyne,
> Yet in the feld of pite, out of peyne,
> That highte Elisos, shal we ben yfeere,
> As Orpheus with Erudice, his fere."   (*Tr* 4. 785–91)

> So bittre teeris weep nought, as I fynde,
> The woful Mirra thorugh the bark and rynde. . . .   (*Tr* 4. 1138–39)

> To bedde he goth, and walweth ther and torneth
> In furie, as doth he Ixion in helle. . . .   (*Tr* 5. 211–12)

Sorrow, complaint, tears, and torment. And when these are seen in conjunction with the allusions to the Furies (4. 22 ff.), the "doom" of Minos (4. 1188), the Fates (4. 1208, 1546; 5. 1–7), the sufferings of Athamas "Eternalich in Stix, the put of helle" (4. 1540), and the torments of the Manes (5. 892), it is clear that Chaucer is insisting in the high style that love's suffering and sorrow are a psychological and moral hell.[16]

Despite their focus on the infernal, these mythic materials are not predictive of damnation; they do not represent a judgment of righteousness announcing that suffering lovers get what they deserve for their passion. Chaucer was no Miss Prism, writing how "the good ended happily, and the bad unhappily." Rather, these allusions are part of a wide-ranging context in which Chaucer insists on painting a double picture of earthly love—just as he does in the gold and black gate-signs in the *Parliament of Fowls*, or in the Knight's playful comment on the conditions of lovers: "Now in the crope, now doun in the breres, / Now up, now down, as boket in a welle" (*KnT* 1532–33). In short Chaucer was not as much concerned with praise and blame as with the typical and actual, pathetic and silly, tragic and comic *conditions* of lovers in the real world. He implies moral purpose or judgment, but his first aim is to create the life of lovers to show *how they fare*. By itself that says a great deal. The mythical allusions from the classical underworld are a means to that end, for they stand against another cluster of joyous mythical allusions which suggest that earthly love is like paradise.[17] And these, too, are expressed in the high style, not only of classical but of Christian allusion: "This joie may nought writen be with inke; / This passeth al that herte may bythynke" (3. 1693–94). Earthly love seems to be heaven; but it is also hell on earth.

For mannes hed ymagynen ne kan,
N'entendement considere, ne tonge telle
The cruele peynes of this sorwful man,
That passen every torment down in helle.   (*Tr* 4. 1695–98)

In what we have seen thus far there are obvious indications that Chaucer sought variety in his use of myth: the tone may be familiar and relaxed, as when allusion enhances the historical setting, or it may be solemn and awesome in a lofty style. The two can also be mixed. The fact that the entry into love may become a venture in infernal sufferings is, for example, implied in Pandare's mythic oath to the three-headed dog at the gate of hell: " 'To Cerberus yn helle ay be I bounde, / Were it for my suster, al thy sorwe, / By my wil she sholde al be thyn to-morwe' " (1. 859–61). If not at once clear, the infernal implications grow evident within a few lines.

But tho gan sely Troilus for to quake
As though men sholde han led hym into helle,
And seyde, "Allas! of al my wo the welle,
Thanne is my swete fo called Criseyde!"   (*Tr* 1. 871–74)

The lover suffers a hell, no doubt, but here and throughout the first three books of the *Troilus* the narrator and Pandare express an attitude toward those sufferings which lacks austerity and immediate seriousness. Both of them encourage us to take a *laissez-faire* stance toward the action. Their language and allusions sometimes plant the seeds of a seriousness to come, but in context they seem "light" or comic.

Consider, for example, the cluster of mythic allusions which suggest treachery; they also, incidentally, imply hell or suffering. At the opening of Book Two Pandare wakens to a reminder of his promise to win Criseyde for Troilus. He hears the song of the swallow (Procne) telling how her husband, Tereus, raped her sister (Philomela).

The swalowe Proigne, with a sorowful lay,
Whan morwen com, gan make hire waymentynge,
Whi she forshapen was; and ever lay
Pandare abedde, half in a slomberynge,
Til she so neigh hym made hire cheterynge

> How Tereus gan forth hire suster take,
> That with the noyse of hire he gan awake,
>
> And gan to calle, and dresse hym up to ryse,
> Remembryng hym his erand was to doone
> From Troilus, and ek his grete emprise. . . .   (2. 64–73)

Pandare of course aims to "take" his niece for Troilus: this is his "grete emprise" and the point of the allusion. In anticipation of the undertaking, the narrator prays to Janus—the god of the entrances or "beginnings" (2. 77), who may also suggest two-faced deception—and then goes on to Pandare's arrival at his niece's house. Pandare, we are told, interrupts the reading of "the siege of Thebes" which Criseyde and her ladies have heard past the point where Oedipus kills his father, and now they are just beginning the account of Amphiaraus' death. They are, in other words, reading tragic stories and the one they are about to start tells how Amphiaraus, betrayed by his wife to join the Argive forces, rides his battle chariot straight to hell.

> "This romaunce is of Thebes that we rede;
> And we han herd how that kyng Layus deyde
> Thorugh Edippus his sone, and al that dede;
> And here we stynten at thise lettres rede,
> How the bisshop, as the book kan telle,
> Amphiorax, fil thorugh the ground to helle."   (*Tr* 2. 100–105)

This is surely not the kind of atmosphere that Pandare has in mind and so he quickly changes the subject: " 'But lat be this, and telle me how ye fare. / Do wey youre barbe, and shewe youre face bare; / Do wey youre book, rys up, and lat us daunce, / And lat us don to May som observaunce' " (2. 108–12). That's the spirit!

The allusions to Procne and Tereus (and Philomela, by implication), and those to Laius, Oedipus, and Amphiaraus invite an uncertain reader reaction, for although they point to deception and tragedy—which will inevitably come—nevertheless the context and the atmosphere do not encourage the reader to take them seriously. At least not now. The same is true of a later reference to Tantalus. As Pandare makes every effort to assure Criseyde that her reputation will be safe if she comes to dine ("soupen" [3. 560]) at his house, he takes a fulsome oath which is so comically exaggerated that the

rhetoric alone is suspect. Troilus will not be there, and there will be
no occasion for gossip.

> He swor hire yis, by stokkes and by stones,
> And by the goddes that in hevene dwelle,
> Or elles were hym levere, soule and bones,
> With Pluto kyng as depe ben in helle
> As Tantalus!—what sholde I more telle?
> Whan al was wel, he roos and took his leve,
> And she to soper com, whan it was eve. . . .   (*Tr* 3. 589–95)

The mythic allusion is perfectly appropriate, but it invites further
suspicion because Tantalus was condemned to hell—unable to reach
food or drink—for deceitfully serving the gods a blasphemous
meal;[18] in other words, Pandare is saying, "If I betray you at my
supper, may I suffer the same fate as that famous dining-room
traitor of legend." The oath and allusion are learnedly funny—witty
if you will.

Not until later when the situation is serious may we reflect on the
smiling face of betrayal, but reflect we will. And in the process we
may recognize that the force of the mythical allusions to treachery
will change from light to dark as Fortune's favor changes. We heard
early in the story, for example, that Criseyde's father was "traitour"
to the town (1. 87), and later we heard her uncle reflect on his own
treachery toward his niece (3. 267–80). Then, in her sorrowful
complaint about her separation from Troilus, we learn that
Criseyde's mother's name was "Argyve," or Argia (4. 762)—the same
as Polyneices' wife (5. 1509), who possessed the fatal "broche" of
Thebes and who helped her husband to the war which brought his
death. Her attractively poisonous brooch, made by Vulcan as a
vengeful gift for the offspring of Mars and Venus, was for Chaucer a
sign of treachery and tragedy;[19] the fact that Criseyde is related to it
through her mother's name is a minor detail, of course, but it is
another part of the more serious context for love's disaster and
betrayal which becomes evident with the change in the face of
Fortune, who

> . . . semeth trewest whan she wol bygyle,
> And kan to fooles so hire song entune,
> That she hem hent and blent, traitour comune!   (4. 3–5)

Several later allusions fit this same beguiling pattern. Criseyde's overflowing oath of fidelity, for example, calls down on her head the torment which Juno inflicted on Athamas, "a type of the 'falsitori,'" who betrayed his wife (4. 1534–40);[20] she then appeals to every deity, large and small, with a rhetoric that wants desperately to be true but which suspects itself of lying.

> "And this on every god celestial
> I swere it yow, and ek on ech goddesse,
> On every nymphe and deite infernal,
> On satiry and fawny more and lesse,
> That halve goddes ben of wildernesse;
> And Attropos my thred of lif tobreste,
> If I be fals! now trowe me if yow leste!"   (*Tr* 4. 1541–47)

The emphasis falls on the sensuous deities of the woods (nymphe, satiry, fawny); on hell and death, and on "trowe me if you leste." In fact, as Chaucer so often does with material like this, the language has a cosmic sweep which encompasses all creation Catholic style: the heavens (celestial), the earth (wildernesse), and the underworld (infernal).

Muted, by comparison, is the mythical song which Troilus hears on the morning he expects Criseyde to return. The narrator has just finished making explicit her change of heart and love to Diomede (5. 1023–99) when the scene shifts back to Troy.

> The laurer-crowned Phebus, with his heete,
> Gan, in his course ay upward as he wente,
> To warmen of the est see the wawes weete,
> And Nysus doughter song with fressh entente,
> Whan Troilus his Pandare after sente;
> And on the walles of the town they pleyde,
> To loke if they kan sen aught of Criseyde.   (*Tr* 5. 1107–13)

The allusion is an interesting blend. Nisus's daughter had fallen in love with the besieging General, Minos, after seeing him from the city walls of Megara; so her stance and Troilus's are obliquely related. But the key fact in the parallel is that Nisus's daughter betrayed her father and her city.[21] She sings of treachery.

Connected with these are several mythical references that are subsumed by the imagery and significance of the moon, the traditional figure of fickle Fortune. These are at once a means of measuring the ten days between Criseyde's departure and her supposed return, and a means of picturing Fortune's treachery: Criseyde will come back before the moon passes from Aries to beyond Leo.

> "And trusteth this, that certes, herte swete,
> Er Phebus suster, Lucina the sheene,
> The Leoun passe out of this Ariete,
> I wol ben here, withouten any wene.
> I mene, as helpe me Juno, hevenes quene,
> The tenthe day, but if that deth m'assaile,
> I wol yow sen, withouten any faille."   (*Tr* 4. 1590–96)

Lucina is the moon, and so, for that matter, is Juno to whom Criseyde prays; and so is Cynthia a few lines later.

> "Now, for the love of Cinthia the sheene,
> Mistrust me nought thus causeles, for routhe,
> Syn to be trewe I have yow plight my trouthe."   (*Tr* 4. 1608–
>   10)

Prayers to the inconstant moon are ominous, of course, but Chaucer was building up to something richer than an omen. In the following passage Latona is the moon and the time for Criseyde's promised return is measured by its eclipsing light, a natural, dramatic image of Fortune failing.

> And every nyght, as was his wone to doone,
> He stood the brighte moone to byholde,
> And al his sorwe he to the moone tolde,
> And seyde, "Ywis, whan thow art horned newe,
> I shal be glad, if al the world be trewe!
>
> I saugh thyn hornes olde ek by the morwe,
> Whan hennes rood my righte lady dere,
> That cause is of my torment and my sorwe;
> For which, O brighte Latona the clere,
> For love of God, ren faste aboute thy spere!

For whan thyne hornes newe gynnen sprynge,
Than shal she come that may my blisse brynge." (*Tr* 5. 647–
58)

Irony at last compounds the pathos of events, for after the dark
misfortune of the tenth day—the new moon, and Criseyde not
returned—the sky will declare the bitterness of love betrayed: the
new "hornes" of Fortune's cuckold.

The brief mythological allusions in *Troilus and Criseyde* suggest
several things. Almost every allusion has a meaning which is either
immediately obvious in itself (Mars = rashness; Lucina = the
moon) or clear from its context (Fury = muse of torment and
sorrow; Pallas = goddess of widowhood, or wisdom, or battle). Also,
Chaucer seems to have been intent on dispersing his allusions—they
are spread rather evenly through the five books—and on incorporat-
ing them into careful patterns that are basically nonmythological
and thematic. They are *made* unobtrusive by being spaced apart and
then subordinated to action, characterization, and rhetorical structures. If he had wanted, Chaucer could easily have made a mythic
frame from, for example, the story of Mars and Venus, and built on
it the story of Troilus and Criseyde. Much of the language and
action of his *Complaint of Mars* suggest that he did in fact
experiment with astronomy and myth in this way, and that he was
aware of numerous parallels between Mars and Troilus, Venus and
Criseyde. But apparently this sort of broad, mythical analogizing or
"allegorizing" did not really interest him when he wrote the
Troilus. His mind was on other things, and to these he made myth
the handmaid.

At times his concern was focused on internal juxtapositions of
narrative elements, similar to those in the *Book of the Duchess* but
now more broadly and systematically balanced. For example, Pandare's little invocation to Mars and the Furies (2. 435–41) is
intended to suggest tragedy to Criseyde—that her cold reserve will
bring death to him and to Troilus; but this is primarily comical. On
the other hand, the narrator's subsequent invocation to Mars and
the Furies (4. 22–28) is utterly serious. Similarly, Criseyde's apparently sincere prayer to Pallas, when she begs her patroness for help
(2. 421–27), echoes in her later empty oath to the same goddess on

behalf of "faithful" widowhood (5. 977–78). The story of Thebes, which was first heard in the relaxed atmosphere of Criseyde's house (2. 99 ff.), is again heard, and in much greater detail, when Cassandra tells Troilus that he has lost his beloved to Diomede (5. 1457 ff.). And one may recall that the moon—whether mythically labeled or not—was dark on the night of Criseyde's betrayal (on her tenth day away from Troy), after it had earlier been dark on the night when Troilus and Criseyde first consummated their love (3. 547–53, 624). In sum, there are a number of instances where mythic materials are made part of a large pattern of juxtaposition which, as I have noted elsewhere,[22] works in the reader's memory to disclose the deepest of tragic effects by a gradual, continuing contrast between past joy and present sorrow.

> "For of fortunes sharpe adversitee
> The worste kynde of infortune is this,
> A man to han ben in prosperitee,
> And it remembren, whan it passed is." (*Tr* 3. 1625–28)

Besides appearing in echoing contrasts, some of the mythical allusions in the *Troilus* are influenced by a pattern which parallels Chaucer's design for tragedy: "Fro wo to wele, and after out of joie." In some the emphasis rests on the sorrowful or joyful conditions in the narrative: as when we find allusions to Niobe and Tityus (1. 699 and 786) in the context of Troilus's first woe; or to the joys of Venus, Cupid, Hymen, and the deities in love (e.g., 3. 712–35 and 1254–60) when Troilus approaches bliss; and to Oedipus, Proserpina, Minos, Atropos, Orpheus, and Ixion when Fortune leads Troilus to suffering and death. Like similar allusions in the *Book of the Duchess*, these often reflect and elaborate moral or psychological states of turmoil; in other words, irrational behavior brings with it its special torments. The difference in the *Troilus*, however, is that such allusions are more human because they have been made dramatic elements in an ancient setting. They appear less "artificial" (imposed from without by an artist/poet) because they seem to develop from an inner necessity for historical characters to express themselves in ways which are "natural" for them and which satisfy our expectations. Thus Pandare's "lore" is the basis for his mention of Oënone's letter to Paris, and also for his comparison of Troilus to Niobe (1. 652 ff. and 699), and Troilus's relative inexperience is the grounds for his ignorance of both these allusions (1. 657 and 759). In such cases Chaucer's skill and originality come less from rhetorical than dramatic ability—his capacity to imagine "real" speech in "real" action.

The tragic design of action is also reflected in a broad pattern similar to that found earlier in the contrasting allusions to the moon in Book Three (549–50, 624) and to Diana, Juno, Latona, and Cynthia in Books Four and Five. As that design was hidden in the narrative, so too are the bird songs of the poem: often couched in classical legend, they sound notes of a tragic evolution. Thus Procne's song of Tereus's raping Philomela (2. 64–70) turns into the attractive love song of the nightingale (Philomela) when Criseyde dreams of love (2. 918–24) and is later filled with love (3. 1233–39). But with Fortune's change we hear "Escaphilo," the owl who bodes death (5. 316–20), and then the lark—Nisus's daughter—who sings of love's treachery (5. 1110). The songs, in other words, come full circle with the narrative.

A similar development which reflects the overall picture of the tragedy can be found in the mythic statements that introduce the five books of the *Troilus*. All of them sound thematic notes, and they also call attention to themselves since four of them are formal invocations. Moreover, they are tonal, for despite their differences they work together to create a general mood of grandeur which suits a book that would follow in the steps of "Virgile, Ovide, Omer, Lucan, and Stace." Their moods, like their themes, will vary in an orderly and purposeful way.

Tisiphone is the poet's muse of suffering and sorrow for the *whole* poem: "Thesiphone, thow help me for t'endite / Thise woful vers, that wepen as I write . . . (1. 6 ff.). Within the confines of Book One, however, the invocation to the Fury prepares for the early tears and torments of Troilus in love. She accompanies and prefigures the "woo" and "every torment and adversite" which make the "Canticus Troili" (1. 400–20) a "waillynge" and a "pleynte"; she sets the scene for Troilus's sorrow and woe which Pandare will confront and seek to counter. In Book Two the muse becomes Clio, the companion of the rhetorician who "endites" a chronicle and who gives an apparently straightforward account from his Latin source of "how Troilus com to his lady grace" (2. 8–35).[23] Here the muse creates and reflects another mood to come which can be somewhat comical because Clio brings with her a reportorial distance which the poet wants in order to be credible. He himself is uninvolved in love and somewhat amused by it, but he doesn't want to be blamed for his detachment or by those who may think that *they* would not act or talk as Troilus does—" 'so nold I nat love purchace' " (2. 33); thus he takes the position that he is simply stating the facts as he finds them: "Myn auctour shal I folwen, if I konne."

At the beginning of Book Three the poet's attitude has changed again. The full force of love's joy and sweetness comes pressing in upon him and his story so that he must shift from his objective stance and plead for help from Venus ("Plesance of love" [3. 4]) fairly to represent "som joye of that is felt in thi servyse" (3. 42). Because he sympathizes with love's servants ("whos clerc I am"), he seeks aid from the fullness of Venus's power—"in hevene and helle, in erthe and salte see"—as that power influences creation, peace and friendship, the fortunes of fish and finally of lovers. Then to treat love in a proper style he calls on Calliope who was traditionally *the best voice* of the Muses: "thi vois be now present, / For now is nede" (3. 45–46).[24] At the end of Book Three, when the bliss and "wele" of love have been seen, the poet expresses his last thanks and praise— not only to Venus, but to her blind and winged son as well; not simply to Calliope, but to all nine of the Muses.

> Thow lady bryght, the doughter to Dyone,
> Thy blynde and wynged sone ek, daun Cupide,
> Yee sustren nyne ek, that by Elicone
> In hil Pernaso listen for t'abide,
> That ye thus fer han deyned me to gyde,
> I kan namore, but syn that ye wol wende,
> Ye heried ben for ay withouten ende!   (*Tr* 3. 1807–13)

The Muses, too, will "wende" as Fortune turns everything around.

Now the lovely song of Calliope changes to the dark complaints of the Furies, and Venus's joyous pleasure turns to Mars's cruel ire.

> O ye Herynes, Nyghtes doughtren thre,
> That endeles compleignen evere in pyne,
> Megera, Alete, and ek Thesiphone;
> Thow cruel Mars ek, fader to Quyryne,
> This ilke ferthe book me helpeth fyne,
> So that the losse of lyf and love yfeere
> Of Troilus be fully shewed heere.   (*Tr* 4. 22–28)

The suffering and weeping of Tisiphone in Book One will seem like nothing compared to the full sorrow and complaint of all three Furies. Again and again they will sing of "losse" of love; and mingled with their tormented music, angry Mars will tell of "woodnesse," of "rage," of thoughts of suicide and "losse of lyf."[25]

Although the Mars-and-Fury invocation of Book Four is the last of its kind, the opening stanza of Book Five serves a purpose akin to an invocation. It emphasizes in mythic terms the fatal mood of the last book; and it also restates the two themes of Troilus's certain loss of love and life "yfeere."

> Aprochen gan the fatal destyne
> That Joves hath in disposicioun,
> And to yow, angry Parcas, sustren thre,
> Committeth to don execucioun;
> For which Criseyde moste out of the town,
> And Troilus shal dwellen forth in pyne
> Til Lachesis his thred no lenger twyne.   (*Tr* 5. 1–7)

At the conclusion of the story the three Fates are in control, all options seem to be gone ("Criseyde *moste* out of the town"), and the principal characters pathetically find themselves in varying stages of *rigor mortis*. No one can do or say anything more or anything different. Pandare can talk only of past satisfactions and of his hatred for pleasure gone, for Criseyde: " 'I dide al that the leste' " and " 'I kan namore seye.' " Criseyde will continue to slide with the course of events. And Troilus will remain pitifully fixed to a love that is dead and gone.

Overall, the mythological statements which introduce each book of the *Troilus* work together to establish an overt pattern of tragic action: from Tisiphone's woe to Clio's hopeful report and the "wele" of Venus and the Muses; then back to the Furies and Mars, to the Fates and tragedy's double sorrow—the sorrow of having loved *and* the sorrow of having lost.[26] I have suggested elsewhere the possibility that these five mythical statements and the five-book structure of the *Troilus* resulted from Chaucer's adoption (and adaptation) of the book divisions and themes in Boethius's *De Consolatione*.[27] But however closely or loosely one reads those parallels, it should be clear that these particular classical allusions are again subordinated to a nonmythological, indeed, to a philosophical design for tragedy which aims to move its reader through five interrelated moods and themes, and ultimately in two different directions at once: toward sympathy for the tragic protagonist and rejection of the cause of his tragedy. To try to "solve" that paradox in a strictly rational way seems needless, indeed unwise, because that would force one to erase a real ambiguity which the poet himself resolves only with a supernatural act of faith. Troilus's torments (and joys) were, from the first, tied to the natural "blynde lust, the which that may nat laste"; in the end they are "the fyn and guerdoun for travaille / Of Jove, Appollo, of Mars, of swich rascaille!" In other words the pagan deities, the figures from classical legend and the characters themselves are bound from beginning to end by an ancient, naturalistic existence in which human potential is flawed and human vision limited by the absence of supernatural possibilities.

In a substantive way, then, the brief allusions in the *Troilus* are like those in the *Book of the Duchess* in that they reflect (along with occasional joys) the shortcomings and self-deception, the sufferings and self-torments of a "natural life." There is no unfettered joy, no blitheness, repose, or serenity in the classical world which Chaucer's allusions help to recreate from ancient history and its people. As Chaucer saw it, that past, with all its earthly loftiness, was a tottering "through the one transitory instability":

> For as yet, that heavenly doctrine was not delivered unto the world, which, purifying the heart by faith, changes the affection with a zealous piety to desire and aim at the blessing of heaven, or those which are above the heavens, and frees men absolutely from the slavery of those proud and ungracious devils [gods].[28]

Like the Christian world which he portrayed elsewhere, Chaucer's classical world was a composite of joy and suffering; but more than that, and finally, it failed to offer real hope or freedom. Chaucer does not say that. His classical characters say it for themselves, as Troilus does after his death, as Virginia does at the moment of her death in the *Physician's Tale*, and as the Good Women do when they are left alone and abandoned. For all of them, often admirable yet frail, death is in fact the end "of every worldly soore."

3 Myth and Allegory

Two of the principal ways by which classical myth passed from antiquity to the Middle Ages were academic glossings, such as those by Servius on the works of Virgil, and encyclopedic gatherings like the three Vatican Mythographies. These often worked hand in hand so that material from one format moved to the other, and then back again. John the Scot, for example, drew on the handbooks of Fulgentius and Isidore of Seville for his commentary on the *Marriage of Mercury and Philology*, and Paul of Perugia and Thomas Walsingham (centuries later) used the standard handbooks for their commentaries on Persius and Ovid.[1] The result was an academic tradition which had two striking features: (1) a general consistency in mythological interpretations over a period of almost one thousand years, and (2) a broad consistency in purpose. The goal remained the same—to explain or to understand the deities and the legends with which they were associated either in terms of natural physical forces or perennial human behavior. Moreover, by the later Middle Ages, many traditional interpretations of the deities which may seem allegorical to us were so well grounded and familiar that they ceased to be more than figurative expressions, personifications, or metaphors. It was almost a literal rendering, therefore, to indicate that Neptune meant the sea, that Jove stood for order and justice, that Mars referred to aggressive actions, and that the Judgment of Paris represented a choice among human goals—money, learning, and pleasure. The lesson in this is that allegorized myth should not be mistaken for something else, for something which may simply be metaphor, *exemplum*, or analogy. When speaking of allegory and allegorized myth, therefore, I mean a discourse more ample and extended than the classical allusions discussed in the previous chapter; I mean one that develops through the course of narrative, drama, or description in such a way that a reader gradually recognizes the dominance of intellectual patterns.

Like the exegetical readings of the Bible, medievalized mythography may lead to intellectual patterns which are primarily theological, philosophical, or moral. Chaucer had encountered such adaptations of classical myth, naturally enough, in the course of his readings—some of them created by pious, religious impositions upon myth, some by rhetorical and stylistic alterations of traditional materials, and some by extensions in detail and meaning which made an idea (and its attendant notions, causes, circumstances, and effects) the paramount concern. He had apparently read, for example, the imposed theological allegories of the *Ovide Moralisé*; and he certainly knew Boethius's artful reworkings of legends, like that of Orpheus and Eurydice, which develop implicit theological and philosophical purposes and then state them explicitly.

> Allas! whanne Orpheus and his wyf weren almest at the termes of the nyght (*that is to seyn, at the laste boundes of helle*), Orpheus lokede abakward on Erudyce his wif, and lost hire, and was deed. This fable apertenith to yow alle, whosoevere desireth or seketh to lede his thought into the sovereyn day (*that is to seyn, into cleernesse of sovereyn good*). For whoso that evere be so overcomen that he ficche his eien into the put of helle (*that is to seyn, whoso sette his thoughtes in erthly thinges*), al that evere he hath drawen of the noble good celestial he lesith it, whanne he looketh the helles. . . .   (III met. 12)

Again, he had seen Alanus de Insulis's lofty picture of Jupiter the Thunderer in the theological/philosophical allegory of the *Anticlaudian*; also Dante's terrifying picture of the three Furies in the moral allegory of *Inferno*, Canto IX; and the descriptions and dramas of Cupid and Venus in the comic moral allegory of the *Roman de la Rose.*[2]

These and more were not wasted on Geoffrey Chaucer. But if I may be excused for looking ahead momentarily, the surprising thing is the clarity of his response. He showed no interest at all in the imposed theological allegorizations of myth, and almost from the beginning he withdrew from and avoided the sort of moral allegorizing of myth that he had seen in the *Roman de la Rose*. Whether in allegorical or literal contexts, his use of classical legends as exemplary fables tended toward multiple and inverted meanings rather than toward the kind of singular allegorical meanings which he had seen in Boethius.[3] And yet, for several years at least, he was almost a traditionalist. He became particularly interested in the kinds of moral and philosophical allegorizing of myth that he encountered in Dante and Boccaccio, and these he would adapt with some flippancy, and at times some grandeur, in the *House of Fame*, the *Parliament of Fowls*, and the *Knight's Tale*.

In the *Book of the Duchess*, where the Black Knight tells how he became subject to love—how he "fell in love," Chaucer touches one of the most familiar forms of allegorized myth. The passage in question (*BD* 759 ff.) owes a good deal to the *Roman de la Rose*, but, by substituting "love" for Cupid or Amor and "plesaunce" for Venus, Chaucer has demythologized the material and drawn allegory into a realistic context.[4] Thus the Black Knight observes that for several years before he saw his Lady White—when he first had a youthful, natural understanding of what love was—he became "tributarye" and gave "rente" to love,

> ". . . hooly with good entente,
> And throgh plesaunce [Venus] become his [Cupid's] thral
> With good wille, body, hert, and al."   (cf. *BD* 759–68)

This early, indiscriminate stage of the Black Knight's devotion ("Al were to me ylyche good") prepares for the moment when by "hap" or "grace" he thoughtlessly makes his lady the single object of his desire: "I ne tok / No maner counseyl but at hir lok / And at myn herte" (*BD* 839–41).

This part of the Black Knight's autobiography is an adaptation of a convention of moral allegory. The substitutions for Cupid and Venus consciously avoid mythological cliché, but the traditional elements are all here. The Black Knight presents his early adolescent ("teenage") attitude toward love—"Yowthe, my maistresse, / Governed me in ydelnesse"—and then shows it focused and particularized in a mode that is thoughtless ("no maner counseyl"), embarrassingly secretive, and ecstatically or impossibly ideal. There is nothing overwhelmingly romantic in this, however, for although the Black Knight glamorizes the history of his love somewhat, his report is dampened both by the noncommittal response of his audience (Chaucer's seemingly dull narrator) and by the rather ordinary character of the event: the passage through puberty to first love. There is, moreover, nothing especially disastrous in what we read; it is not an account of moral or spiritual bankruptcy which invites condemnation. Indeed, the experience of youth adjusting to desire and then falling in love with love, whether seen in the cynical comedy of an Ovidian context or with Chaucer's sympathetic and amused detachment, has changed little over the centuries in both life and fiction. Chaucer's Knight describes that experience—in one of Theseus's famous speeches—as an adolescent, mindless, marvelous, somewhat silly, and entirely normal experience (*KnT* 1785 ff.). In the *Troilus* such love (Cupid) is identified with the "lawe of kynde," and although it may be cruel, irrational, and disturbing, it is nevertheless a natural force which everyone lives with for better or worse, usually for a while, but in some rare, tragic cases sorrowfully until death. "This was, and is, and yet men shal it see" (*Tr* 1. 245).

The opening of *Troilus and Criseyde* presents a realistic elaboration on the same convention. With his crowd of young friends Troilus enjoys looking at the girls—at *all* of them—"to preise and lakken whom hym leste" (*Tr* 1. 189); but soon the narrator interrupts this familiar action by shifting to an overt mythological allegory just after Troilus makes fun of lovers.

> And with that word he [Troilus] gan caste up the browe,
> Ascaunces, "Loo! is this naught wisely spoken?"
> At which the God of Love gan loken rowe
> Right for despit, and shop for to ben wroken.
> He kidde anon his bowe nas naught broken;
> For sodeynly he hitte hym atte fulle;
> And yet as proud a pekok kan he pulle.   (*Tr* 1. 204–10)

Compared to the mode of the *Roman de la Rose*, or even the *Book of the Duchess*, this Cupid works like lightning. Just one line. And then the poet immediately amplifies on the same event by describing it nonmythologically—as it "really" happened.

> Withinne the temple he wente hym forth pleyinge,
> This Troilus, of every wight aboute,
> On this lady, and now on that, lokynge,
> Wher so she were of town or of withoute;
> And upon cas bifel that thorugh a route
> His eye percede, and so depe it wente,
> Til on Criseyde it smot, and ther it stente.   (*Tr* 1. 267–73)

Although the onomatopoeia of the last line helps Cupid's arrow hit its target, the passage actually translates the earlier brief allegory into familiar drama, and Troilus responds with language that is even more familiar ("Where have you been all my life?"): " 'O mercy, God,' thoughte he, 'wher hastow woned, / That art so feyr and goodly to devise?' " (*Tr* 1. 276–77).

Even more important than Chaucer's humanizing of a conventional allegorical pattern, however, are the comments of both his narrator and Troilus. These interrupt and mingle with the action in such ways that they invite multiple and contradictory reactions in the audience. For example, the narrator first responds with a comment on Troilus's folly in supposing that he is, for some reason, above falling in love ("For kaught is proud, and kaught is debonaire"); next, he focuses on the pragmatic virtue of giving in to love ("Now sith it may nat goodly ben withstonde. . . ."); and then, although he is amazed at Cupid's power (*Tr* 1. 308), he recognizes that the end result can be disastrous since Troilus is "ful unavysed of his woo comynge." Like the narrator, Troilus finds himself at odds. He has already made fun of the folly and suffering of lovers (*Tr* 1. 190–203), but now he is dumbstruck by love's attraction and soon must repeat his mockery to disguise his feelings (*Tr* 1. 330–50). From such full and conflicting reports we have to assume that Chaucer is not so much narrating an event now in an allegorical and now in a realistic mode (although he does this) as he is creating a conflict of perceptions and responses. His imagination does not focus primarily on what happens, and certainly not on a single meaning in what happens, but on the complexities and contradictions inherent in a situation that involves both Troilus's "joie" and "his cares colde" (*Tr* 1. 264).

The adaptations of mythical allegory in the *Book of the Duchess* and *Troilus* are brief indeed, and, as with their appearance in the French tradition from which Chaucer drew them, their concern is with a process of love which can and might be examined in detail—intellectually and microscopically. But Chaucer's interests lie elsewhere, in different matters and modes; indeed, when other opportunities arise to use this allegory he invariably avoids it. Palamon and Arcite are struck by the beauty of Emelye, one stung "unto the herte" and "wounded sore," and the other "sodeynly" slain; but there is no blind Bowboy, no armory of arrows, and none of the classical personifications or other paraphernalia that medieval literature could provide. Nicholas in the *Miller's Tale* simply grabs the nearest lovely, and January in the *Merchant's Tale* rests his mind as "in a commune market-place" and chooses one from among hundreds. The Wife of Bath thinks on Jankyn's "paire / Of legges and of feet so clene and faire"; and two others who fall in love more fastidiously—Ariadne and Phaedra—seem most concerned that they will be "duchesses" and "likly to ben quenes" (*LGW* 2126-29). In fact, where his source includes only the mildest mythological allegory like this—in Virgil's account of Dido's falling in love with Aeneas, when Cupid is disguised as Ascanius—Chaucer excludes it. He omits it from his version in the *House of Fame* and he disowns it outright in the *Legend of Good Women*.

> But natheles, oure autour telleth us,
> That Cupido, that is the god of love,
> At preyere of his moder hye above,
> Hadde the liknesse of the child ytake,
> This noble queen enamored to make
> On Eneas; but, as of that scripture,
> Be as be may, I take of it no cure.   (*LGW* 1139-45)

Still, Chaucer's skirting of one kind of allegory seems to have had no influence on his willingness to accept another.

In place of the continuous love allegory of moral psychology which employs type characterization ("the lover") and its companion mythological figures (Cupid = concupiscence, Venus = delight, Narcissus = self-love), Chaucer turned to a broader, philosophical form which he could isolate as a unit and/or incorporate with other, more realistic modes of discourse. At another time or place he might have found this sort of allegorizing in Plato or Euripides, but its possibilities reached him through his reading of Dante and Boccaccio, and perhaps of Statius and Petrarch. This

other kind of mythological allegory could be architecturally grand
and descriptive—the temples of Venus and Mars in the *Teseida;* and
it could be realistically dramatic—Dante's encounters with Virgil,
with the Furies, and with Statius. For Chaucer the distinguishing
feature of this allegory was its capacity to develop an idea or a
complex of ideas, briefly or extensively, within a literary context
that could be made to appear actual, historical, and individual.
Thus, in the *Parliament of Fowls* he would alter Boccaccio's
mythical allegory on the power of love to create a vignette of love's
tragic pattern; and in the *Knight's Tale* he would broaden Boccaccio's allegorized myth to create a picture of a chivalric ideal. But
first, in the *House of Fame,* he would experiment with everything—
everything from classical *exemplum,* to mythological dramatic
allegory, to partly mythological descriptive allegory. And to these he
would add some epic invocations. Taken altogether, the literary
elements of our classical heritage have never been so comically
cudgeled by an Englishman.

   The *House of Fame* consists of three kinds of material which are
different in mode, but dramatically and thematically related. Book
One centers on the past, on Geoffrey the love poet's memory of
Virgil's epic; it is a disturbing experience. Book Two is a contempo-
raneous allegorical action, a mythological flight of the mind in
which Geoffrey is learning. And Book Three is largely an allegorical
vision, a *pictura* of Geoffrey's developing perception of what earthly
fame has been and will always be. As poet and dreamer, Chaucer
takes us on a journey through a world of learning—much of it
classical—where the legendary past proves decorously arid, the
"scientific" present tediously useful; and where the encompassing
sight of fame proves absurdly grand, unstable, and evanescent.[5]
   As the poet's dream begins he finds himself in what seems to be
the mirror of his mind, within a glass temple where he reflects on
his devotion to the literature of love. He sees Venus and Cupid in
their traditional "portreyture" (*HF* 130-39),[6] images of the love
theme which we learn he has "served so ententyfly" (*HF* 614-19) as
a writer. And he sees Virgil's poem, probably the most renowned of
all the many "another book" that he has studied so tirelessly (*HF*
652-60).

>   "I wol now singen, yif I kan,
>   The armes, and also the man

> That first cam, thurgh his destinee,
> Fugityf of Troy contree. . . . (*HF* 143 ff.)

The recapitulation of the *Aeneid* which follows is actually a double story evenly divided, almost fifty-fifty, between the tragedy of Dido (143 lines) and the exploits of Aeneas (135 lines).[7]

On one hand we see Dido's story of impetuous love (*HF* 239–382) which ends in her rash and pathetic suicide and which survives in her wicked fame: " '. . . my name lorn, / And alle myn actes red and songe / Over al thys lond, on every tonge.' " The narrative and the narrator alike point to the unfairness of it, for Dido was truly deceived (as she deceived herself, no doubt); she was betrayed, abandoned, and shamed by Aeneas, and to top it off she is judged badly by all the world.

> "Eke, though I myghte duren ever,
> That I have don, rekever I never,
> That I ne shal be seyd, allas,
> Yshamed be thourgh Eneas,
> And that I shal thus juged be,—
> 'Loo, ryght as she hath don, now she
> Wol doo eft-sones, hardely;'
> Thus seyth the peple prively." (*HF* 353–60)

Thus Dido. But on the other hand, what of Aeneas? In the past he had been regularly blessed by good fortune (*HF* 143–238; 427–67): he fled and escaped the fall of Troy; he was favored by Jove against Juno's destructiveness; and wandering ashore he was comforted by Venus's intervention and Dido's affection. Now, of course, he sails off again to escape another storm, to be helped by the Sybil, to slay Turnus and win Lavinia. The "book," says Chaucer briefly, excuses Aeneas "fullyche of al his grete trespas," but what does this mean against the persistent accusations of treachery? Indeed, the narrator's long list of analogs (*HF* 383–426) from other stories almost comically belabors Aeneas as false: as false as Demophon to Phyllis, Achilles to Briseis, Paris to Oënone, Jason to Hypsipyle and Medea, etc., etc. Still, at journey's end this shifty Trojan prince finds favor from the "goddys celestials" and approval from the heavens (*HF* 459–67). He has not only "acheved al his aventure," but he is thought well of to boot!

If there is a sensible conclusion to this redaction of the *Aeneid*, it is that the noble worlds of antiquity and poetic report are surely madcap worlds. They cannot be trusted. Aeneas the lucky and protected traitor—"Thumbs up!" says Fame, and Virgil too. But what of Dido, the tragic victim of passion? "Thumbs down!" says Fame, and the *Aeneid* proves it. The issue, then, is not love and fortune, although they are relevant; and it is certainly not earthly as opposed to heavenly fame. The point is simply that fame, supported by literary record, is entirely irrational and unfair. The "noble temple" of ancient love literature which Geoffrey has devoted himself to may be filled with rich artistic decorations (*HF* 121 ff.; 468–73), but outside it lies a desert which elicits fear and then a plea for help. There is surely something absurd in this. For although Geoffrey would like to believe that he has experienced a nightmare, "fantome and illusion" (*HF* 482–94), or a dream of no account, he has, ironically, seen a truth which he cannot or will not accept. The proud and jaunty narrator who had begun to tell his dream with all the assurance he could muster has now been reduced to a figure of terrified uncertainty—and even prayer!

Although part of a psychological dream allegory, the classical material in Book One of the *House of Fame* cannot properly be called allegorized myth. The brief portraits of Venus and Cupid with which the dream begins help to identify the temple of glass as Chaucer's palace of art, of *love* literature, but in this role they are figural labels rather than allegorized deities. Furthermore, the retelling of the *Aeneid* does not constitute an *allegoria* in which characters and incidents represent something other, or something more than they are; like the story of Ceyx and Alcyone in the *Book of the Duchess*, it is a skewed *exemplum:* a historical legend whose meaning is not specified and whose significance can be deduced only from its context. Be that as it may, Book Two does use classical myth as its allegorical vehicle. Jove's eagle swoops down and seizes Geoffrey. It carries him off to the mansion of Fame, and in the process it lessons him in the scientific nature of Fame and in the relevant laws of physics. Jove and his eagle, then, are more than simply representations of ideas—emblems, if you will; they are dramatic figures in an allegorical action, one offstage and the other acting for him.

The suggestion has already been made that we might interpret Jove as the Christian God and, from that basis, understand that his eagle represents something like the force of divine wisdom or insight.[8] However, when such "wisdom" expresses itself in a parody of a scholastic lecture in natural philosophy on such mundane matters as *place, sound,* and *motion,* and when it deposits Geoffrey in a middle-world of noise and confusion, we have good reasons for doubting any lofty meanings. Moreover, if we look to classical and medieval precedents (in conjunction with Chaucer's context), there is ample evidence for our being satisfied with allegorical meanings that are less than theological. From both glosses and mythological compendia there is a long tradition which associated "Jove" with the created laws of nature, and which accordingly had him represent those laws that govern the natural generation and continuation of life, and the right, just, and benevolent ordering of earthly things.[9]

From the perspective of this tradition Jove's considerate attitude toward Geoffrey makes good sense. The god has seen Geoffrey labor attentively at love poetry, but with no results. He knows how Geoffrey has written of love without having had a share in love; and he knows how he has praised love and "furthered" love's folk without even a report to show for it. As the eagle says at length, Jove knows that Geoffrey has not been treated squarely.

> "Certeyn, he hath of the routhe,
> That thou so longe trewely
> Hast served so ententyfly
> Hys blynde nevew Cupido,
> And faire Venus also,
> Withoute guerdon ever yit,
> And never-the-lesse hast set thy wit—
> Although that in thy hed ful lyte is—
> To make bookys, songes, dytees,
> In ryme, or elles in cadence,
> As thou best canst, in reverence
> Of Love, and of hys servantes eke. . . ."   (*HF* 614 ff.)

Thus Jove aims, at long last, to render justice. He will redress an imbalance and he will repay the poet "in som recompensacion / Of labour and devocion"; he "wol with som maner thing the quyte" (*HF* 661–71). And his means for doing this—the eagle and the flight—are neither divine nor highly philosophical.

Indeed, it is fair to say that with whatever else it may embody,

Jove's eagle represents a naturally intelligent and rather obvious insight into human and physical problems. It is, I think, Geoffrey's own experiential, practical thinking. It has no concern whatever for the illusions of poetry or of the past: for Venus, Cupid, and the Muses, or for Aeneas, Dido, and Virgil. Its style reflects its being. Simple and long-winded, it is that faculty or force which perceives the dull, unvarnished truths of common life, of nature, and of comedy. It speaks with a funny sort of inflated simplicity.

> "Withoute any subtilite
> Of speche, or gret prolixite
> Of termes of philosophie,
> Of figures of poetrie,
> Or colours of rethorike. . . .   (*HF* 855 ff.)

None of the "noblesse of ymages, ne such richesse" of art as Geoffrey saw and told about in Book One! And in substance, Geoffrey's bookish memories from Virgil and Ovid—or now from the likes of "Boece," "Marcian," and "Anteclaudian" (*HF* 972–90)—contrast sharply with what the eagle presents. It shows Geoffrey the thing itself—physical reality in all its luminous existence. And the experience is almost too much. As one who has scarcely ever bothered about what was going on with his next-door "neyghebores," Geoffrey finds this eagle trip partly mind-shattering and partly a bore. At its beginning he had had a grand "fantasye" (*HF* 593) of flying like Enoch or Elijah, like Ganymede or Romulus, and becoming a star—wow! He was wrong then, and he is wrong again now when he thinks he is on the "fetheres of Philosophye" piercing beyond the elements to the highest region of the heavens. That too is just another "fantasye" (*HF* 992), for although the eagle's wings take Geoffrey up, he attains no more than a vision of where things really stand and how they really are: of the clouds, the mists, the rains, the winds, the constellations of the sky, and finally, bathetically, human fame or some of the sounds which people make.

Geoffrey has read much, but now he actually sees things. In the process he learns one of "Jove's" great laws: EVERYTHING IN CREATION HAS ITS PROPER PLACE; and he is taught a comic corollary of that law: fame is nothing more than "broken air" (*HF* 765)—a cosmic flatus[10]—which tends upward and comes to rest in its own peculiar natural place. Although Geoffrey shows some comic reluctance to perceive what stands before his eyes, his practical, experiential mind prevails. Toward the end he will be well satisfied to recognize the simple fact that he (of all people!) knows best his own condition, the place where he stands, but that will happen only after he has viewed the grand fatuousness of all worldly reports.

The last book of the *House of Fame* incorporates a good deal of classical legend and myth, adapted in allegorical pictures and allegorical action, to help illuminate the nature of Fame. In the "hous," the "kynde place" or "mansioun" of Fame, figures from classical antiquity become part of a decorative panorama of meaning. Historical chronology, geographic range, and "great themes" all come together in a deliriously mock-heroic allegory. And everyone creates illusions: musicians, magicians, *poets, and historians!* Those in the outside niches of the place either played or tricked their way to fame: harpers from the mythical Orpheus, Arion, and Chiron to the medieval Breton, Glascurion; pipers from the ancient "Atiteris," "Pseustis" of Athens, and Marsyas, to young and old "pipers of the Duche tonge"; and martial trumpeters from Misenus of the *Aeneid* and Theodomas of Thebes to those who used the clarion "in Cataloigne and Aragon." Like the little harpers with whom they are portrayed, all of them play a game of make-believe in imitation of nature, "and countrefete hem as an ape, / Or as craft countrefeteth kynde" (*HF* 1212-13). And the facade concludes with illusionists of various sorts—"jugelours, / Magiciens, and tregetours," "wicches, sorceresses," and clerks who "craftely doon her ententes / To make, in certeyn ascendentes, / Ymages. . . ." They are all crafty magicians, *artists* if you will, and like their musician predecessors, they appear chronologically from the classical to the near-contemporary, from Medea, Circe, and Calypso to the Biblical "Limote" and Simon Magus, and conclude with England's very own "Colle tregetour."

Inside this gaudy structure where the glasslike walls, the "ymageries" and "richesse" all recall the earlier temple of Venus, a noisy crowd idolizes its goddess; the nine Muses sing her glory in parody of the angelic salutation to Mary, " 'Heryed be thou and thy name, / Goddesse of Renoun or of Fame!' " Fame, herself a classical allegorical grotesque drawn largely from the *Aeneid* (IV. 173 ff.), displays her meaning: both tiny and tall denote the extent of her power; her countless eyes, tongues, and ears declare that she comes from all that is seen, said, and heard. Her feathered feet indicate her travels through the air, and her shoulders sustain Hercules and Alexander who epitomize the "large fame" of physical prowess on one side and of imperial magnificence on the other.[11]

If the outside of Fame's house illustrates how one enters its precincts—by play, art, illusion, or trickery—the inside shows how perilously it stands. Suitable metal pillars line the hall, on top of which stand authors, on top of whom stand the great fames of peoples, places, and conditions: "Jewerye" on Josephus, Thebes and Achilles on Statius, Troy on top of six contending authors (from Homer to Geoffrey of Monmouth), Aeneas on Virgil (whom we know about already), Love or Cupid on Ovid, Caesar, Pompey, and Rome on Lucan and others, and finally on Claudian the fame of hell—of Pluto and Proserpina who "quene ys of the derke pyne" (*HF* 1512). The architectural and allegorical plan creates a thoughtfully ambiguous effect. It gives a grand impression in its sweeping history and catalog of the illustrious, but it also manifests a perverse, comic message: first because of the uncertain *standing* of any fame which must rest on the shoulders of untrustworthy writers who nestle at the tops of pillars, in a mansion on top of ice; and second, because of the "narrative" order of the construction which moves from "Jewerye" to "Romes myghty werkes," only to end suspiciously in hell (*HF* 1507–12). The effect is an epical bathos which we have seen several times before, for example, in the long list of figures outside the "hous" which concluded with a monstrous anticlimax—a windmill under a walnut shell (*HF* 1280–81).[12] All in all the glorious place is marvelously unstable and unreal. Its minstrels "tellen tales," its musicians feign nature, its magicians work tricks, and its poet-historians play a grand game of circus acrobatics.

Obviously this is the right place for the allegorical actions of Lady Fame and her agent, "the god of wind," for they will now dispense renown without any discrimination or care, and certainly with "no justice" (*HF* 1820). There is no "Jove" in this place! But whether smelling of roses or stinking of hell as it flows from Aeolus's "clariouns," fame is finally (and only) noisy air—prepared, as we discover, in a "queynte hous," built by a classical trickster, Daedalus, and blown to the four winds. Having learned this much, Geoffrey, who had first fancied himself as a poet above reproach and then as ready for stardom, finds himself quite content to know himself and how he stands.

The *House of Fame* is a pyrotechnic display of Chaucer's comic powers. Restricting our view to classical legend and myth, we find that he adapted these materials to allegory in such ways that (1) a classical epic, the *Aeneid*, embodies the "problem" of the poem, (2) a mythical eagle, borrowed from Dante, serves the cause of justice and dramatizes an intellectual process, so that (3) some grand catalogs of classical and other references can give historical scope and meaning to a piece of foolish grandeur. And with all its amazing variety the poem still consistently subordinates its mass of detail to several interrelated lines of thematic development.

Parts of that development can be seen in the classical allusions which serve as formal signposts to the way the poem evolves. Like the invocations used later in the *Troilus*, but more complicated, those which introduce the three books of *Fame* sound like chords that introduce both theme and tone. The first is partly pagan and partly Christian: it is addressed to Morpheus, "the god of slep," and then to the true God, "he that mover ys of al." Although skeptical of Morpheus's power (*"Yf* every drem stonde in his myght" [italics added]), Geoffrey prays to him "With special devocion" for help to report his dream "aryght." This classical note may sound somewhat serious, even pious, but it soon turns sour and rather ominous when we read that the "unmerie" Morpheus dwells "in a cave of stoon / Upon a strem that cometh fro Lete, / That is a flood of helle unswete" (*HF* 70–72). It is not an auspicious beginning. But as it goes on the Christian part of Geoffrey's invocation becomes flippant, almost blasphemous, as it asserts his self-importance as a poet. The mode of expression, like that at the beginning of the *Troilus* (1. 29–51), is a parody of the "Bidding Prayer" in the Mass, but here the effect is more comically and dramatically ironic. In paraphrase it goes like this:

> May the Lord Himself give joy to the audience which hears this dream.
> May He help all of you to stand in love's grace, or wherever you would like to stand.
> May He watch over those who hear me, and protect them, and give them all that they desire, unless . . .
> *Unless* they treat this dream badly, or scorn it, or misjudge it, or criticize it because of hate, or envy, or villainy, or whatever.

> In such cases, then, O Lord, grant that they be overwhelmed
> with harm.
> Let 'em be hanged, and let 'em deserve it!
> "I am no bet in charyte!"   (*HF* 81–108)

This seems absurd enough, but a comparison of the two parts of the
invocation gives a totally ridiculous effect because their form and
content are inverted. Geoffrey's attitude toward his art—and his
critics—is nothing if not aggressively vainglorious, but to assert
himself as an artist he invokes the Lord God. On the other hand, to
achieve the truth ("My sweven for to telle aryght") he invokes a
dubious deity, on behalf of an "unmerie" story of Dido and Aeneas
which will leave him, the poet, in an appropriate sort of hell: alone
in a wasteland, like Ariadne (*HF* 416–17) deserted in sleep.

To help recognize the contrast and complete turnaround in
Geoffrey's position and tone, consider his invocation to Book
Three. The goal is clear: to describe the House of Fame (*HF* 1105) as
a means of expressing a single idea—the dubiousness of human
glory. The point is simple. Moreover, the mood is quiet and humble.
He calls on one deity, Apollo, not as chief of the Muses surely, but as
a representation of the power of human understanding. Apollo is
the god of "science," or the *scientia* which has been learned from
Jove's eagle and which will be shown and seen in the allegorical
picture of Fame that follows. He embodies the ability to perceive
and communicate with a clarity and "lyght" that contrast with the
darkness of Morpheus's hell; and under his direction Geoffrey
purposes to create nothing elaborately poetical to satisfy his vanity,
but only a simple report on a single idea.

> Nat that I wilne, for maistrye,
> Here art poetical be shewed;
> But for the rym ys lyght and lewed,
> Yit make hyt sumwhat agreable,
> Though som vers fayle in a sillable;
> And that I do no diligence
> To shewe craft, but o sentence.   (*HF* 1094–1100)

Neither are there any curses on anyone. If Geoffrey succeeds
"sumwhat," as he says, he will thankfully hurry to kiss the first
laurel tree that he sees since "hyt is [Apollo's] tree." Comedy has

certainly not disappeared in this passage, but the perception has changed from darkness to light and the pride which suffused the opening of Book One and the anxiety which had worried Book Two have dissolved; we now see Geoffrey the writer, "your humble servant." The tone, too, has shifted dramatically from the foolish arrogance of the first invocation to an amusingly sympathetic self-restraint. Then, incongruously of course—for Chaucer is given to such tricks—the poetry of Book Three turns out to be the richest and most elaborate in the whole work; rich and ironically sensible.

Between the others, the invocation for Book Two naturally enough looks both ways. It shows traces of Geoffrey's earlier pride in his art ("Now herkeneth, every maner man") and also of his patronizing treatment of learning, since *his* dream is obviously more wonderful than those of Isaiah, Scipio, Nebuchadnezzar, Pharaoh, Turnus, and "Elcanor" (*HF* 512–17). No matter whose, Geoffrey's is better. But now his language lacks the fulsomeness of his offhand treatment of dreams at the beginning of Book One, and his two-part invocation is much briefer. The first, to Venus and the Muses, recalls the discredited art world of Venus's temple, of the *Aeneid*, and of other ancient love stories, even as it prepares for the eagle's amusing report on Geoffrey's unrewarded and perhaps unrewarding devotion to his own love poetry.

> Now faire blisfull, O Cipris,
> So be my favour at this tyme!
> And ye, me to endite and ryme
> Helpeth, that on Parnaso duelle,
> Be Elicon, the clere welle. (*HF* 518–22)

This is surely tame. And with it comes an equally brief prayer to Thought ("To tellen al my drem aryght") which helps provide a gloss on the eagle that was descending upon Geoffrey at the end of Book One to carry him to the learning that follows, and finally to the "science" and "lyght" of Apollo.

A perceptive reader should expect that the classical invocations in the *House of Fame* make sense, that is, that they relate to their contexts and to each other. And indeed they do if one looks less for immediate "deep meanings" and more for a network of surface meanings. Morpheus, Thought, and Apollo serve the same function, to help the poet put his story on paper; but each is invoked in its place because it suits something else in the narrative: Morpheus the destitute suffering of Dido, of other abandoned women, and of the narrator; Thought the learning process which the eagle conducts; and Apollo the clarity of genuine understanding. Moreover, each invocation says something different about Geoffrey's changing attitudes as he shifts from loudmouthed hauteur to uncertain brevity—almost silence, and then to a humility that carries with it some real self-assurance. These and other developments in genre and in time—like that from a poetic narrative of the past, to a dramatic dialogue in the present, to a parodic apocalyptic vision—are particularly evident in the poem's classical and mythic materials.[13] But all this material is not allegorical in itself. The retelling of the *Aeneid* may be part of an *allegoria* of memory, of Geoffrey's recollection of a great poetic report; and the classical and mythological details which are parts of Fame's mansion have surely been adapted to an allegorical picture. But the strictly allegorical myth in the *House of Fame* consists only of the eagle and his offstage master, Jove, together with Lady Fame and her special agent, Aeolus. The actions and words of these "characters" are direct representations of natural or human activities which relate variously to nature, to Geoffrey, and to the essence of earthly fame. With them Chaucer has breathed a new life of realism into old allegorical forms.

The brief uses which Chaucer had made of allegorized myth in the French mode suggest, as has been noted, his early reluctance to follow what tradition might have dictated. He humanized allegorized myth in the *Book of the Duchess*, used it perfunctorily in the *Troilus*, and then dropped it. In the *House of Fame*, however, he showed that he could adapt all sorts of things to an allegorical frame—the classical stories of Virgil and others, invocations, allegorized myth, science, architecture, history, and the languages of the court, the classroom, and the street. The result is much more comedy and a good deal less philosophy (or theology), more art and less disorderly learning than many scholars have allowed. At the end Chaucer might have said, with Bottom the Weaver,

> The eye of man hath not heard, the ear of man hath not seen, man's hand is not able to taste, his tongue to conceive, nor his heart to report, what my dream was. . . . it shall be called Bottom's Dream, because it hath no bottom.

But from here Chaucer would move to more serious business.

The *Parliament of Fowls* is all about Love, the lord of paradox. In a concentrated fashion, but like the *House of Fame*, its parts appear at once discrete in source, subject, and style, and yet are wedded to a single theme. Within this mixture classical mythology plays two roles. It provides the central figures for an allegorical excursion through one aspect of love;[14] and second, by invocations, it plays a part in establishing the theme and tone of the poem. In both its roles, like everything else in the *Parliament*, the mythical is subordinated to a comic, philosophical view of love which may be summarized but not resolved.

One long passage (*PF* 211–94) which precedes the convention of Dame Nature and her birds finds Cupid forging and filing his arrows beside a well; it ends with a list of tragic lovers. As a combination of classical deities (Cupid, Priapus, and Venus), classical *exempla*, and figures from medieval moral psychology (Will, Pleasure, Lust, etc.), it constitutes a major mythical and allegorical contribution to the poem. Its construction resembles that of a "Progress" or "Triumph" of love and, given its allegorical genre, it overflows with life, pleasure, danger, and sorrow.

> Under a tre, besyde a welle, I say
> Cupide, oure lord, his arwes forge and file;
> And at his fet his bowe al redy lay;
> And Wille, his doughter, temprede al this while
> The hevedes in the welle, and with hire file
> She touchede hem, after they shulde serve
> Some for to sle, and some to wounde and kerve.
>
> Tho was I war of Plesaunce anon-ryght,
> And of Aray, and Lust, and Curteysie,
> And of the Craft that can and hath the myght
> To don by force a wyght to don folye—
> Disfigurat was she, I nyl nat lye;
> And by hymself, under an ok, I gesse,
> Saw I Delyt, that stod with Gentilesse.   (*PF* 211 ff.)

The instinct of desire, "Cupide," works on arrows (or what we would call "looks") with which to make his mark; "Wille" strengthens and sharpens them, presumably by assenting to desires, and thereby makes them deadly or morally harmful. After desire and decision come the circumstances of the game of love, the courting which logically follows. Some of these circumstances personify stages of love, and others the necessary conditions of love. There are pleasures ("Plesaunce"), attractive clothes ("Aray"), and delightful manners ("Delyt, that stod with Gentilesse"); there are physical beauty and adolescent fun and games ("Beute withouten any atyr, / And Youthe, ful of game and jolyte"). Yet this love must be a mixed blessing for it also involves some ugly connivance ("Craft . . . Disfigurat"), abetted by a fair share of foolishness, boldness, flattery, yearning, letter writing, and bribery. The first part of the process ends, then, with things not to be mentioned: probably touching, kissing, and sexual intercourse.

Desire has run its initial course, and now our eye shifts to a "temple" where it is devoutly maintained and revered. Outside this place of worship loose women ("in kertels, al dishevele") dance about, and on it sit hundreds of pairs of doves, the common emblems of sexual congress. Before the church doors, on an insecure hill of sand, sit figures of external or apparent quietude and discretion ("Pees" and "Pacience"), while a gaggle of artful promises ("Byheste and Art") can be heard as they enter and exit the temple. Then inside there are the passionate sighs, the jealous sorrows, and, at the center in a "sovereyn place," Priapus with *penis erectus* being "besyly" garlanded by the fresh orgasmic flowers of men. At this point sexual pleasure stands at its delightful but somewhat frustrating height, for Priapus is seen "as whan the asse hym shente," that is, when the ass by its braying awakened everyone to the sight of the god and prevented him from taking his pleasure. Next, off to the side in a secluded alcove lies the perennial Playboy's coney, Venus, having fun ("in disport"): secretive, sensual, pleasure filling.

> Hyre gilte heres with a golden thred
> Ibounden were, untressed as she lay,
> And naked from the brest unto the hed
> Men myghte hire sen; and, sothly for to say,
> The remenaunt was wel kevered to my pay,
> Ryght with a subtyl coverchef of Valence—
> Ther nas no thikkere cloth of no defense.   (*PF* 267–73)

Dining and drinking ("Ceres" and "Bacchus") serve as companions, to keep love "in heat," for according to the old proverb, "Venus

freezes without Ceres and Bacchus." And a youthful couple kneel
in prayerful pleading to their goddess.

From its beginning this picture of love's evolution invites a wary
response: its joy mingles with ugliness and its pleasure with anxiety
and failure. Although it has a strong dose of flippant bawdiness, it
also reaches a serious conclusion with its accounting of the
wretched aftermath of love's servitude: the trophies of those who
wasted their maidenhood, and the portraits of notables who died
for love.

> Semyramis, Candace, and Hercules,
> Biblis, Dido, Thisbe, and Piramus,
> Tristram, Isaude, Paris, and Achilles,
> Eleyne, Cleopatre, and Troylus,
> Silla, and ek the moder of Romulus:
> Alle these were peynted on that other syde,
> And al here love, and in what plyt they dyde.   (*PF* 288–94)

As an allegorical drama of a love which moves from desire, looks,
and assent to the heights of pleasure and devotion, and now finally
to ruination, the passage also represents a change from its source,
Teseida Book Seven. Where Boccaccio emphasized love's power,
concluding with the figure of lordly Cupid, Chaucer alters things so
as to focus on love's tragic conclusion. Moreover, while this new
patterning may call to mind the design of the *Troilus* or the plot of
the *Complaint of Mars*, as it stands in the *Parliament* it is only one
part of a complex unit.

By itself the passage offers a dire comment on the joy of love, and
thereby fulfills the earlier warning in the poem—the black-lettered
verses on the gateway to life which spoke of the "mortal strokes,"
the barrenness, the sorrows, and the self-imprisonment of love (*PF*
134–40). But that is not all, for the passages which immediately
precede and which immediately follow the allegory of love's tragedy
portray two contrasting scenes that are full of joy and harmony.
Before Cupid appeared at the well, working on his arrows, the
Edenic garden had been replete with life and song, with fish and
birds, the conies, "hert and hynde," the gentle breezes, and the "ay
cler day."

> Of instruments of strenges in acord
> Herde I so pleye a ravyshyng swetnesse,

> That God, that makere is of al and lord,
> Ne herde nevere beter, as I gesse.
> Therwith a wynd, unnethe it myghte be lesse,
> Made in the leves grene a noyse softe
> Acordaunt to the foules song alofte.   (*PF* 197–203)

Everything is in concord, heavenly. Then too, after the picture of love's progress and the "plyt" and deaths of love's victims, fair Nature ("noble emperesse") prepares to hold her customary court (*PF* 295 ff.) and every sort of bird crowds comfortably into parliament, each in "his owne place." Again the sights and sounds tell of the fullness of life in harmony as each one "dide his besy cure / Benygnely to chese or for to take, / By [Nature's] acord, his formel or his make."

Elsewhere I have sought to show that the rhythm of these scenes—from order to disorder to order—is part of a continuous pattern in the *Parliament*, and that it reflects the mysterious rhythm of the created world and its love.[15] This love and its earthly harmony (or is it chaos?) puzzle the narrator of the poem from beginning to end. And as they were seen in the descriptive allegories of the garden (or later in the dramatic allegory of the parliament scene) so they appear in the poem's two mythological invocations. The first of these, addressed to lord Cupid, constitutes a list of extreme and contrasting observations about earthly love: short and long, tough and sharp, dread and joy, float and sink, books and experience, miracles and cruel behavior. Love on earth: "A paradox! A paradox!"

> The lyf so short, the craft so long to lerne,
> Th'assay so hard, so sharp the conquerynge,
> The dredful joye, alwey that slit so yerne:
> Al this mene I by Love. . . .   (*PF* 1–4)

And the paradox heightens when the narrator refers to his reading of Cicero's "Drem of Scipioun," a book which affirms that heavenly harmony is the source of earthly love and accord: it is the "welle . . . of musik and melodye / In this world here, and cause of armonye." But how? Concord may be a fine thing for the heavens and the afterlife, the poem seems to say, but where is "armonye" in this world and its love? That central question never does find an answer. Indeed, it is reiterated in the second invocation (*PF* 113–19), this time to Venus, who appears as "blysful lady swete" in one line, and in the very next line terrifies whomever she pleases ("That with thy fyrbrond dauntest whom the lest"). A fine "lady" she turns out to be! And the poet emphasizes his own ambiguous feelings by asking for her best "helpe" while she, as a planet, is in an unpropitious position in the sky.[16]

Thus, both of the mythological invocations in the *Parliament*, first to Cupid and then to Venus, suggest anxiety, extremes of power, and disorder within the earthly frame; and yet they, in turn, surround the classic statement of ideal order and balance found in Scipio's dream (*PF* 29–84). In other words, the invocations in their context reflect a similar concern for the juxtaposition of discordancy and harmony that one also finds in the allegorical drama of love in its context. By such means Chaucer forces his reader to recognize the puzzling character of love and, indeed, of all this world and its life. Small wonder that the narrator has difficulty understanding his materials or that critics have trouble understanding his report. Given the disposition of its details, one must do violence to the *Parliament* in order to impose a "solution" on it or extract a solution from it. For the mystery of love and life, earthly and human, is precisely what the work explores and discovers. Like some of the philosophers and theologians of the later Middle Ages, Chaucer apparently recognized an irrational human condition, one which he could query in relative calm without needing to be assured of an answer.

Important though it is in Chaucer's poems on fame and love, allegorized myth *qua* allegory really does not dominate these works. As we have seen before, Chaucer tends to humanize allegory—to create an unusual balance between the details of external reality and the universality of allegorical conceptions. He asks his reader to accept both of these simultaneously. Jove's eagle, for example, serves as a convenient hook on which to hang a university lecturer *and* as a dramatic representation of a psychological process; also, with all her gaudy trappings Lady Fame (as others have observed) is as much a fishwife as she is an awesome *figura* from classical antiquity; and the allegorized mythology in the *Parliament* begins by being subordinated to a broad, uncertain philosophical excursion, and ends by being balanced with the grand comedy of the parliament of birds itself. Only in the *Knight's Tale* does allegorized myth come close to having a major, governing role. One hint of this comes from the fact that although Chaucer cut back on almost everything in his primary source, the *Teseida*, he nevertheless restructured and amplified Boccaccio's mythological temples. To those of Venus and Mars he added a third, a "church" for Diana; then he incorporated all three as oratories in a grand, circular "noble theatre" which Theseus constructs for the tournament of Palamon and Arcite.

Like the house of Lady Fame and the temple of Priapus, the chapels of the three divinities in the *Knight's Tale* express a pattern of ideas, but rhetorically and architectonically they function in a rather different way. They represent natural and potentially destructive aspects of the soul, but joined together (in the theater of which they are parts) they suggest a broad picture of human nature as an ordered, balanced whole—in a wholeness which has harmony and stability. Thus, while the mansion of Fame embodies an encyclopedic summation of an idea and while the mythic allegory in the *Parliament* serves as one element in a complex motif, Theseus's allegorical theater stands as a central statement. Its meaning, to borrow R. E. Kaske's language, hovers over everything that happens: all that was said and done before its construction and all that follows after. Or to take a different perspective: the allegories of the eagle's flight and of love's progress follow typical patterns of *action*—one educative and the other tragic, but the mythological theater says something grand and all-encompassing about the human soul in its ideal natural *condition*.

Critics generally agree that the Knight tells a carefully wrought tale, notable for its balance and order.[17] The story opens with the resolution of two struggles: one between Duke Theseus's Athenian forces and the Amazonians led by "queene Ypolita"—a struggle which concludes with the victory of Theseus and his peaceful political marriage to the queen; and the other between Athens and Thebes, which ends in Theseus's conquest of the wrathful tyrant, Creon, the utter destruction of his city, and the burial of the Theban dead. All these events are compressed into the first 140 lines of the narrative and they constitute, as it were, a prologue to the tale. As others have noted, too, these events will be balanced by the actions which conclude the tale: the burial of Arcite, the reconciliation of Athens and Thebes, and the affectionate political marriage of Palamon and Emelye. What interests us here, however, are the ways in which the introductory passage prepares the ground for Theseus's mythological theater.

As the Knight begins we learn at once that his is a classical story: "Whilom, as olde stories tellen us. . . ." Although there is little mythology at the onset, the forces which myth comes to embody and represent appear implicitly in the language and action of legendary history. For example, in Thebes, the city of Mars and Venus, a Mars-like tyrant, blinded by a merciless wrath, refuses to bury a large part of the Theban dead.

> "And yet now the olde Creon, weylaway!
> That lord is now of Thebes the citee,
> Fulfild of ire and of iniquitee,
> He, for despit and for his tirannye,
> To do the dede bodyes vileynye . . .
> Hath alle the bodyes on an heep ydrawe,
> And wol nat suffren hem, by noon assent,
> Neither to been yburyed nor ybrent,
> But maketh houndes ete hem in despit."   (*KnT* 938–47)

All the emphatic words—"ire," "despit," "dede bodyes," "yburyed"—even the detail of the dead being eaten by "houndes," suggest that Creon is himself ruled by that irascible appetite which will be allegorized in the oratory of Mars.

Similarly but less obviously, the Amazonians whom Theseus defeats were traditionally governed by a harsh and fierce restraint. They were the "aspre [harsh] folk of Cithe" in Chaucer's *Anelida;* warrior women of "the regne of Femenye" according to the Knight. Because they scorn the household and all "normal" relationships with men, the wedding of their "hardy" queen to Theseus ("lord and governour") signifies both their subjugation and their restoration to a "reasonable," Athens-like life of order. Later, in the oratory of Diana, we will see an allegorization of that insensitive restraint which Theseus had overcome by a victory and a marriage.

Lastly, the prologue gives a good deal of information about the character of Theseus, about the qualities or ideals by which he seeks to govern himself and others. Thus he acts as a martial figure, a "conquerour" who leads his army to a "Victorie"—complete and absolute—against Thebes.

> He faught, and slough [Creon] manly as a knyght
> In pleyn bataille, and putte the folk to flyght;

And by assaut he wan the citee after,
And rente adoun bothe wall and sparre and rafter. . . .   (*KnT*
987–90)

He can be fierce, obviously, but he also shows mercy, kindness, even
love. In his defeat of the Amazons, for example, he brings peace with
conquest, "melodye" with "victorie" (*KnT* 872); and he marries
Hippolyta, "the faire" Queen. Then, at the height of his triumphant
return to Athens, his brusqueness (" 'What folk been ye, that at
myn homcomynge / Perturben so my feste' ") melts to sympathy
for the Theban widows who beseech his "mercy and socour" at the
temple of Clementia.

"Have mercy on oure wo and oure distresse!
Som drope of pitee, thurgh thy gentillesse,
Upon us wrecched wommen lat thou falle."   (*KnT* 919–21)

Theseus's responses, as we can see, reflect his capacity to soften
martial vigor with those qualities traditionally associated with
Venus: gentility, pity, comfort, and heart.

This gentil duc doun from his courser sterte
With herte pitous, whan he herde hem speke.
Hym thoughte that his herte wolde breke,
Whan he saugh hem so pitous and so maat,
That whilom weren of so greet estaat;
And in his armes he hem alle up hente,
And hem conforteth in ful good entente. . . .   (*KnT* 952–58)

Theseus is androgynous.
    Moreover, he not only acts with the firmness of Mars and the
affection of Venus but, as "lord and governour," he seeks to rule
with a pervading sense of order and justice which weighs one action
against another. This is implicit in what has already been observed:
in the way he balances victory with peace and marriage—in the
process wedding one who is both "hardy" *and* "faire" (*KnT* 882); in
the way he balances his victorious return with mercy and clemency
toward the widows, and then balances that benign action with his
harsh defeat of Creon. His character becomes clearer still as the
narrative proceeds, for he becomes increasingly linked to the

mythological figure of order and justice, Jupiter. And finally, Theseus has been called a man of "wysdom" (*KnT* 865), of perception. He has, or at least comes to have, that prudential understanding of things which constitutes the intellectual prerequisite of all just and virtuous behavior. His insignia, in fact, already tell of his ideals.

> The rede statue of Mars, with spere and targe,
> So shyneth in his white baner large,
> That alle the feeldes glyteren up and doun;
> And by his baner born is his penoun
> Of gold ful riche, in which ther was ybete
> The Mynotaur, which that he slough in Crete.   (*KnT* 975–80)

Red Mars on a shining white Venusian flag; and with it a pennon of gold (wisdom) to memorialize his conquest of bestiality.[18]

This is not to say that Theseus simply represents a static ideal; rather that he inclines toward and emulates an ideal. His defeat of Thebes, for example, seems needlessly absolute, uncompromising. His treatment of Palamon and Arcite, the sole survivors of the Theban royal house, seems excessively severe: no ransom at all and perpetual imprisonment! Then too, his response to the request of his friend, Duke Pirithous, seems out of balance: singularly over-generous in the release of Arcite "withouten any raunsoun," but insensibly strict (or blind) toward Palamon, who must remain imprisoned for seven years before he escapes on his own. When Theseus encounters Palamon and Arcite trying to kill each other in the grove, he moves toward a new, balanced resolution; but even here (as in his initial reaction to the Theban widows) his first instincts sound harsh—violent and deadly.

> And at a stert he was bitwix hem two,
> And pulled out a swerd, and cride, "Hoo!
> Namoore, up peyne of lesynge of youre heed!
> By myghty Mars, he shal anon be deed
> That smyteth any strook that I may seen."   (*KnT* 1705–9)

Perhaps boldness had been necessary in the midst of strife, but hardly in the aftermath when Palamon foolishly begs for his own execution, and for Arcite's as well.

"This is a short conclusioun.
Youre owene mouth, by youre confessioun,
Hath dampned yow, and I wol it recorde;
It nedeth noght to pyne yow with the corde.
Ye shal be deed, by myghty Mars the rede!"   (*KnT* 1743–47)

Theseus is rash, but Theseus listens as he had listened to the Theban widows; and the tearful pleas for "mercy" from Hippolyte, Emelye, and the other women soon soften his "ire" so that in his "resoun" he pardons Palamon and Arcite.

Til at the laste aslaked was his mood,
For pitee renneth soone in gentil herte.
And though he first for ire quook and sterte,
He hath considered shortly, in a clause,
The trespas of hem bothe, and eek the cause,
And although that his ire hir gilt accused,
Yet in his resoun he hem bothe excused. . . .   (*KnT* 1760–66)

Wisely and compassionately he comments on the folly of Palamon and Arcite's love for Emelye; but he goes beyond this balancing of his own disposition by purposing to resolve the lovers' strife with a justice that will render each his due: " 'As I shal evene juge been and trewe' " (*KnT* 1864).

The tournament which Theseus decrees is only one of many efforts to achieve a balanced judgment and to show fair-handed justice; he also builds his ideals into the allegorical theater for the tournament. Besides painters and sculptors, he hires "crafty" men who know "geometrie or ars-metrike" (*KnT* 1898) for he wishes everything to be carefully planned and precisely measured. The works cover the "circuit" of a mile "aboute, / Walled of stoon, and dyched al withoute."

Round was the shap, in manere of compas,
Ful of degrees, the heighte of sixty pas,
That whan a man was set on o degree,
He letted nat his felawe for to see.   (*KnT* 1889–92)

At each of three points on the compass stands a gate, and above each gate an altar and a chapel: due east for Venus, west for Mars, "and

northward, in a touret on the wal"—cold, guarded, and embattled—
"an oratorie, riche for to see, / In worshipe of Dyane of chastitee." It
is "a noble theatre" (*KnT* 1885), "wroght in noble wyse" (*KnT*
1913), partly because of its "noble kervyng" and other rich decorations, but more importantly because of its noble conception.

Our view of that conception begins problematically in Venus's
chapel. Here we first see the conditions associated with falling in
love: the "broken" sleeps, the cold sighs, the sacred tears, and the
fiery "strokes" of desiring; then the personifications of "alle the
circumstaunces" of love such as had been seen in the *Parliament:*
Pleasure, Hope, Desire, Foolishness, Beauty, Youth, Lying, Flattery,
and the rest. Next we have a brief glimpse of "the mount of
Citheroun," where "Venus hath hir principal dwellynge"—with
some overtones of body imagery—and joined to that the conventional garden of love leading to a catalog of love's victims: Narcissus,
Solomon (!), Hercules, Medea, and so on. The list is exemplary, of
course, and we are told its purpose: to show the broad power of
Venus to affect the lives of tremendous numbers of people, all quite
different.

> Thus may ye seen that wysdom ne richesse,
> Beautee ne sleighte, strengthe ne hardynesse,
> Ne may with Venus holde champartie,
> For as hir list the world than may she gye.   (*KnT* 1947–50)

This gloss on the chapel declares that the decorations show the
power of sensuous pleasure (Venus) over all creation and, sadly, its
capacity to ruin those who have been pictured and "a thousand
mo" who could be mentioned. The narrative structure also points
to the same conclusion, for the passage ends with an impressive,
albeit conventional, allegorical picture: Venus asea on her shell,
with roses and doves; and standing before her, Cupid, the lordly
figure of desire.[19]

The details of Venus's oratory may recall the tragic allegory of love
in the *Parliament*, since the source in Boccaccio is the same. But the
poetic structures actually differ as their themes differ. The picture
of love's progress had ended with the wretched fate of lovers—the
sorrowful effect; but this one ends with the figure of fickle and blind
desire—the powerful cause.

> Biforn hire stood hir sone Cupido;
> Upon his shuldres wynges hadde he two,
> And blynd he was, as it is often seene;
> A bowe he bar and arwes brighte and kene.   (*KnT* 1963-66)

Thus the allegory in the *Knight's Tale* builds from love's conditions and circumstances, and the range of its effects and influences, to focus finally on the natural force behind all these: the human instinct "to have" or to possess what is attractive. In the jargon of medieval moral psychology, it is the concupiscible appetite.[20]

The description of the chapel of Mars, which immediately follows, allegorizes the other part of the sensitive soul—the irascible appetite. The order of details differs slightly from those in Venus's chapel, and the weight given to the different kinds of details varies somewhat, but we again see the dwelling of the deity with its surrounding geography. The place is "colde" and "grisly"; the landscape a gnarled and barren forest filled with a tempestuous rumbling ("As though a storm sholde bresten every bough"). From the entrance to the god's abode "a rage" and stormy blast comes whirling, shaking the very gates, so that everything seen and heard suggests the violent, fierce, coldhearted mood of angry and impetuous behavior. And the temple of Mars itself, "wroght al of burned steel," looks tough and inflexible; it provides no glimmer of clarity or understanding, only a "northren lyght" at the gate and darkness within: "For wyndowe on the wal ne was ther noon, / Thurgh which men myghten any light discerne." Everything is heavy, hard, and strong.

> The dore was al of adamant eterne,
> Yclenched overthwart and endelong
> With iren tough; and for to make it strong,
> Every pyler, the temple to sustene,
> Was tonne-greet, of iren bright and shene.   (*KnT* 1990-94)

Within the temple the central figure, "Meschaunce," and everything around it tell of the misfortunes associated with Mars and the various kinds of destructive behavior that follow from his influence. Felony, thieving, suicide, killing, and "the colde deeth"; the town destroyed, the burning ships, the strangled hunter, the child eaten in its cradle by a sow—"noght was foryeten by the infortune of Marte." These widespread effects overwhelm the scene as, mingling with them, a group of personified "circumstaunces" engage in martial strife—the "crueel Ire," "Contek, with blody knyf," Madness ("Woodnesse"), Violent Excess ("Outrage"), and finally "Conquest" sitting in precarious honor under the sword of Damocles and painted 'round with a few *exempla* of massive battle slaughter. The scene of horror then concludes, like the previous chapel scene, with the picture of the deity. Mars stands armed on a cart, looking grim and crazy ("grym as he were wood"), and at his feet a red-eyed wolf devours a man.[21] As an allegory on the force and impact of man's natural, instinctive irascibility, the whole passage has an awesome ugliness.

To the oratories which Theseus has constructed over the east and west gates, he adds a third. Like the chaste goddess, Diana, whom it honors, this chapel suggests a cold protectiveness in its location ("northward, in a touret"); and its building materials ("of alabastre whit and reed coral") combine the hardness of Diana's chastity with the colors of her purity and modest shamefacedness. Like the other oratories, too, this one represents an arational and destructive force, for the legendary *exempla* which are painted all about (*KnT* 2056–74) and which dominate the passage have all to do with various cruel, spiteful actions on behalf of chastity: Callisto turned into a bear because Diana "agreved was with here"; Daphne turned into a tree rather than lose her maidenhood; Acteon turned into a hart and eaten by his hounds "for vengeaunce that he saugh Diane al naked"; and Meleager shown hunting the boar, "for which Dyane wroghte hym care and wo." These painful scenes lead to the brief picture of the goddess (*KnT* 2075–88), which—though it begins with the traditional chaste huntress—turns downward to emphasize her infernal and tormenting character.

> Hir eyen caste she ful lowe adoun,
> Ther Pluto hath his derke regioun.
> A womman travaillynge was hire biforn;
> But for hir child so longe was unborn,
> Ful pitously Lucyna gan she calle,
> And seyde, "Help, for thou mayst best of alle!"   (*KnT* 2081–
> 86)

In this conclusion a victim of Diana-Proserpina's unreasonable restraint against the senses, and against a normal process, pleads for help; and for relief she prays to a higher aspect of the same deity,

Diana-Lucina, or the moon, the patroness of childbirth.

Looking back at the allegorical oratories in Theseus's theater, one cannot help but sense a problem. Each oratory defines and elaborates upon a natural instinct which is seen to be the cause of widespread ruin and destruction. The seductive pleasures of Venus mingle with various forms of unhappy and unflattering behavior; the aggressiveness of Mars appears, for all its strength and power, as heartlessly gruesome; even Diana's chastity shows itself in actions which are mean and cruel. Given a medieval context, one might assume that the goddess of chastity, at least, would seem virtuous; but she has instead been made the embodiment of that flight from *all* bodily delights which Aristotle and the medieval schoolmen judged to be "insensitive or savage."[22]

Where are we, then? The Knight in various ways has assured us of the nobility of Theseus's theater, but the details that we have seen offer some overwhelming evidence of just the opposite. Or is all this a parody, another sort of House of Fame which undercuts and mocks nobility? It would appear not. The mood of the Knight's story, the attitude of the narrator, the response of its audience—all these suggest otherwise. Most important, however, we have been looking narrowly at the parts of an allegory. Those parts declare without qualification that one or another sort of instinctive, natural behavior—unrestrained or unassuaged by any other natural instinct—leads to nothing less than chaos and ruin. But the total construction, the whole allegory, says something quite different. It represents, in fact, an ideal of human nature on the natural level, for in each oratory an instinctive tendency receives its proper place, its due and complete honor; it then finds itself balanced by other, equally valued instincts, and is finally bound in or controlled by "a just circle" which makes the whole construction a noble work. The theater, in other words, reflects the moral virtue of justice. It gives each one, each thing and, in this instance of moral allegory, each aspect of the soul its due place. Moreover, as tradition says of justice, the theater embodies two other moral virtues because it binds in and controls the instincts so that temperance may act as a mean between unrestrained desire for sensual pleasure and the savageness that rejects all pleasures; and so that fortitude may find the mean between cowardly softness and ruthless aggression.[23]

Despite, or perhaps because of, its ambiguities, Theseus's theater expresses a noble conception. Moreover, it finds its rationale neither

in classical mythology nor in Arabian astrology and the powers of
the heavens, but in a cluster of conventional notions drawn from
Aristotle and from medieval moral philosophy. From this perspective, too, one may look back at the "prologue" of the *Knight's Tale*
and see that it is only the first part of a condensed history of
Theseus's efforts toward just, balanced behavior: moving now
toward Mars's role, then toward Venus's and back again, all the time
governing himself and others as best he can. Naturally enough,
Theseus does not achieve the ideal; that, after all, is not what ideals
are for. But his forward movement is constant. He releases Arcite for
reasons of friendship, and later he entirely forgives the trespasses of
both Palamon and Arcite ("every deel"). He tries to arrange a fair
contest by battle, and he later improves on that by establishing rules
which will avoid needless bloodshed and death. In short, Theseus
grows toward the moral ideal which he has displayed in the allegory
and architecture of his theater.

However, Theseus is not the only one concerned. He has built the
theater for a tournament, we may recall, and three other characters
have a stake in it. In their prison tower Palamon and Arcite fall in
love with Emelye as she strolls in the nearby garden; but they fall in
love in different ways. Palamon responds in Venus-Cupid fashion as
he sees someone pleasing, fair, and desirable whom he wants to
have, to possess.

> "I noot wher she be womman or goddesse,
> But Venus is it soothly, as I gesse."
> And therwithal on knees doun he fil,
> And seyde: "Venus, if it be thy wil
> Yow in this gardyn thus to transfigure
> Bifore me, sorweful, wrecched creature,
> Out of this prisoun help that we may scapen."   (*KnT* 1101–7)

By contrast, Arcite responds to the same stimulus with the deadly,
impetuous language of Mars.

> "The fresshe beautee sleeth me sodeynly
> Of hire that rometh in the yonder place,
> And but I have hir mercy and hir grace,
> That I may seen hire atte leeste weye,
> I nam but deed; ther nis namoore to seye."   (*KnT* 1118–22)

For Arcite the love of Emelye is, and will prove to be, less a matter of affection than a contest ("Contek"), a fight. Whereas Palamon worships Emelye and will do what he must to have her, Arcite will be content to "stryve" for her, to "seen hire atte leeste weye," and to prevent Palamon from having her. His speech is aggressive and bellicose, but not possessive or even gentle toward Emelye.

> "We stryve as dide the houndes for the boon;
> They foughte al day, and yet hir part was noon.
> Ther cam a kyte, whil that they were so wrothe,
> And baar awey the boon bitwixe hem bothe.
> And therfore, at the kynges court, my brother,
> Ech man for hymself, ther is noon oother."   (*KnT* 1177–82)

The different ways in which Palamon and Arcite fall in love lie at the heart of the subsequent ironic situation when Theseus frees Arcite from prison on the condition that he never return. Now whom can he fight with over Emelye? And how can he see her? On the other hand, Palamon must remain imprisoned where he can see Emelye but where he is helpless to win her. Again their words disclose their differences: Arcite thinks that Palamon has achieved a "victorie" (*KnT* 1235)—as though a battle had been won—because he has the "sighte" (*KnT* 1231, 1239) of Emelye and may even, given the fluctuations of Fortune, someday "atteyne" to his desire. But tormented by love's jealousy, Palamon assumes that Arcite has "the fruyt" of their dispute because he can gather an army and, one way or another, *have* her as his own: "by som aventure or some tretee / Thow mayst have hire to lady and to wyf" (*KnT* 1288–89).

In an important sense, Arcite has his reward after he returns to Athens in disguise, as "Philostrate," and lives in Theseus's court where he may "seen his lady wel ny day by day"; more than that, he will actually win when he gets a chance to fight for her. But now at the end of seven years, he still mouths the same deadly language of Mars when he makes his complaint and when Palamon overhears him.

> "And over al this, to sleen me outrely,
> Love hath his firy dart so brennyngly
> Ystiked thurgh my trewe, careful herte,
> That shapen was my deeth erst than my sherte.

Ye sleen me with youre eyen, Emelye!
Ye been the cause wherfore that I dye." (*KnT* 1563–68)

Ironically but understandably, Palamon wants to gather some forces
and, if need be, fight to the death; but only because he feels he must
do this to "wynnen Emelye unto his wyf" (*KnT* 1486). He may be
"sik and wood for love," but he will battle to have her, and Arcite (as
chance would have it, rather than Theseus) eagerly accommodates
him with a double load of martial "harneys," along with bedding,
food, and drink. These cousin-brothers have reverted to where they
were in prison, or worse, for they are up to their ankles in blood
when Theseus stops them.

No doubt Palamon and Arcite have a stake in Theseus's temple:
Palamon for his devotion to Venus and Arcite for his to Mars. Soon
enough, too, we discover in the prayer of Emelye that she has her
proper place as well. All along she has apparently wanted to remain a
maiden and avoid Diana's "ire."

"Chaste goddesse, wel wostow that I
Desire to ben a mayden al my lyf,
Ne nevere wol I be no love ne wyf.
I am, thow woost, yet of thy compaignye,
A mayde, and love huntynge and venerye,
And for to walken in the wodes wilde,
And noght to ben a wyf and be with childe." (*KnT* 2304–10)

From this prayer, offered in Diana's vengeful setting, and all that has
gone before, one might conclude that Palamon, Arcite, and Emelye
directly reflect the deities whom they honor and the behavioral
instincts which those deities represent. But not so. As in the
Troilus, the relationships between characters and deities in the
Knight's Tale do not appear to be simple. Palamon, Arcite, and
Emelye are not just allegorical extensions of ideas—of concupiscence, irascibility, and insensitivity—for the obvious reason that
each one proves more generous, more human, and more complicated than any single abstract notion.[24]

Their prayers give assurance of this. For although the deities
surely stand for the dominant passions of character, each character
suggests something more, indeed something better, than the embodiment of a blind, destructive force. Palamon, for example, knows

that he has suffered the torment and befuddlement of love: he is
"confus"; he has no care for "victorie," "ne veyne glorie / Of pris of
armes." More than life itself he wishes for Emelye to be his wife: to
"have fully possessioun / Of Emelye"; to "have my lady in myne
armes"; to "wel have my love." The drive of concupiscence *to have*
could scarcely be clearer, but at the same time Palamon shows
nothing at all of the lying, deceit, trickery, vanity, flattery, or
"Bauderie" portrayed in his oratory. He is in love and, like Theseus,
we are persuaded to sympathize with his plight. Emelye, too,
sympathizes with him—and with Arcite as well. She would prefer to
remain a maiden, independent and free of cares, but her desire
shows none of the fierceness of her Amazonian heritage or the
meanness of Diana. She prays for peace between her contending
suitors; and if destiny cannot fulfill her wish she hopes (as no
complete devotee of the goddess could hope) that her husband may
be the one who desires most to have her (*KnT* 2322–25). Lastly, like
Palamon in his prayer, Arcite elicits our sympathy by alluding to his
sufferings and sorrows, his youthfulness and his "unkonnynge." He
prays for "victorie," for the "myght," and for the "strengthe" to
"wynne" Emelye, but now he makes no mention of his cousin's
death and shows none of the crazy impetuosity which characterizes
his god and which characterized some of his own earlier actions.

> "Now, lord, have routhe upon my sorwes soore;
> Yif me victorie, I aske thee namoore."   (*KnT* 2419–20)

The language and the aim of all three characters, then, express the
thoughts of complex, changing, "living" people; they are not
identical with the unequivocal forces which their deities represent,
and in time they will change still more. Saturn, as a figure for Time
and Fortune,[25] will see to it that the prayers of each—Palamon,
Arcite, and Emelye—will in one sense be answered "yes," and in
another sense denied.

> . . . the pale Saturnus the colde,
> That knew so manye of aventures olde,
> Foond in his olde experience an art
> That he ful soone hath plesed every part.   (*KnT* 2443–46)

In time things will change. Palamon "shal have his lady," Mars "shal
helpe his knyght" to victory, and Emelye will have "hym that moost

desireth" her. With the appearance of Saturn the mythological allegory of the *Knight's Tale* concludes and the narrative itself will work out the implications of that allegory.

As the Knight begins the fourth part of his story, he returns to the romance genre. The shift is not entirely abrupt, however, because the broad concepts which myth has embodied continue to appear intermittently. Before the tournament Theseus holds a great "feeste" in Athens, one which assures that "Venus" will receive her reasonable honors and that the pleasures of life should have their time and place.

> Greet was the feeste in Atthenes that day,
> And eek the lusty seson of that May
> Made every wight to been in swich plesaunce
> That al that Monday justen they and daunce,
> And spenden it in Venus heigh servyse.   (*KnT* 2483–87)

A bit of Mars's jousting mingles with the revelry just as, on the following day, Venus's "mynstralcie" (*KnT* 2524) joins the more pervasive sounds of Mars: the "hors and harneys noyse and claterynge"; steeds and steel and armory.

> . . . and eek squieres
> Nailynge the speres, and helmes bokelynge;
> Giggynge of sheeldes, with layneres lacynge
> (There as nede is they weren no thyng ydel);
> The fomy steedes on the golden brydel
> Gnawynge, and faste the armurers also
> With fyle and hamer prikynge to and fro . . .
> Pypes, trompes, nakers, clariounes,
> That in the bataille blowen blody sounes. . . .   (*KnT* 2502–12)

Then like a figure of Jove himself, Theseus appears at a window before the throng, "as he were a god in trone."

A herald reads his lord's decree on the rules of battle. To avoid the destruction of "gentil blood," Theseus, "of his heigh discrecioun," declares a ban against deadly weapons in the tourney. The force of Mars, as pictured in his chapel, will be abated; as far as possible death will be eschewed.

> "Wherfore, to shapen that they shal nat dye,
> He wol his firste purpos modifye.

> No man therfore, up peyne of los of lyf,
> No maner shot, ne polax, ne short knyf
> Into the lystes sende, or thider brynge;
> Ne short swerd, for to stoke with poynt bitynge,
> No man ne drawe, ne bere it by his syde." *(KnT* 2541–47)

The people rejoice "with murie stevene," joyous cheers that reach the heavens. Next comes the procession of knights from both sides, as orderly and balanced as the theater itself—"evene, withouten variacioun" *(KnT* 2588).

> For ther was noon so wys that koude seye
> That any hadde of oother avauntage
> Of worthynesse, ne of estaat, ne age,
> So evene were they chosen, for to gesse.
> And in two renges faire they hem dresse. *(KnT* 2590–94)

Again the balanced justice of "Jove" shows itself, this time in pageant fashion; for the forces of Venus, now tempered and restrained, pass through the east gate with their "baner whyt" and join the forces of Mars, now mollified and controlled, as they pass through the west gate with their "baner reed" *(KnT* 2580–86). The rule of the just governor, the "evene juge . . . and trewe," appears manifest in the equitable distribution of "two renges faire."

However, at this point in the *Knight's Tale* another force comes into play. Twice we had been advised of its coming. First, when Theseus announced his original plan for resolving the dispute between Palamon and Arcite in a battle which Fortune would govern *(KnT* 1860–61), and then later in Saturn's discourse where he declared that the strife between Venus and Mars would be settled by the intervention of his influence—we had been warned. Now time, bad fortune and death will run their course.

> "My cours, that hath so wyde for to turne,
> Hath moore power than woot any man.
> Myn is the drenchyng in the see so wan;
> Myn is the prison in the derke cote;
> Myn is the stranglyng and hangyng by the throte,
> The murmure and the cherles rebellyng,
> The groynynge, and the pryvee empoysonyng;
> I do vengeance and pleyn correccioun. . . . *(KnT* 2454–61)

The tournament field, as events devolve, soon turns into the place of Saturn rather than of Jove: the place of chance events, confusion, and mishap rather than of natural order. With the capture of Palamon, Theseus halts the strife in full expectation that impartial justice has been done.

> He cryde, "Hoo! namoore, for it is doon!
> I wol be trewe juge, and no partie.
> Arcite of Thebes shal have Emelie,
> That by his fortune hath hire faire ywonne." (*KnT* 2656–59)

For a brief moment fortune looks like justice. But only for a moment. It has brought defeat to Palamon, and then almost immediately it defeats Arcite as well. Even as he receives the plaudits of victory and the friendly look of Emelye ("the favour of Fortune"), Arcite is thrown from his horse and mortally injured. The result: complete frustration for everyone involved! Theseus comforts both sides and calls for friendship between them. He calls attention to the power of "aventure" (*KnT* 2703) and he assures everyone that no shame should be attached to being overthrown in battle, and certainly none to being thrown from a horse: " 'For fallyng nys nat but an aventure' " (*KnT* 2722).

On the face of it this is cold comfort in the midst of an ironic situation. Palamon's love has been for naught; Arcite's victory for naught; Theseus's planning, the theater, the tourney, even Emelye's acceptance of a destiny not preferred—all for naught. On the verge of death Arcite poses a central question, a perennial one in fact.

> "What is this world? what asketh men to have?
> Now with his love, now in his colde grave
> Allone, withouten any compaignye." (*KnT* 2777–79)

The futility and sadness of the scene impress the narrator as much as does the irony of events: "Infinite been the sorwes and the teeres / Of olde folk, and folk of tendre yeeres." Still, a resolution comes—a forward movement. For Saturn, who had prefigured these misfortunes—indeed, all misfortunes and deaths—also embodies the means for understanding them. He had said that he represents more than ill luck and ruin, for (although it is against his nature) he also stands for the virtue of prudence,[26] which should rule the intellect as justice should rule the will, by wise deliberations and perceptions. With his age, experience, and wisdom he finds the right path for human well-being even in the face of adversity.

> As sooth is seyd, elde hath greet avantage;
> In elde is bothe wysdom and usage;
> Men may the olde atrenne and noght atrede.
> Saturne anon, to stynten strif and drede,
> Al be it that it is agayn his kynde,
> Of al this strif he gan remedie fynde.   (*KnT* 2447–52)

This allegorized mythology from the close of Part Three now finds its narrative fulfillment in the philosophy of Theseus's aged father, Egeus, who "knew this worldes transmutacioun, / As he hadde seyn it chaunge bothe up and doun, / Joye after wo, and wo after gladnesse."

Sometimes cited for its connection with a pilgrimage motif in the *Canterbury Tales*, Egeus's brief speech has more obvious significance in its immediate context: in the natural fact of death and in the wisdom of humankind's need to place this last of all human misfortunes in a reasonable perspective.

> "Right as ther dyed nevere man," quod he,
> "That he ne lyvede in erthe in some degree,
> Right so ther lyvede never man," he seyde,
> "In al this world, that som tyme he ne deyde.
> This world nys but a thurghfare ful of wo,
> And we been pilgrymes, passynge to and fro.
> Deeth is an ende of every worldly soore."   (*KnT* 2843–49)

Egeus's melancholy words are, in point of fact, wise and comforting; he speaks "To this effect, ful wisely to enhorte / The peple that they sholde hem reconforte." And Theseus responds at once. With "al his bisy cure," he arranges the construction of a sepulchre for Arcite and then a magnificent funeral ceremony. The details for this long section of the narrative (*KnT* 2853–2966), which Chaucer drew from the funeral of Archemorus in the *Teseida* and ultimately from Book Six of Statius's *Thebaid*, have often puzzled readers, but in point of fact they are simply a logical extension of Egeus's speech. The living must pay their honor and their service to the dead: to Death, the last of "every worldly soore." And in his customary fashion Theseus ensures that this service will be just as "noble and

riche" (*KnT* 2888) as the theater he had built and the tourney he
had held. He chooses the same site where Arcite first fought with
Palamon for love; the same site where the tournament was held
(*KnT* 1862, 2857-64). He has the same grove ("swoote and grene")
where love's "hoote fires" burned stripped of all its growth to make
another blaze: "a fyr in which the office / Funeral he myghte al
accomplice." Everyone and everything laments. Tearful Palamon
and "wepynge" Emelye accompany three white steeds, sump-
tuously dressed out and bearing Arcite's shield and spear and bow;
the "nobleste of the Grekes" shoulder the bier through the black-
draped street, escorted by Egeus on one side and Theseus on the
other bearing golden vessels filled with funeral offerings of "hony,
milk, and blood, and wyn." With this sumptuous ritual of sorrow
Arcite receives his last honors and the living have the comfort of
their grief.

The *Knight's Tale* ends with the equivalent of an epilogue of
almost the same length (142 lines) as the "prologue" (143 lines)
with which it began. It provides a summary statement on the
significance of the events, as Theseus sees them, particularly in the
light of human misfortune and death. And more than that, it offers
a specific, natural example of what should follow from his theoreti-
cal summation. First, Theseus's philosophical discourse—drawn
from Boethius—both countervails and encompasses the wisdom of
Egeus's speech.[27] It addresses itself to life rather than to death; in
mythical terms its words are jovial rather than saturnine, prudent
but joyous. Thus it tells how the "faire cheyne of love" binds all the
disparate elements of creation in an established order, in a harmo-
nious rhythm which joins birth to death. Everything in "this
wrecched world," Theseus says, is limited, measured, and finite:
"Certeyne dayes and duracioun / To al that is engendred in this
place, / Over the whiche day they may nat pace." But everything
also finds its source of being in a Power which is "parfit," "stable"
and "eterne" and which sees to the endurance of creation "by
successiouns."

> "And therfore, of his wise purveiaunce,
> He [the Firste Moevere] hath so wel biset his ordinaunce,
> That speces of thynges and progressiouns
> Shullen enduren by successiouns,
> And nat eterne, withouten any lye."   (*KnT* 3011-15)

Theseus then proceeds to particularize the fact that death is intrinsic not only to the life of man, but to all earthly things (*KnT* 3017–34); it is not a *dis*order, but a part of the natural order of Jupiter who is the figure of Nature's rule.

> "What maketh this [the harmony of death] but Juppiter, the
>   kyng,
> That is prince and cause of alle thyng,
> Convertynge al unto his propre welle
> From which it is dirryved, sooth to telle?
> And heer-agayns no creature on lyve,
> Of no degree, availleth for to stryve."   (*KnT* 3035–40)

Instead of encouraging despair, therefore, death should persuade the prudent to recognize and live content within the natural bounds of existence.

> "Thanne is it wysdom, as it thynketh me,
> To maken vertu of necessitee,
> And take it weel that we may nat eschue,
> And namely that to us alle is due."   (*KnT* 3041–44)

Not to "take it weel"—to complain and "grucche" about the human condition, misfortune, and death—is not simply a waste of time; it is willful shortsightedness.

From this it follows that Theseus proposes neither a denial of death and woe nor a supernatural leap over death and woe, but an acceptance of the normal rhythm of human existence: death with life, sorrow with joy.

> "What may I conclude of this longe serye,
> But after wo I rede us to be merye,
> And thanken Juppiter of al his grace?"   (*KnT* 3067–69)

The pathos of Arcite's death and the grief of his friends have proved real enough, but so is the honor of his name ("goode Arcite, of chivalrie the flour"), and so is the goodness of continuing life. Therefore, "of sorwes two," of the griefs of Emelye and Palamon, Theseus recommends "o parfit joye, lastynge everemo." His characteristic optimism may be showing again, but Theseus's heart and mind are in the right place. He will "bigynne," he says, by amending the griefs of those who sorrow most. If Emelye will show her "wommanly pitee," and if Palamon will "com neer, and taak [his] lady by the hond," there will be another new start and a "merye" celebration of life.

> And thus with alle blisse and melodye
> Hath Palamon ywedded Emelye.
> And God, that al this wyde world hath wroght,
> Sende hym his love that hath it deere aboght. . . . (*KnT*
>   3097–3100)

As Saturn had predicted: a perfectly happy ending. Mars has been honored in battle, death, and funeral, and now Venus rejoices in the "blisse and melodye" of love's wedlock. In contrast to the uncertain ending of the *Parliament*, where no contestant wins, the *Knight's Tale* concludes with everyone somehow a winner. A "remedie" has been found and it "hath plesed every part" (*KnT* 2446, 2452).

But in what does the remedy lie? Certainly not in an escape from reality, or in luck and the mere passage of time, or in the self-congratulatory assurance that good has somehow triumphed over evil. The *Knight's Tale* simply does not work in these ways. Its special character, as many critics have variously observed, consists of a series or network of dual, balancing parts. Personages are balanced against each other: Palamon and Arcite. Rhetorical units balance each other: the lovers' complaints and the lovers' prayers. Events balance each other: Theseus's Amazonian victory and wedding; Theseus's Theban clemency and destruction; the funeral of Arcite and the wedding of Palamon. There are clear signs, too, that just as the parts of the allegorized mythology balance each other—Mars and Venus, Saturn and Jupiter—so do the vocabularies associated with the deities. The language of Venus, for example, has to do with "having" and possessing, with jealousy, loveliness, and pleasure, with feasting, joy, and melody, with kindness, mercy, and pity; and the language of Mars has to do with "fending off," with violence, anger, and blaring sounds, with hardness, strength, victory, strife, and death.[28] Thus the following excerpt from Theseus's speech to Palamon and Arcite, with its paired arrangement of words, suggests that a linguistic analysis may very well reaffirm the results of other kinds of criticism.

". . . but nathelees
I speke as for my suster Emelye,
For whom ye have this strif [Mars] and jalousye [Venus].
Ye woot yourself she may nat wedden [Venus] two
Atones, though ye fighten [Mars] everemo.
That oon of you, al be hym looth [Mars] or lief [Venus],
He moot go pipen in an yvy leef;
This is to seyn, she may nat now han bothe,
Al be ye never so jalouse [Venus] ne so wrothe [Mars]." (*KnT*
1832–40)

In a style that is akin to decorative gothic, the *Knight's Tale* makes
its point over and over again, in analogous shapes and patterns: not
only in allegory, but in structure, characterization, and style.

Because allegory functions most obviously in the realm of ideas,
it provides some of the best clues for comprehending the philosophical rationale which "hovers over" the *Knight's Tale.* Throughout
this discussion I have been implying that the "golden mean" and, in
particular, Aristotle's conception of the four moral virtues lie at the
heart of what the story says and, indeed, how it is expressed.
Excluding all else, for the moment, the allegory addresses itself to
two dual human forces: to concupiscence and irascibility in the
sensitive soul, and to will and intelligence (to use the scholastic
terminology) in the intellective soul. When these forces balance
each other in a dramatic way—changing and altering as circumstances change—then the condition of virtue prevails. Temperance
rules the concupiscible appetite, fortitude the irascible appetite,
justice the will, and prudence the intellect.[29] Not only does the
Knight's Tale embody this philosophical commonplace in a mythological allegory wherein Venus represents both concupiscence and
temperance, Mars irascibility and fortitude, Jupiter will and justice,
and Saturn intellect and prudence, but it reflects these associations
in other artistic modes and even in the story's largest structural
pattern, its four-part division.

Apart from the introductory "prologue" which deals with the
exploits of Theseus, Part One of the Knight's story focuses primarily
on the action of Venus: on Palamon and Arcite's falling in love with
Emelye, on their arguing over love, and on their complaining for
love. Indeed, it ends with the unanswerable lover's question: "Yow
loveres axe I now this questioun: / Who hath the worse, Arcite or
Palamoun?" Another kind of action begins Part Two. Arcite returns

to Athens in disguise and Palamon at last escapes from prison. The action gradually builds up to the outrageous battle in the grove where the Theban lovers of Part One (*KnT* 1328–33) now take on the role of Theban warriors (*KnT* 1542–62) engaged in internecine battle, pleading to be put to death, and rejoicing at the prospect of yet another fight within the year. Part Three, dominated by the mythological allegory of justice, shows how Theseus arranges everything in an ideal balance which gives human appetites their appropriate place and simultaneously binds them within the just circle of the theater; and it ends with the oddly benevolent assurance (odd because it comes unnaturally from Saturn) that everything will turn out right. And finally, apart from its "epilogue" resolution, Part Four focuses upon human misfortune, suffering, and death; on the "aventure" of tourneying, the accident of Arcite's death, and on the only natural means that prudence can perceive for coping with them—the ritual of funereal sorrow.

To suggest that Chaucer had an idea in mind when he divided the *Knight's Tale* as he did does not imply that he imposed on it a rigid philosophical formula, in the style of Dante, let us say. There are too many other things going on in the various parts of his story—too much interweaving and crisscrossing—for one to believe that each of four parts "stands for" something in a numerological game between the poet and his readers. At the same time Chaucer must have been thinking about what he was doing, and it is at least a reasonable possibility that he gave the *Knight's Tale* something like what he gave the *Troilus* when he modeled its five-book structure on Boethius's five books of the *De Consolatione:* [30] an allusive form of what Panofsky calls *manifestatio,* an ordering of parts which tends to make content and theme somehow palpable and explicit. [31] The four parts of the *Knight's Tale* would then constitute an appropriate shape which helps enhance what the story already does in its various pairing of twos and twos.

Chaucer's excursion into the realm of allegorized mythology ended with the *Knight's Tale.* What he did with it cannot be summarized in any simple fashion because he had so absorbed the natural and moral traditions of classical myth in the Middle Ages, and so subordinated them to the intricacies of a highly mannered art that it would be perverse to simplify the process. Still, two things can be said with some assurance. First, even when he adopted allegorized myth, Chaucer did so with the clear understanding that in its most elaborate forms it belonged to the naturalistic levels of

physical reality and human behavior. But those limits were generous, for they allowed Chaucer ample opportunity to create a
composite image of the chivalric ideal of the "verray, parfit gentil
knyght" who seeks to be and to exemplify in story the nature of a
"whole person." That ideal was not dominated by one part or
another, by the instincts of Venus or of Mars; nor did it deny its
parts, but governed them with a just balancing of strength and
kindness and, finally, by prudently perceiving a path by which just
conduct may proceed (with a stability that renews itself) through
the fluctuations of time and changing human conditions. The
nobility of this ideal, and ultimately of the Knight's entire story,
does not derive from any single part—from "any partie or cantel of a
thyng"—but from the wholeness and fullness of its nature.

Last, a somewhat disturbing thought. Over a period of years
criticism has often wrestled with the fact that Chaucer was inclined
to humanize his allegorical sources, adapting "characterizations"
out of the *Roman de la Rose*, for example, in such ways as to create
striking individuals like the Pardoner and the Wife of Bath. In
general, critics have respected this tendency of Chaucer's, as though
some special approbation were due to one who was divesting
himself of the medieval past. On occasion, too—the *Clerk's Tale*
being a notable example—criticism has found it difficult to accept
Chaucer's mixing of realism and allegory, apparently assuming that
he can have one or the other, but certainly not both at the same
time. Instead of easing this situation, some recent allegorical
criticism of Chaucer's work has tended to magnify the division
between realism and allegory, the letter and the spirit. But what if
Chaucer aimed to do precisely what many readers seem to think
impossible? What if he was consciously, insistently mixing things?
The allegorical mythology in the *Knight's Tale* suggests that this is
what he did in one story, at least. For given the straightforward and
loosely wrought narrative of the *Teseida*, written in what Boccaccio
must have conceived of as the grand style, Chaucer pared his source
drastically and then supported it with an allegorical frame—with
Theseus's theater at the center, and with the influences of morally
allegorized deities radiating out into the structure, the language,
and the characterization of the whole story. It is a curious phenomenon, indeed, to see Chaucer *adding allegory* to a historical
romance as though his overall goal was to create a blend in which
the letter and the spirit are one and the same thing.

4 The Classical Scene: Ancient Place and Natural Time

Chaucer's art, as Paull Baum has noted,[1] shows little concern for the details of real settings and real geography. On numerous occasions Chaucer had stopped at Dover and Calais, and had made the Channel crossing; he was in Reims as a prisoner of war, in Paris on business, and might easily have visited St. Denis, the locale of the *Shipman's Tale*, and Poperinghe, the "birthplace" of Sir Thopas. He had been to Genoa, Florence, and Milan, and had doubtless seen some of Europe's loveliest countryside.[2] But for all that, his description of the Po River and its beautiful valley (a rarity in his works) comes borrowed and reduced from his source for the *Clerk's Tale*. Although he may not have traveled as far and wide as his Canterbury Knight or Wife of Bath, Chaucer had seen a great deal of his world and has told us practically nothing about it. Even his descriptions of home, of London and of England, are chary. We may deduce the city scene from the Cook's fragment and the tale of the Canon's Yeoman, but we actually see very little; and the same is true for the rest of England—a few fleeting topographical allusions, like those to Richmond, Greenwich, and "Bobbe-up-and-doun." High hedges may account for limited vistas up to a point, but the obvious conclusion lies elsewhere.

Aside from certain domestic details in the fabliau tradition—the location of windows and beds in the Miller's and Reeve's tales, or the plumbing and room arrangements in Pandare's house—"setting" was for Chaucer largely a matter of metaphor and symbol. In this he resembled those classical poets who conceived of "place" as a literary *topos*, a motif to suit what happens: to emphasize a moral condition or to amplify an idea. Like Ovid, whose settings are exemplary and depend on the connotations of history and literary tradition,[3] Chaucer used places as parallels or contrasts for his narrative themes. The tormenting cave of Alcyone's mind, the Edenic garden in the *Parliament* or in January's story, the rugged coast of Brittany—which seems real enough—are all primarily portraits of internal, human problems or conditions; and it matters not in the least whether Chaucer's own imagination or his sources concocted them, or whether external reality affirmed them. Setting *meant* something. Moreover, its meaning could be read in descriptive details themselves and in their context so that, for example, the poor widow's "narwe cotage" in the *Nun's Priest's Tale* serves, like her "diete" and her "cote," to describe a humility which contrasts with the proud barn "yeerd" kingdom that regal Chauntecleer holds in "governaunce" for his "plesaunce."[4]

Classical history and myth had given Chaucer several ancient settings, most obviously the Troy scene of the *Troilus*. Although many of its specifics will suggest that Chaucer modeled his Troy on fourteenth-century London, we will also see that he carefully adapted his story to a pattern of tragic action. When he dealt with Rome in three of the *Canterbury Tales*, his treatment varied: he blurred the city from recognition in the story of Virginia, converted it from its pagan past in the legend of Saint Cecilia, and then overlaid it with spiritual meaning in the tale of Custance. There are ancient settings in the *Knight's Tale* as well—Scythia, Thebes, and Athens. And although their importance does not approach that of the prison tower, the grove, or the arena, it is clear that Chaucer was familiar with their connotative meanings and used them to suit his purposes.

The Scythia of the *Knight's Tale* and *Anelida* refers to an ill-defined region north of the Black Sea, extending from the mouth of the Danube in the west to the Caucasus Mountains in the east. For us the precise location matters less than some traditional associations: the fact that Scythia "meant" a bitterly cold climate, cruel behavior, and a barbarous culture. Thus the account from Herodotus, mentioned by Tertullian,[5] describes the Scythians and their neighbors as plunderers and cannibals. They scalped their enemies and drank their blood; they used human skulls for drinking bowls—apparently in a more familiar manner than the Gauls. Their worship of Diana, the chief deity of the Tauri, included, according

to an anecdote in Ovid (*Ex Ponto* III. ii), the blood sacrifice by
Scythian maidens of those unlucky male strangers who happened
on their shores. The legendary Amazons[6] were one of the Scythian
tribes to share the hated reputation of the region. As fierce warriors
of a cold and snowy clime, they were thought to have made a
practice of slaying or abandoning their male children, of requiring
the killing of a man in battle before receiving allowance to bear
children, and of removing a breast (their name: *a-mazo*, by one
etymology) to enable them to handle the bow and arrow with ease.
Tradition would suggest, then, that Theseus had no easy conquest
in his encounter with the "regne of Femenye": Statius and Boccaccio treat it as a serious struggle, and even Chaucer's minimal
redaction makes clear that Theseus's victory had followed upon a
lengthy war, a "grete bataille," and finally a siege (*KnT* 875–81).
Still, the bloody and heartless background of Scythia seems far
removed from the *Knight's Tale* when one considers the joyous
entry into Athens of Theseus's Amazonian bride, Hippolyta, or her
lovely sister, Emelye, picking flowers near the prison of Palamon and
Arcite. It would be far removed, too, were it not for the fact that
Chaucer's Scythian and Amazonian allusions, though brief, provide
his only forewarning of (or background to) the bloody, vindictive
portrait of Diana in Theseus's theater. The goddess's ruthlessness
was part of mythic history before Chaucer made it part of allegory.
And the same was also true of Mars and Venus, two of the major
deities of Thebes.

   In a characterization which dates back to classical antiquity,
Chaucer's Man of Law associates Thebes with "strif" (*MLT* 200).
Dicaearchus, for example, had observed in the *Descriptio Graeciae*
that the insolent pride of Thebes and its inhabitants was such that
they were "always ready to settle their disputes by fighting rather
than by the ordinary course of justice"; Tertullian's brief remark,
with its ring of proverbial prejudice, follows similar lines: "It is said
that Thebans are born stupid and brutal, and Athenians most
skillful in learning and speech."[7] Sweeping generalizations like these
were supported, of course, by a mythical history which Chaucer
had learned primarily from Ovid, Statius, and Boccaccio;[8] perhaps,
too, from a "romaunce" of Thebes like the one Criseyde and her
ladies hear in Troy (*Tr* 2. 100–105). At its root was the legend of the
city's founding by Cadmus who slays a dragon and then sows its
teeth; armed warriors immediately grow out of the earth and begin

to slaughter each other. The survivors become the "city fathers," and the history of their settlement constitutes a series of wild and bloody episodes marked by internecine war, illicit behavior, and treachery. Oedipus slays his father and marries his mother; his sons, Etheocles and Polyneices, break their pledge concerning the city's governance and engage in a furious civil war which ends in mutual fratricide; their successor, the "tiraunt Creon," appears at the beginning of the *Knight's Tale* where he refuses the Theban widows the right to bury their slain husbands. This is Thebes. And as if family chaos were not enough, the city was also noted as a favorite haunt for philandering Jupiter: here he bedded with Alcmena, the mother of Hercules, and then with Semele, the mother of Bacchus, thus arousing the anger of Juno against a criminal and adulterous city. That characterization also reached back to the founding of Thebes, to Cadmus's wife, Harmonia, the illegitimate offspring of the affair between Venus and Mars. Her parents' crime, too, had ravaged the city, for to spite his cuckoldry Vulcan had given Harmonia the legendary Brooch of Thebes as a wedding gift—a token which would inspire feminine greed and treachery.[9]

Taken altogether the Theban scene could exemplify a number of unhappy themes, for example, the history of old tragedies, as it does in the *Troilus*, or a history of Mars unleashed and of Venus unrestrained, as it does in the *Knight's Tale*. Thus Palamon and Arcite survive as worthy heirs of two unhappy traditions of the "blood roial" of Thebes (*KnT* 1018–19). Despite their sworn brotherhood, or perhaps because of it since they are Thebans, they respond to falling in love with Emelye by breaking their oath to each other and by engaging in a senseless argument, a "greet . . . strif," which the passing of years only exacerbates. Like their forebears, Etheocles and Polyneices, they thrive on fighting and on mutual accusations of falsehood and treachery. Looking for someone or something to blame, they look outside themselves: to Theseus, to the "crueel goddes" who govern the world, to bad Fortune (Saturn), and above all to their lineage and history. Moreover, as they comment on the past they align themselves with it in slightly different ways, for Palamon emphasizes the Thebes of intemperate love where Juno personifies jealousy and Venus inspires it.

> "But I moot been in prisoun thurgh Saturne,
> And eek thurgh Juno, jalous and eek wood,

> That hath destroyed wel ny al the blood
> Of Thebes with his waste walles wyde;
> And Venus sleeth me on that oother syde
> For jalousie and fere of hym Arcite." (*KnT* 1328–33)

Arcite, however, finds his kinship in the Thebes of violence: in Juno's cruel warring against Thebes, in Cadmus the founder, and in Mars's ire.

> "How longe, Juno, thurgh thy crueltee,
> Woltow werreyen Thebes the citee?
> Allas, ybroght is to confusioun
> The blood roial of Cadme and Amphioun,—
> Of Cadmus, which that was the firste man
> That Thebes bulte, or first the toun bigan. . . .
> Allas, thou felle Mars! allas, Juno!
> Thus hath youre ire oure lynage al fordo,
> Save oonly me and wrecched Palamoun. . . . (*KnT* 1543–61)

In a sense they do not recognize, Palamon and Arcite are right to blame Juno/Venus and Juno/Mars because the two cousins share a Theban penchant for uncontrolled passions—for the desire and the ire which have practically destroyed the "blood of Thebes," and which threaten to destroy the two of them in a fraternal battle or in the double execution they invite from Theseus. Being "ybroght . . . to confusioun" is an old art of Thebans, being merciless to themselves and to each other. It also spills over to the heavens where the mythological metaphors of passion continue the fighting.

> And right anon swich strif ther is bigonne,
> For thilke grauntyng, in the hevene above,
> Bitwixe Venus, the goddesse of love,
> And Mars, the stierne god armypotente,
> That Juppiter was bisy it to stente. . . . (*KnT* 2438–42)

The political and moral enemy of Theban extremes and Scythian barbarity is Athens, the traditional setting for wise, just, and philosophical behavior. The city had its name from its patron goddess of wisdom which means that it was, etymologically, the locale of the arts, philosophy, and letters.[10] Echoing Cicero, Saint Augustine would repeat a familiar notion: Athens was "the mother and the nurse of liberal doctrines, and of so many and so great philosophers, than whom Greece had nothing more famous and noble."[11] For Chaucer, too, the history of philosophy meant at least the names of honored Greeks, such as Plato, Socrates, Anaxagoras, Zeno, and "Aristotle and his philosophie"; or it meant Athens, which (like a university city) had a place for academic discourse, the Porch, *"that is to seyn, a gate of the toun of Athenis there as philosophris hadden hir congregacioun to desputen";*[12] it was *the* ancient place of study, for "lernynge philosophie" (*LGW* 1894-99). And in the *Knight's Tale*—as in Statius and Boccaccio—it was also the setting for mercy, because the "temple of the goddesse Clemence" (*KnT* 928) stood near the entrance to the town. Thus the "duc" who governs Chaucer's Athens conquers by "wysdom" as well as chivalry (*KnT* 865). He makes peace, fairly or firmly, with defeated enemies; he grants "mercy" to destitute widows, generous favors to a dear friend (Pirithous), and complete forgiveness to an escaped prisoner and a forsworn exile. He builds for his city a noble theater, rules its tournament with gentle justice, comforts the overthrown and the sorrowing, and heeds the counsel of a father who speaks "wisely." He honors the dead, rules in the wise English way, with the advice of "parlement," and from "his wise brest," like a philosopher king, he discourses on the nature of creation—of human life and death. For such lordship Athens is the proper scene.

Taken separately and together, the ancient places of the *Knight's Tale* have a direct relationship to the moral allegory which mythological allusion helps sustain: Scythia and harsh Diana, Thebes and the dissonance of Venus and Mars, Athens and the philosophical aspects of Saturn and Jupiter. Each place and its history represent a tendency to act along specific lines. Like the deities who settle their disputes in time, and the characters who finally reach accord, the three locales become part of an analogous, unified political order: Athens subjugates Scythia and placates it by royal wedlock; Athens lays waste Thebes and, in the end, restores it by "alliaunce" to "have fully of Thebans obeisaunce" (*KnT* 989-90, 2972-74). In sum, the reconciliations of characters and moral tendencies develop in parallel with political and historical reconciliations. Within this network it is clear that the ancient settings of the Knight's story are more akin to ideas than to real places. We *see* nothing at all of Scythia and scarcely anything of Thebes except its "olde" or "waste walles wyde"; and although nearly all the action occurs in and around Athens we have no sense of it as a place. We know only that the Temple of Clemence stands near the town and that a neighboring grove provides enough space for a tournament field and for burial ceremonies and games.[13] Had Chaucer not been condensing his materials and had he wanted us to imagine a "real place," he obviously could have done so—as he does when he amplifies his source in the *Troilus*. He could have created a "classical" scene which not only embodied meaning, but made its meaning all the more impressive by being a part of a living, historical reality.

The Trojan scene of the *Troilus* can be visualized despite the prevalence of vague domestic settings. Inside the walls of Troy are several temples, including one for Pallas Athena and the "palladion," where Troilus first sees Criseyde, and another apparently for Apollo (*Tr* 1. 162 ff.; 3. 539–46). Houses or palaces—the terms are used interchangeably—serve as the residences of Troilus, Criseyde, Deiphebus, and Pandare. The palaces have "halles" (which may be dining areas as well), chambers for sleeping, and small rooms or "closets" where one can sit alone and think in quiet, or write a letter, or sleep on occasion (*Tr* 2. 599, 1215; 3. 663). A bedroom may be small enough to be easily crowded by one or two, or large enough to accommodate a group of people staying overnight; it may even have a "chymeneye" and a "secre trappe-dore" (*Tr* 2. 1646–47; 3. 666–67, 759, 1141); and stairs from it may lead to a garden or an "herber" for relaxation and strolling (*Tr* 2. 814, 1705). There are gates at the city walls, for Troilus and Hector return triumphant through the Gate of Dardanus; Criseyde departs from an unnamed "yate," and near a gate at the walls Troilus looks for her return. Finally, outside the walls lies a "valeye"—perhaps the "feld" for battles—and beyond that a hill; then the Greek camp, which has a view of Troy in the distance. These physical details may seem imprecise, but they do give an overall impression of familiarity, as though Troy were very much like medieval London.[14] But over all else, Troy has an atmosphere. Kittredge described it as a doomed place and therefore a suitable setting for the doomed love of Troilus and Criseyde. Although questions have been raised about this view,[15] it has validity, especially when broadened to include the spectrum of Trojan history, from joy to woe. For what Chaucer did was to adapt the story of Troy, the tragedy of Troy, as a suitable background for the tragedy of Troilus. He made the characters, the careers, and the fortunes of both the city and his protagonist parallel and analogous.

According to a persistent tradition, which was both classical and medieval, the fall of Troy was ascribed to foolish pride and criminal lust.[16] The city freely and mistakenly followed a course of action which brought it not only great prosperity, but collapse and ruin as well. Its history was a civic or corporate tragedy, in particular a tragedy of love, for by Paris's rape of Helen and the subsequent determination of the city to defend that crime, Troy subjected itself to a woman and to the caprice of Fortune.[17] That Chaucer knew about the tradition of Troy's tragedy is clear, for when his Aeneas speaks of the city's fall he couches his remarks in the familiar language of medieval tragedy.

> "Allas, that I was born!" quod Eneas;
> "Thourghout the world oure shame is kid so wyde,
> Now it is peynted upon every syde.
> We, that weren in prosperite,
> Been now desclandred, and in swich degre,
> No lenger for to lyven I ne kepe."   (*LGW* 1027–32)

It is also likely that Chaucer was aware of identifications between the city and his hero: by etymology Troilus literally means "Little Troy," and his principal source, Boccaccio's *Filostrato*, had told him that Troilo was afflicted by the same love that had doomed all Troy to destruction.[18]

If we turn to the *Troilus* itself we can best see how Chaucer has adapted these traditions. In Book One, like Boccaccio, he begins by immediately setting the scene. A thousand Greek ships have come to Troy to avenge the rape of Helen, and Calchas, learning that the city will be destroyed, flees and leaves behind his widowed daughter, Criseyde. Of the war between the Trojans and the Greeks, Chaucer remarks only in passing what was commonplace—Fortune is in control.

> The thynges fellen, as they don of werre,
> Bitwixen hem of Troie and Grekes ofte;
> For som day boughten they of Troie it derre,
> And eft the Grekes founden nothing softe
> The folk of Troie; and thus Fortune on lofte,

And under eft, gan hem to whielen bothe
Aftir hir course, ay whil that thei were wrothe.   (*Tr* 1. 134–40)

But with the "gestes" and the details of how Troy fell, the poet will not concern himself. He will concentrate, instead, on the story of Troilus, and he advises those who are interested in the long history of the city and its battles to read elsewhere, "in Omer, or in Dares, or in Dite." Although this initial outline of the Trojan scene is brief, and drawn largely from the *Filostrato*, it is still significant. In a few stanzas it gives a threefold picture of the Troy story—the rape, the rule of Fortune in the ensuing war, and the destruction to come—a picture which is comparable to the narrator's three-part outline of Troilus's own story in the introduction to Book One, "Fro wo to wele, and after out of joie."

From the twenty-first stanza of Book One until the beginning of Book Four, no mention is made of the destiny of Troy or of its fall. With perhaps one exception, everything that we read seems favorable.[19] At the feast of the Palladion we see the gaiety of spring and a crowd of Trojan knights and maidens at ease and well arrayed (*Tr* 1. 155 ff.). Later we hear two brief allusions to women of Troy, Helen and Polyxena (*Tr* 1. 454–55, 676–79), renowned for their beauty. In addition, Pandare quotes a portion of Oënone's letter to Paris (*Tr* 1. 652–65), an illustration of his craft in love—despite his failures, but also a reminder of Troy's concern for love. Moreover, there are suggestions of victories by Troy and Troilus (*Tr* 1. 470–83): for "in armes so he spedde, / That the Grekes as the deth him dredde"; Pandare jokes about the siege (*Tr* 1. 558–60); and at length we learn that Troilus plays the lion amid the Greek host after Pandare promises to help him in his cause (*Tr* 1. 1072–75).

Amid this relaxed and prosperous setting, Troilus, like Troy, becomes devoted to a woman and subject to the whims of Fortune. "Ful unavysed of his woo comynge," he determines with full assent, "Criseyde for to love, and nought repente." He is willing to offer his full service to love and to deny his royal lineage, if need be; no longer will he fight for the city, or his family, or his own self-respect, but rather "to liken hire the bet for his renoun." Also, with his new devotion comes all the uncertainty of a love dependent upon Fortune (*Tr* 1. 330–50). Even the bright future that Pandare foresees is closely tied to the movement of the goddess's turning wheel: if you are now in sorrow, he tells Troilus, take comfort in the fact that Fortune changes.

"Woost thow nat wel that Fortune is comune
To everi manere wight in som degree?
And yet thow hast this comfort, lo, parde,
That, as hire joies moten overgon,
So mote hire sorwes passen everechon." (*Tr* 1. 843–47)

Such comfort will be small when we hear it again under different circumstances (*Tr* 4. 384 ff.), but at this point there are no worries about the war, nor will Troilus need to worry about his love. All is well as Pandare leads the way: "Tho Troilus gan doun on knees to falle, / And Pandare in his armes hente faste, / And seyde, 'Now, fy on the Grekes alle! / Yet, pardee, God shal helpe us atte laste' " (*Tr* 1. 1044–47).

If the pleasant and increasingly optimistic Troy setting is significant at this early stage of the narrative, it becomes more important in Books Two and Three. Here we encounter the joyful, mannered scene at Criseyde's house where the women listen, at their leisure, to the romance of Thebes, and where Pandare urges Criseyde to forget the austerity of her widow's life and to go out and enjoy the usual "Trojan" May games (*Tr* 2. 78 ff.). There is also the garden scene where Antigone sings of love, " 'in alle joie and seurte,' " and where Criseyde and her nieces amuse themselves so "that it joye was to see" (*Tr* 2. 813 ff.); and there are the parties, first at Deiphebus's house and then later, in Book Three, at Pandare's. Moreover, while the Trojans are happy at home, they continue to be fortunate in battle. Pandare, for example, tells of Troilus's victories (*Tr* 2. 190–203) and how the "Grekes fro hym gonne fleen"; he says, too, that he and Troilus spent half a day relaxing in the palace garden and discussing a plan for defeating the Greeks (*Tr* 2. 505–11). Moreover, there is another victory when Criseyde watches Troilus return triumphant from having "put to flighte the Grekes route" (*Tr* 2. 610–44); and later, in Book Three, part of the plan for deceiving everyone on Troilus's first night of bliss is the fabricated story that he is at a temple waiting for an omen from Apollo, "To telle hym next whan Grekes sholde flee" (*Tr* 3. 533–44).

But let us go back for a moment to Chaucer's most colorful addition to the bright picture of Troy, the party at Deiphebus's house which Helen attends. There is nothing of this in Chaucer's sources, and its effect is to enhance the joy, beauty, and easy pleasures that we have already seen in the city. At Pandare's urging

Deiphebus agrees to host a dinner for those who want to "protect" Criseyde; but when he asks about inviting Helen his reason has its own interest because it provides a background of male subservience at a particularly crucial time: " 'What wiltow seyn, if I for Eleyne sente / To speke of this? I trowe it be the beste, / For she may leden Paris as hire leste.' " At the gathering that takes place Helen holds the center stage and, along with Pandare, dominates the conversation. After Troilus's illness is mentioned, she complains so "that pite was to here"; and when Pandare explains that Criseyde needs help, Helen rises to the occasion with a speech that echoes with ironic associations between the two women—of harm done to them, of sorrow and truth.

> Eleyne, which that by the hond hire [Criseyde] held,
> Took first the tale, and seyde, "Go we blyve";
> And goodly on Criseyde she biheld,
> And seyde, "Joves lat hym nevere thryve,
> That doth yow harm, and brynge hym soone of lyve,
> And yeve me sorwe, but he shal it rewe,
> If that I may, and alle folk be trewe!"   (*Tr* 2. 1604–10)

Everyone at the dinner then determines to be Criseyde's friend in the suit brought against her by the traitorous straw man, Poliphete. But before the matter is dropped Helen and Deiphebus invade Troilus's sickroom to elicit his aid and to give us a glimpse of the gracious allurement of Menelaus's wife, whose actions are a prologue to Criseyde's.

> Eleyne, in al hire goodly softe wyse,
> Gan hym salue, and wommanly to pleye,
> And seyde, "Iwys, ye moste alweies arise!
> Now, faire brother, beth al hool, I preye!"
> And gan hire arm right over his shulder leye,
> And hym with al hire wit to reconforte;
> As she best koude, she gan hym to disporte.   (*Tr* 2. 1667–73;
>   cf. 3. 168, 1128–34)

Without much prodding Troilus consents to help defend Criseyde, greatly to Helen's pleasure; then he deceives his brother and sister-in-law with a letter and a document which he asks them to examine and which they take to a nearby garden.[20] Finally, after the secret meeting of the lovers and the miracle of Criseyde's first kiss, they return, and "Eleyne hym kiste, and took hire leve blyve, / Deiphebus ek, and hom wente every wight."

As R. D. Mayo has observed, the references to the Trojan scene through most of Book One, and all of Books Two and Three, show that Chaucer made no effort to direct attention to the final destruction of the city. And yet the picture of Troy is still important as a scene of prosperity. No mention is made of the fall of the city because Chaucer is describing Troy in good fortune, and this background suits the growing prosperity and good fortune of Troilus in love. With "wordes white" Pandare works hard to undermine Criseyde's status as a widow. He arranges the details of Troilus's success: the exchange of letters, the "chance" encounter at Criseyde's window, the first meeting of the lovers, and their nights of joy. And like Troy, Troilus becomes more deeply involved in a game of chance for worldly bliss—a game in which everything depends on the roll of the dice (*Tr* 2. 1347–49). Lucky occasions and properly calculated times mean a great deal in this play for, as Pandare says, "worldly joie halt nought but by a wir . . . Forthi nede is to werken with it softe." Thus, as the paradisiacal imagery accumulates in the last part of Book Three and as the narrator finds himself caught up in the joys of love which he describes, the reader is regularly reminded of the inconstancy of earthly affections.[21]

Then, at the beginning of Book Four, we learn that fickle Fortune is about to overturn Troilus and to take away his joy.

> But al to litel, weylaway the whyle,
> Lasteth swich joie, ythonked be Fortune,
> That semeth trewest whan she wol bygyle,
> And kan to fooles so hire song entune,
> That she hem hent and blent, traitour comune!
> And whan a wight is from hire whiel ythrowe,
> Than laugheth she, and maketh hym the mowe.   (*Tr* 4. 1–7)

Immediately after the proem, and as an impetus and backdrop for Troilus's misfortune, we learn that Troy, too, has come upon bad days. For the first time the Trojan forces suffer a setback: Hector and "ful many a bold baroun" go out to battle and, after the long day's struggle, it is they who flee and feel the pinch of sorrow.

But in the laste shour, soth for to telle,
The folk of Troie hemselven so mysledden
That with the worse at nyght homward they fledden.

At which day was taken Antenore . . .
So that, for harm, that day the folk of Troie
Dredden to lese a gret part of hire joie.   (*Tr* 4. 47–56)

In the Greek camp Calchas is soon pleading that Antenor be
exchanged for Criseyde, and he reiterates at length the prophecy
that we had heard at the outset: Troy shall be "ybrend, and beten
down to grownde"; Troy will turn "to asshen dede"; "The town of
Troie shal ben set on-fire" (*Tr* 4. 71–126).

A parliament in Troy must next decide whether to accept the
Greek terms of exchange. And here Chaucer alters and expands
Boccaccio's account as he ironically describes the foolish self-
betrayal of the people, who "sholden hire confusioun desire" by
seeking the deliverance of Antenor, "that brought hem to meschaunce": "For he was after traitour to the town / Of Troye; allas,
they quytte hym out to rathe! / O nyce world, lo, thy discrecioun!"
With this mistake on top of the defeat in battle, the atmosphere of
the Troy scene grows dark and foreboding, and treachery lurks in
the background.

Faced with the dilemma of disclosing his love for Criseyde or
losing her, Troilus abandons his self-control. He batters himself
about and roars useless complaints against Fortune and Cupid (*Tr* 4.
260–90). But even now, when all attention seems fixed on the
internal struggles of Troilus, we do not lose sight of the city. In his
lament Troilus wonders why Fortune has not slain him, or his
brothers, or his "fader, kyng of Troye"—eventualities which will
come soon enough. And when he cries against the trick that
Fortune has played on him, Pandare offers several cures: a different
gift of Fortune, another woman; or failing that, there is the example
of Paris, the cause of Troy's predicament.

"Go ravisshe here ne kanstow nat for shame!
And other lat here out of towne fare,
Or hold here stille, and leve thi nyce fare.

"Artow in Troie, and hast non hardyment
To take a womman which that loveth the,

> And wolde hireselven ben of thyn assent?
> Now is nat this a nyce vanitee?''   (*Tr* 4. 530–36)

But Troilus thinks this will not do. Another rape would be intolerable during the present misfortunes: " 'First, syn thow woost this town hath al this werre / For ravysshyng of wommen so by myght, / It sholde nought be suffred me to erre, / As it stant now, ne don so gret unright' " (*Tr* 4. 547–50). And, besides, Criseyde's "name" is at stake. Still, Pandare goes right on, recalling how Paris has solaced himself and asking Troilus why he should not do the same: " 'Thenk ek how Paris hath, that is thi brother, / A love; and whi shaltow nat have another?' "

The bad fortunes of the city and their cause have now begun to matter; and later, when the lovers are together for the last time, Criseyde highlights that fact in her frenetic list of ways by which they may be reunited, mentioning, among other things, a current peace rumor. If Helen, the cause of the war, were restored to her rightful husband, then their situation—as well as Troy's—would change for the better.

> "Ye sen that every day ek, more and more,
> Men trete of pees; and it supposid is
> That men the queene Eleyne shal restore,
> And Grekis us restoren that is mys.
> So, though ther nere comfort non but this,
> That men purposen pees on every syde,
> Ye may the bettre at ese of herte abyde."   (*Tr* 4. 1345–51)

Toward the end of her exhortation Criseyde implies, as Troilus had before, that Troy is faring badly; she urges Troilus to forget about fleeing the city with her, " 'syn Troie hath now swich nede / Of help.' "

In Book Five Chaucer not only continues to paint the declining picture of Troy with an eye on his failing hero, but he effectively identifies the two. The weeklong feast at Sarpedoun's (*Tr* 5. 428–501), with its wine, women, and song, pathetically recalls the bright and joyous parties in the Troy of Books Two and Three; the letters which Troilus reads in seclusion recall the happier times when they were written. The vanity of Troy's and Troilus's past pleasures grows ever more apparent. On returning to the city and its haunting memories, he laments his own fate and that of Troy—both subjects of love's desire: " 'Now blisful lord [Cupide], so cruel thow ne be / Unto the blood of Troie, I preye the, / As Juno was unto the blood Thebane, / For which the folk of Thebes caughte hire bane.' " Like Fortune, Cupid's desire is cruel and blind, and it will—so to speak— destroy not only Troilus but all the "blood of Troie."

Even more pointed are the comments of Diomede and Criseyde in the Greek camp. Diomede's persuasive love talk, for example, is shot through with an insistent dual purpose: Greeks are stronger than Trojans—he will be a better lover than any Trojan; the Greeks will destroy Troy and every Trojan—including Criseyde's lover. The high point of his argument comes when he declares that those imprisoned in the city will suffer unmercifully for the rape of Helen.

> "Swiche wreche on hem, for fecchynge of Eleyne,
> Ther shal ben take, er that we hennes wende,
> That Manes, which that goddes ben of peyne,
> Shal ben agast that Grekes wol hem shende.
> And men shul drede, unto the worldes ende,
> From hennesforth to ravysshen any queene,
> So cruel shal oure wreche on hem be seene.
>
> "What wol ye more, lufsom lady deere?
> Lat Troie and Troian fro youre herte pace!"   (*Tr* 5. 890–96, 911–12)

With unerring insight into Criseyde's heart, Diomede ties the failing fortune of the city to that of Troilus. She, too, we may recall, had reminisced on the past joys of Troy and Troilus (*Tr* 5. 729–35); and in anticipation of Diomede's success the narrator had observed that "bothe Troilus and Troie town / Shal knotteles thoroughout hire herte slide; / For she wol take a purpos for t'abyde" (*Tr* 5. 768–70). By this point, it would appear that Diomede, Criseyde, and the narrator are all explicitly aware that Troy and Troilus are one.

Meanwhile, waiting vainly for Criseyde's return, Troilus dreams that his love has been taken by a boar. In the *Filostrato* Troilo understands that Diomede is the boar and that he has lost his beloved, but Chaucer's Troilus remains unsure. He asks the advice of his sister, Cassandra, who tells him that to understand the dream—and, by implication, his own tragic condition—he must learn its background: " 'Thow most a fewe of olde stories heere, / To purpos, how that Fortune overthrowe / Hath lordes olde. . . .' " The sketch of Theban history which follows (*Tr* 5. 1464 ff.) consists primarily of tragedies, and it concludes by showing that Diomede is the boar and that Troilus's lady (whom Cassandra by a smile suggests she knows) is gone: " 'This Diomede is inne, and thow art oute.' " The immediate effect of introducing Cassandra from the Trojan scene is to have her provide, in panoramic fashion, some concrete analogies to the condition of Troilus as a tragic victim of Fortune. Her speech is a historic or mythic counterpart of the Boethian philosophic discourse in Book Four. The latter deepens our insight into Troilus's psychic failure, but this extends the implications of his trust in Fortune beyond even the Trojan setting and prepares for the ultimate vision (of the past, present, and future) in the closing stanzas of the poem.

Now near the end, and in anticipation of Troilus's death, the narrator turns to the city, which is on the verge of suffering its worst misfortune.

> Fortune, which that permutacioun
> Of thynges hath, as it is hire comitted
> Thorugh purveyaunce and disposicioun
> Of heighe Jove, as regnes shal be flitted
> Fro folk in folk, or when they shal be smytted,
> Gan pulle awey the fetheres brighte of Troie
> Fro day to day, til they ben bare of joie.   (*Tr* 5. 1541–47)

The brightest feather of Troy is plucked when Hector is slain. Now the inevitable is at hand for Troy—and Troilus too, for soon after Hector's death Troilus sees the captured "cote-armure" of Diomede and on it finds the brooch he gave Criseyde. Fortune has played a game with him as well: "Gret was the sorwe and pleynte of Troilus; / But forth hire cours Fortune ay gan to holde. / Criseyde loveth the sone of Tideüs, / And Troilus moot wepe in cares colde. / Swich is this world, whoso it kan byholde" (*Tr* 5. 1744–48). Again, foreground and background intertwine: the imperial dominion will pass from Troy to Greece, as Criseyde passes from Troilus to Diomede; and as Fortune's tragic movement ends for Troilus, the poem anticipates the city's fall in the background.

Thus, in the last two books of the *Troilus*, the initial analogies between the loves and fortunes of Troy and Troilus reach a classically symmetrical resolution. The change in the city's fortune, which comes with the capture and exchange of the traitorous Antenor, is simultaneously the occasion for the change of Troilus's fortune and an anticipation of Criseyde's betrayal. In addition, the disenchantment regarding the war and the rape that caused it becomes a minor motif in the complaints of the lovers. In the thoughts of Criseyde and in the persuasive speeches of Diomede we find an insistent identification of Troy with Troilus; and at the end there are the last explicit analogies between Fortune's shift from Troilus to Diomede, from Troy to Greece. Troy and Troilus, then, have become one in misfortune as they had been one in prosperity.

The similarities between the foreground and the background of Fortune's activities in the *Troilus* constitute the best evidence for concluding that Chaucer has made the tragedy of Troy akin to the tragedy of Troilus in both substance and contour. At the center of that kinship rests a perception concerning the individual and the commonweal which one medieval humanist expressed with uncompromising austerity.

> The beginnings of desire are sweet beyond honey and the honeycomb; but its end is more bitter than any wormwood. For what is the end of idle tale-telling, feasting and sated desire but the blazing pyre which scatters the burning brands of desolation over all the citizens?[22]

Such harsh moralizing may sound unfriendly to us, but it was not so foreign to the ears of Chaucer and his audience; indeed, for all his gentle sympathy Geoffrey Chaucer could write something similar in two of the concluding stanzas of the *Troilus*.

> Swich fyn hath, lo, this Troilus for love!
> Swich fyn hath al his grete worthynesse!
> Swich fyn hath his estat real above,
> Swich fyn his lust, swich fyn hath his noblesse!
> Swich fyn hath false worldes brotelnesse!

> Lo here, of payens corsed olde rites,
> Lo here, what alle hire goddes may availle;
> Lo here, thise wrecched worldes appetites. . . .   (*Tr* 5. 1828 ff.)

If there is a problem with these lines, it does not arise from the fact that they lack logic or philosophical validity, but that their tone seems jarring. And it jars because, unlike other moralizing passages in the *Troilus*, these lines are addressed from outside the narrative and reflect on the protagonist seriously and directly.[23] Elsewhere Chaucer's method has been sympathetically indirect. His "moralite," buried in the facts, comes by implication. It is his usual mode, his best, and the Trojan scene can serve as a paradigm of it because that scene is so unobtrusively shaded and colored with the hues of the foreground that it calls no attention to itself as a source for preachment or as something intellectually separable and distinct from the fictional life of its inhabitants. The analogies, in brief, are implicit and vital, sensed or felt but never once directly stated.

Moreover, the similarities between Troy and Troilus are arranged so that they disclose what Eric Auerbach might call an "intrahistorical" action. In the *Troilus* the fortunes of an individual are viewed within the setting of a whole society enmeshed in similar fortunes; thus, what Troilus does—and what happens to him—seems in no way extraordinary, "especially arranged," or "outside the usual course of events." The instability of Fortune in his case "results from the inner processes of the real, historical world" where he appears as a real, historical figure.[24] Unlike the ancient scenes of the *Knight's Tale*, which are suitable in only nominal ways, the setting for the *Troilus* has a literal, historical reality which gives an added dimension to the story. It is so disposed that one can turn it around and recognize Troilus's personal tragedy as a particular, pathetic example of a corporate tragedy enacted by a great people long ago. Furthermore, Chaucer apparently thought that his story of Troilus and old Troy would recreate a past which might have a special impact upon the "New Troy"[25] of England's London and on its "yonge, fresshe folkes." For like its significance to "he or she," the story's history was somehow still alive.

In his customary way Chaucer did not tempt success. But even if the classical scenes matter relatively little in his later ancient stories, some account should be taken of the fact that three of the *Canterbury Tales* are variously set in Rome: the old Rome of Livy's story of Appius and Virginius; the Rome of Christian persecution where Saint Cecilia is martyred, and the Rome of Christendom where an emperor marries his daughter to a distant sultan of Syria. Although it is difficult to be sure what Chaucer's assumptions about Rome may have been, certain traditions were readily available. From his reading in Virgil, Lucan, and Valerius Maximus—and perhaps in parts of Livy, Suetonius, Sallust, Augustine, and Jerome—he would have known of the city's old political and military greatness, the Roman *imperium*. In addition, with the greatness of its rule he would have found a mixture of characteristic virtues and vices: on one side, a stern sense of duty like Aeneas's, social and political justice such as Scipio describes, personal integrity like Seneca's "moralitee," Cato's austerity, Lucrece's chastity, and Caesar's "estaatly honestee"; and on the other side, cruel pride like Tarquin's, luxury and unnatural viciousness like Nero's, and over all a sense of glory and self-esteem which Sallust praised and Augustine often mocked.[26] It is a curious mixture, and at best rather heartless. In Christian times, moreover, this picture was replaced by the notion of Rome as the Chair of Saint Peter, the center and home of Christianity—a matter of special interest to the English court after 1378 and the beginning of the Western Schism.[27] This shift from one time to another, from ancient past to Christian present, will be a minor motif in Chaucer's three Roman stories.

At the uncertain center of the *Physician's Tale* there is an old Roman assumption that virtue is in some sense physical and material, and that immortality arises from what people think, from human respect. For more than a hundred lines, before he actually begins his story, the Physician describes how "just governance" and Nature are his primary concerns. Nature, the "vicaire general" of God (who is Himself "the formere principal"), has in its "sovereyn diligence" created an ideal young woman. Like "othere creatures," Nature has made Virginia "to the worshipe of [its] lord," but *she* stands above all as Nature's own "delit": beautifully hued, with golden hair that "Phebus dyed"; chaste, virtuous, and wise "as Pallas"; quiet, gentle, but busy to avoid "Bacus," "Venus," and the follies that appear "at feestes, revels, and at daunces." At some length, then, the Physician presents an ideal picture of a chain of command—God's lordly governance of Nature, Nature's "sovereyn" rule over creation, and finally Virginia's, the best of creatures, rule of herself: "With alle humylitee and abstinence, / With alle attemperaunce and pacience, / With mesure eek of beryng and array" (*PhysT* 5–66). Moreover, the Physician knows very well that what Nature proposes, man disposes; therefore he goes on to point out the responsibilities of governesses to govern their charges and of parents to govern their children (*PhysT* 72–104).

But herein lies a major problem of his story. At its start the unjust

and lecherous judge Appius, who "governour was of that regioun,"
lusts after Virginia and decrees that she is actually the property of
his cohort in crime, the false "cherl" Claudius. Appius orders her
father, Virginius, to turn her over to the court. His corruption of
governance by his "sentence" and "juggement" is self-evident, but
the problem of human control is compounded by the subsequent
"sentence" of Virginia's father, who decides to kill his daughter to
save her honor.

> "O doghter, which that art my laste wo,
> And in my lyf my laste joye also,
> O gemme of chastitee, in pacience
> Take thou thy deeth, for this is my sentence.
> For love, and nat for hate, thou most be deed;
> My pitous hand moot smyten of thyn heed."   (*PhysT* 221–26)

A curious situation this, especially since the Physician had earlier
warned against *leniency* with children: "Under a shepherde softe
and necligent / The wolf hath many a sheep and lamb torent."
Virginia must surely be the "sheep and lamb" of her story, but who
is the wolf? Can it be both a cruel, lecherous governor *and* a stern,
loving father? It would seem so, for Virginius's incapacity to see
beyond physical, temporal, and natural virtue leads him to proceed
in the ancient fashion: "Hir fader, with ful sorweful herte and wil, /
Hir heed of smoot, and by the top it hente, / And to the juge he gan
it to presente" (*PhysT* 254–56). To paraphrase Augustine, we may
commend and feel sympathy for Virginius's—and Virginia's!—
"greatness of spirit," but never their soundness of judgment.[28]

To search out a "solution" for the *Physician's Tale* would seem to
be a waste of time, and perhaps irrelevant. On one hand the
generous work of Nature, the laudatory portraits of Virginia and
Virginius, and the climactic pathos of the scene between father and
daughter are designed to catch our hearts; but the facts of the story
force us to question natural, human governance just as the entropic
movement in the *Parliament* forces us to question human love. And
if this is true up to the point of Virginia's death, the concluding
judgments of the story only emphasize our doubts. Thus the people
imprison Appius and he commits suicide—his fate not unlike
Virginia's; Claudius was "demed" to be hanged but, although he
was equally guilty, Virginius ("of his pitee"!) pleads for his life and

he is exiled; and then the accomplices in crime—whom we have heard nothing of till now—are summarily hanged: "The remenant were anhanged, moore and lesse, / That were consentant of this cursednesse." With such indiscriminate judgments, "moore and lesse," with such governance in disarray, the story proper ends— only to be followed by two more "sentences." First the Physician, the critic of the legal system, as Beryl Rowland has shown, says that his story shows the superiority of *God's* judgment: it proves that sin gets its reward and that the "worm of conscience" secretly terrorizes the wicked. "Heere may men seen how synne hath his merite. / Beth war, for no man woot whom God wol smyte / In no degree. . . ." Of that pious conclusion and its impious implication (was it also God who "smoot" Virginia?) neither the Physician nor we have any assurance. This, in turn, is followed by Harry Bailly's judgments that put the blame on almost everyone: the "fals cherl" (Claudius), the "fals justise" (Appius), all such "juges and hire advocatz," and finally Nature!

> Algate this sely mayde is slayn, allas!
> Allas, to deere boughte she beautee!
> Wherfore I seye al day that men may see
> That yiftes of Fortune and of Nature
> Been cause of deeth to many a creature.
> Hire beautee was hire deth, I dar wel sayn.   (*PardT* 292–97)

With this simpleminded summary the whole tale boomerangs and goes back to the initial portrait of Nature's ideal and loving rule. Nature, like Appius and Virginius, has become a destroyer.

Just what is one to think or feel about such contrariness? If one is not puzzled it would appear that Chaucer's craft has failed. Nor need one be surprised that this was Chaucer's purpose: to give an artfully confused picture of the way the world goes. He had done this before and would do it again. Still, the classical setting does help to make things clearer, for although Virginia's story comes ultimately from a Roman historian, "Titus Livius," and although it could be used to explain the fall of the Roman Decimvirs and a major change in Roman government, Rome is not mentioned once and has absolutely no role. Instead the scene has been made intentionally vague: it is a pagan "toun" and "regioun" where a maiden visits a "temple, with hire mooder deere"; it is a place where the mythological metaphors of Nature—"Phebus," "Pallas,"

"Bacus," and "Venus"—are as much at home as the comparisons with ancient artisans like "Pigmalion," "Apelles," and "Zanzis," who are counterfeiters of Nature (*PhysT* 11–18). The *Physician's Tale* has, in other words, been given a natural setting to suit a natural story about natural activities. It is also factual, "no fable, / But knowen for historial thyng notable." Rather than expressing any peculiarly Roman characteristics, the story serves as the occasion for an elaborate, general comment on the uncertainties of the whole human natural condition. Like Nature's most loving and lavish efforts, a loving parent's natural affections fail to achieve what they desire; they are frustrated in much the same way that an evil "juge" and a corrupt legal system are frustrated. Thus both good and evil, everyone and everything in the *Physician's Tale* conspire in a failure to govern reality and to judge it aright. In the end, as Fortune or fate would have it, they have all worked to the destruction of goodness in a natural world.

Entirely different conditions prevail in the *Second Nun's Tale* where the purpose and setting are clearly defined. Here Rome is a battlefield and bright Cecilia, "comen of Romayns, and of noble kynde," represents "the feith / Of Crist" conquering the darkness of pagan idolatry and the empty power of a Roman prefect, Almachius. Unlike her submissive counterparts, Custance and Griselde, Cecilia speaks out like a warrior saint—"boldely," "stedfastly," and "al openly"; and in Almachius she meets the materialistic force and the myopia of a paganism firmly committed to the gods of classical mythology. It is the only example in Chaucer's works where the false deities are pitted against the true God. Almachius would constrain the Christians to worship the "ymage of Juppiter" with "sacrifise" (*SNT* 360–66): when Cecilia's husband, Valerian, and his brother, Tiburce, refuse they are beheaded; and when Almachius's own officer, Maximus, converts to Christianity and himself succeeds in converting "many a wight," he is beaten to death "with whippe of leed" (*SNT* 393–406). Then Cecilia.

> And after this, Almachius hastily
> Bad his ministres fecchen openly
> Cecile, so that she myghte in his presence
> Doon sacrifice, and Juppiter encense.   (*SNT* 410–13)

And "incense" Jupiter she does, for in the confrontation which follows Cecilia derides the limited, mortal power of Almachius and of all men: their strength is like "a bladdre ful of wynd" that goes with the nick of needle point. Almachius acts as nothing more than a "ministre of deeth"; he is a silly ("nyce") creature, "a lewed officer and a veyn justise." He lacks not only spiritual vision, but physical sense as well since he cannot see what is right before his eyes—a stone idol, and nothing more.

> ". . . for thyng that we seen alle
> That it is stoon,—that men may wel espyen,—
> That ilke stoon a god thow wolt it calle.
> I rede thee, lat thyn hand upon it falle,
> And taste it wel, and stoon thou shalt it fynde,
> Syn that thou seest nat with thyne eyen blynde." (*SNT* 499–504)

It is a ludicrous situation to Cecilia—almost a parody of Saint Thomas's encounter with the risen Christ—and a reminder, too, of the traditional view which linked the pagan gods to physical force and nature: their "ymages" may "noght profite"; they are not "worth a myte."

The Roman setting of Cecilia's story has both specificity and historicity. The old idolatry really existed, and the Roman *imperium*—that bladder full of wind and minister of death—included city prefects, their clerk ("corniculer"), "ministres," "sergeantz of the toun of Rome," and an executioner ("the tormentour"). Pope Urban, too, really lived near to the "povre folkes," just outside the city, three miles by the "Via Apia" (*SNT* 172–75) among the catacombs ("the seintes buryeles"). Cecilia's compatriots actually lived at Rome and died there for their faith; and Cecilia's house still stands, a church which Pope Urban made at her request.

> Hir hous the chirche of Seint Cecilie highte;
> Seint Urban halwed it, as he wel myghte;
> In which, into this day, in noble wyse,
> Men doon to Crist and to his seint servyse. (*SNT* 550–53)

As a minor motif, the Rome of the *Second Nun's Tale* is more than a scene of battle between the material and spiritual; like the changes and conversions which dominate the tale,[29] the Roman setting also converts. From a place of darkness, vain power, and idols it becomes a place of Christian worship where "men doon to Crist and to his seint servyse" even "into this day."

In the *Man of Law's Tale* the struggle at Rome has ended and the city has become the center of Christianity—the home not only of bishops, lords and ladies, and knights of renown, but of the papacy, a Christian "Emperour of Rome" and his fair "yonge doghter," Custance. The "toun" where Custance lives proves to be the place of "hooly chirche": the arrangements for her marriage to the sultan of Syria are made "by the popes mediacioun, / And al the chirche, and al the chivalrie"; and it is accomplished for the sake of destroying foreign idolatry and increasing "Cristes lawe deere" (*MLT* 233–38). Having sailed to the east to bring about the conversion of one nation, and having that work aborted by the "olde" sultaness's murderous ways, Custance again takes ship to be carried to the other end of the world, "fer in Northhumberlond." Here she reaffirms Christianity to a few "olde Britons" and, by miracles and wedlock to King Alla, converts the "payens" who had conquered Britain. At the midpoint of her story she is both "an Emperoures doghter" and—by formal declaration—"the doghter of hooly chirche" (*MLT* 655, 675). But again frustrations come when Custance's satanic mother-in-law arranges her third debarkation, now on the same rudderless ship[30] which had brought her to England. Her homeward journey, interrupted by a lecherous apostate "that hadde reneyed oure creance," brings Custance's story and pilgrimage back where it began. At the end home and Rome become emblems of reconciliation.

Thus the senator of the "Romayn Emperour" recovers Custance from the sea when he returns "homward to Rome" (966) with the army that had avenged, in Syria, "the slaughtre of cristen folk, and dishonour / Doon to [the Emperor's] doghter." "To Rome-ward" he sails when he takes Custance aboard, and "bryngeth hire to Rome."[31] "To Rome" King Alla comes in pilgrimage for having slain his treacherous mother, "to receyven his penance; / And putte hym in the Popes ordinance." And when all are peacefully restored—Custance, King Alla, and their son, Maurice; then Custance and "hire fader"—we are assured that young Maurice will follow in his mother's steps, for he was later made emperor "by the Pope, and lyved cristenly; / To Cristes chirche he dide greet honour" (*MLT* 1122–23). Finally, after a brief time in England with King Alla, the widowed Custance comes home again to Rome—to Rome.

> And dame Custance, finally to seye,
> Toward the toun of Rome goth hir weye.
>
> To Rome is come this hooly creature,
> And fyndeth hire freendes hoole and sounde;
> Now is she scaped al hire aventure.
> And whan that she hir fader hath yfounde,
> Doun on hir knees falleth she to grounde;
> Wepynge for tendrenesse in herte blithe,
> She heryeth God an hundred thousand sithe.   (*MLT* 1147–55)

This last of several happily pathetic scenes in the *Man of Law's Tale* suggests once more that "Rome" means more than Custance's home or the home of the Church. It has become the beginning and end of the Christian adventure.

Although spiritual Rome has taken us far from the classical scene, it nevertheless provides a point of departure for examining a last aspect of Chaucer's ancient settings, namely, their times. For to Chaucer, and medieval writers generally, the most elemental fact about the pagan past was its exclusion from the fruits of Christ's redemption.[32] To use the words of Virginia, antiquity was literally and spiritually an era of "no grace . . . no remedye" (*PhysT* 236). Even for the best intentioned among those who lived in old Thebes or Troy, in Athens or in Rome, the highest achievement was to live with—and love—the law of Nature, "the lawe of kinde" (*BD* 56); to act with "resoun" and "compassioun" (*KnT* 1766, 1770). The *Knight's Tale* shows that Chaucer thought this to be no mean accomplishment.[33] And yet, at its noblest, Chaucer's classical world lacked the supernatural possibilities that were available to even the poorest and clumsiest of his medieval pilgrims. While this Christian view may seem solemn, it actually helps to explain Chaucer's widest-ranging sympathies. For in all his fictions where the scene encompasses the New Dispensation, he can consistently allow for the hope which accompanies a loving faith: the Reeve, the Friar and Summoner, the Wife of Bath, and especially the Pardoner may judge themselves or each other—but Chaucer the poet surely does not. For him all travel the road to Canterbury unsure, except for grace. But the same cannot be said of Chaucer's classical characters, dead and gone. At their worst they inspire contempt—Nero, Creon, and Jason; and at their best, like Theseus in Athens, they elicit a respect for natural reason or, like Lucrece at Rome, a compassion for a natural commitment and a sorrow, sadly untouched by the mingling joys or hopes of Christian heroines—Custance or Griselde.

Chaucer's approach to classical antiquity often resembles Jerome's approach to virtuous pagans in *Against Jovinian*. He was not concerned with "payens corsed old rites" as such, but with natural virtue in the pathetic, tragic context of ancient life. Furthermore, with the exception of Troilus, Chaucer most frequently fixed his attention on classical women, not in order to portray them as grand and noble ladies, but as spiritually and morally helpless people. Their strongest efforts to be true or virtuous within the natural condition invariably end in failure, often in a disappointing, empty kind of death. Chaucer's treatment of Alcyone, for example, proves her wifely fidelity, first through grief at Ceyx's absence and then through her gentle, submissive prayer to Juno.

> "Helpe me out of thys distresse,
> And yeve me grace my lord to se
> Soone, or wite wher-so he be,
> Or how he fareth, or in what wise . . .
> And but thow wolt this, lady swete,
> Send me grace to slepe, and mete. . . .   (*BD* 110 ff.)

The sadness of Alcyone's condition actually intensifies as her prayer generates several reminders of a Christian perspective which she herself cannot share. The form of her plea, with its piously alternative petitions, resembles a Christian prayer; her "lady swete" denotes Juno, but to Chaucer's audience it would connote the Blessed Mother; and the two requests for "grace," to know the physical fact of Ceyx's whereabouts or to sleep and dream about him, imply another "grace" unavailable and unknown to her. When Alcyone learns that her "worldes blysse" has passed away, her only relief from sorrow comes with death. She is told her loss, and she perceives nothing more: "hir eyen up she casteth / And saw noght.

'Allas!' quod she for sorwe, / And deyede within the thridde morwe" (*BD* 212–14). Indeed, within her limited ken, Alcyone truly has nothing to live for; and the Christian assumptions of the narrator, who "knew never god but oon," together with the overtones of her prayer only magnify the pathos of her condition.

Alcyone does not choose to die; death simply overwhelms her. She is almost entirely passive, like several of the Good Women in Chaucer's *Legend*:[34] like Hypsipyle, abandoned by Jason and dying "for his love, of sorwes smerte"; like Ariadne, left on the desert island by Theseus and too fearful to do anything on her own behalf (" 'I can myselven in this cas nat rede' "); and Hypermnestra, forgotten by her fleeing husband and "caught and fetered in prysoun" by her own father. Not all of Chaucer's classical heroines are so helpless, however. Cleopatra seizes her fate as though it were a bargain, leaping into the grisly serpent pit "with ful good herte" and "with good cheere." She has made a pledge to share Anthony's "wel or wo," his "lyf or deth" (692); and she "wol fulfille" that pledge with a death that more than matches his. Thisbe also acts in an aggressive way, albeit with some innocence: she sees herself as the "felawe and cause" (895) of Pyramus's death, and she can no more depart from him in such a little thing as death than she can in life.

> "And thogh that nothing, save the deth only,
> Mighte thee fro me departe trewely,
> Thow shalt no more departe now fro me
> Than fro the deth, for I wol go with thee." (*LGW* 896–99)

For her part the Dido of the *Legend* cares little about the dilemma—ill fame or death—that dominated her story in the *House of Fame*; here she is the generous giver from whom Aeneas has taken everything—coursers, steeds, palfries, "sakkes ful of gold," rubies, falcons, hounds, and cups of gold (*LGW* 1114–24); his survival, her heart, and now her life. Dido has said that " 'al my love and lyf lyth in his cure,' " but when the time comes for decision the one thing Aeneas refuses to take is the one thing he has promised, " 'to wyve me to take,' " " 'me now to wive take' " (*LGW* 1304, 1319). He leaves her pregnant with his child, abandoned to her political enemies and to the "goddes . . . contraire"; he gives her his infidelity, and (by accident in haste) a "cloth" and a "swerd"—and she takes them both, the one for her "soule" and the other for her "herte." And

Lucrece, too, will seize her fate, partly from her own shame, but partly so "hir husbonde shulde nat have the foule name" of that same shame.

All of Chaucer's Good Women of antiquity have been victimized by treacherous men, by treacherous fate, or (looked at in another way) by their own strong faith in something or someone who, from the very nature of things, will prove unstable or transitory. They believe in men who kill themselves or flee, or in lovers who beguile; they believe in worldly reputation or physical honor. They search for truth, grace, mercy, and steadfastness, but in the world which Chaucer creates for them there are neither theological nor rational alternatives. Even when his Women try to think things out, as it were—Cleopatra arranging Anthony's "shryne," Dido weighing her alternatives in the *House of Fame* or luring Aeneas's love in the *Legend*, Hypsipyle and Medea planning to save Jason's life as Ariadne and Phaedra plot on Theseus's behalf, and Lucrece considering her guilt and her forgiveness—all of them are ruled by their hearts and their affections. Nor is there any special irony in this, for although Chaucer does not entirely exculpate his Women, he makes them understandable and he focuses our attention on what they had: human faith, trust, truth, and love. He turns them into Nature's Covenanters who bind themselves in various devout ways to natural goods which cannot be secure. With Anthony gone, Cleopatra's only source of "grace" (*LGW* 663) is Octavius Caesar, who is not worth the asking; moreover, she has a "covenaunt" with Anthony (*LGW* 688, 693). In spite of "wrecchede jelos" fathers, hindering friends, a "wikkede" wall, and a "wilde lyonesse," Pyramus and Thisbe plight their "trouthe" fully in their faith ("here fey") and keep their "covenaunt" (*LGW* 778, 790) in death. Dido's only source of "mercy" and "pite" (*LGW* 1324) is Aeneas, but "truste" in him turns into winds and running water: " 'For thilke wynd that blew youre ship awey, / The same wynd hath blowe awey youre fey.' " And so it is with the others who, literally and historically, cannot find a faith that "nyl falsen no wight, dar I seye": Lucrece begging "grace" of bestial Tarquin, receiving the "forgyvyng" of husband and friends, but naturally unable to forget and forgive; Ariadne begging "routhe" of Theseus after he had violated their "covenaunt" (*LGW* 2139, 2200); Phyllis trusting in Demophon's treacherous lineage, his "fayre tonge" and false tears. With all their yearning for truth and security, each one of these women finds, like Phyllis, "no fey certeyn" or, like Hypermnestra, "non other grace."

To read into Chaucer's treatment of his dark and troubled Good Women an implied satire or a series of neat ironies would be perverse in the extreme. It would require that we overlook the obvious intent of language, rhetoric, and selection of details in order to attend to what Chaucer has carefully overlooked or changed. Cleopatra's abandonment of a sea battle is nothing strange: "No wonder was she myghte it nat endure." Medea's murderous barbarism has no place in the *Legend*, and her black magic has even been raised to wisdom (*LGW* 1599) and to a "sleyghte" of "enchauntement" which saves Jason's life and gives him honor as a conqueror. There is no hint that Hypermnestra (by other accounts) had forty-nine murderous sisters, or that Procne and Philomela slew the child, Ithys, and fed him to his father. Even the reader who knows and remembers the *City of God* (I. 19)— where Lucrece's suicide is criticized—will find Augustine flipped on his head for the sake of a Good Woman.

> But he that cleped is in oure legende
> The grete Austyn, hath gret compassioun
> Of this Lucresse, that starf at Rome toun. . . .   (*LGW* 1689–
>   91)[35]

Chaucer is not playing games with Lucrece, but with Augustine, and he concludes by crediting her with a kind of sainthood, according to her own ancient lights and law. Her death brought an end to royal tyranny and oppression, and its date became a "holy day" in the Roman calendar.[36]

> Ne never was ther kyng in Rome toun
> Syn thilke day; and she was holden there
> A seynt, and ever hir day yhalwed dere
> As in hir lawe. . . .   (*LGW* 1869–72)

One need not unstring the *Legend* or go far to find the irony and satire which relieve its elegiac tone and heighten its effects. The objects of Chaucer's barbs are men[37]—the great heroes of antiquity and, by implication, their lineal descendants in fourteenth-century England, including Geoffrey Chaucer himself (*LGW* 2561). Even the most respectable of them comes off second best. Anthony, for example, had betrayed a woman (*LGW* 592–95) before he killed himself "for dispeyr out of his wit"; and Pyramus, late for his appointment (*LGW* 824), does not think twice about Thisbe's bloody "wympel," but hastily stabs himself and dies a most unflattering death ("betynge with his heles on the grounde"), dumb as any stone.

> This woful man, that was nat fully ded,
> Whan that he herde the name of Tisbe cryen,
> On hire he caste his hevy, dedly yen,
> And doun agayn, and yeldeth up the gost.   (*LGW* 883–86)

But if the "good men" are badly upstaged, the rest are no more than a pack of cowardly villains: Aeneas the pillager of a kingdom and a woman; Tarquin the mighty beast (*LGW* 1788), "a wolf that fynt a lomb alone", Minos "wikkedly" abandoning Nisus's daughter; Theseus pledging his "lyf or breth" in the most groveling servitude (*LGW* 2027–73), and then slithering off; Tereus committing incest with rape, then cutting out his "sister's" tongue and weeping feigned tears that she had died; Demophon, like his father—dead but for a woman—swearing and betraying in lineal descent; and "Lyno" out the "wyndow," taking to his heels as though the only virtue were speed (*LGW* 2709–22)—the son of a lecher, leaving his new wife to the mercies of her own lecherous, murderous father. It is a grand and various group which Chaucer mocks, and Jason is only the foulest of the lot.

> Thow rote of false lovers, Duc Jasoun,
> Thow sly devourere and confusioun
> Of gentil wemen, tendre creatures,
> Thow madest thy recleymyng and thy lures
> To ladyes of thy statly aparaunce,
> And of thy wordes, farced with plesaunce,
> And of thy feyned trouthe and thy manere,
> With thyn obeÿsaunce and humble cheere,
> And with thy contrefeted peyne and wo. . . .
> Have at thee, Jason! now thyn horn is blowe!   (*LGW* 1368 ff.)

There is no mistaking what Chaucer has done in the *Legend;* he creates his usual mix of contrasts. And the way in which he has divided his characterizations between Good Women and bad men radiates out in a cluster of other divisions: in tone between sympathy and contempt; in genre between elegy and satire; and in effect between tears and laughter (cf. *LGW* F89–93).

Within the framework of classical time, Chaucer took advantage of Nature's limitations and "hir lawe." He did not criticize his pagan women for being pagan rather than Christian—for that would have been truly anachronistic and beside the point. Instead, he praised his women for their natural trust and hope and love, in spite of and perhaps because of the sad fates that their virtues brought them; and he blamed the men for their unnaturalness—their perfidy, their unanchored flightiness, their selfishness—in spite of and perhaps because of their heroics, their successes, and survival. Although these polarizations may be thought of as Chaucer's penance from Queen Alceste, to make a "gloryous legende" of Good Women who "were trewe in lovynge al here lyves" and to "telle of false men that hem bytrayen" (*LGW* G471–79), Chaucer actually followed similar procedures in several of his earlier works. His juxtaposition of Dido and Aeneas, together with that of other heroines and their betrayers in the *House of Fame*, centers on the "untrouthe" of men and the "routhe" of women (*HF* 383–84, 395–96) in a sort of prologue to the Prologue of the *Legend.* And the contrast surfaces most obviously in the *Anelida and Arcite* where the lovely and pathetic Anelida serves as a classical model of truth and steadfastness in love: "For, as of trouthe, is ther noon her lyche, / Of al the women in this worlde riche" (*Anel* 76–77); and her counterpart, the "fals Arcite," appears as the ultimate example of duplicity ("double in love"), "kunnyng," and false swearing.

> Alas, the while! for hit was routhe and synne,
> That she upon his sorowes wolde rewe;
> But nothing thinketh the fals as doth the trewe.   (*Anel* 103–5)

Anelida is honest and open ("pleyn"); she languishes and begs for "merci." But Arcite is "subtil"; he has his way and cares not whether she "flete or synke." The recurrent plaintive theme tells of human truth's—womanly truth's—encounter with a hopelessly faithless world which has no living "Truth."

> For thogh I hadde yow to-morowe ageyn,
> I myghte as wel holde Aperill fro reyn,
> As holde yow, to make yow be stidfast.
> Almyghty God, of trouthe sovereyn,
> Wher is the trouthe of man? Who hath hit slayn?   (*Anel* 308–
>   12)

Indeed, if we go back to the earliest years of Chaucer's career, when he translated the *De Maria Magdalena* (*LGW* G417–18), we will find a Christian original for the Good Women standing steadfast at the tomb of her beloved. Peter has betrayed Him and the disciples have fled, but Mary, who "understood nothing but love and, for her love, knew nothing but sorrow," stands firm, alone, in tears.[38]

Finally, like these earlier writings, Chaucer's Prologue to the *Legend of Good Women* foreshadows and prepares us for a generally sympathetic reading of his legendary heroines. It does this, first, by addressing itself to the same problem that engages his Women, human faith and trust. From its opening lines the Prologue invites us to believe all we can from the past, even in the absence of certitude.

> But Goddes forbode, but men shulde leve
> Wel more thyng than men han seyn with ye!
>
> Thanne mote we to bokes that we fynde,
> Though whiche that olde thynges ben in mynde,
> And to the doctryne of these olde wyse
> Yeven credence, in every skylful wyse,
> And trowen on these olde aproved storyes. . . .   (*LGW*
>   G10 ff.)

The logical, or at least persuasive inference from this premise is that we should give "credence" to the stories we will soon hear from old "autoritees."

> But wherfore that I spak, to yeve credence
> To bokes olde and don hem reverence,
> Is for men shulde autoritees beleve,
> There as there lyth non other assay by preve.
> For myn entent is, or I fro yow fare,

The naked text in English to declare
Of many a story, or elles of many a geste,
As autours seyn; leveth hem if yow leste!   (*LGW* G81-88)

As audience, then, we are being placed in a position analogous to
that in which the Good Women find themselves—trusting in what
we hear. But will we, too, be betrayed?—"leveth if yow leste!" Well,
that is a chance *we* will have to take. And as we do we are forced to
accept a "mirroring," sympathetic stance toward the later heroines.

But the Prologue goes further. It draws us into the context of
Nature's old era, with its "olde bokes," its "olde stories," and "the
doctryne of these olde wyse."[39] It asks us to prescind, for the
moment, from "our" Christian assumptions, to forget about the
"current" literary strife between the Flower and the Leaf, and to
accept the fact that "this werk is al of another tonne, / Of olde story,
er swich strif was begonne" (*LGW* G79-80). Moreover, as this
happens, the Prologue increases our willingness to believe and to
stand by our Women. As in the *House of Fame* (1068-83), the
waking words of the poet become the realities of his dream. The
Daisy which Chaucer had reverenced in the fields—which he loves
even more than his "olde bokes"—now enters as the beautiful
Queen Alceste. Are we to reject her, the model of all Good
Women?—the "calandier" of "goodnesse" and of "fyn lovynge, / ·
And namely of wifhod the lyvynge" (*LGW* G533-35). Now that
hardly seems possible. In the creation formed "by kynde" (*LGW*
G178) she is *the* daisy, the epitome of all naturally trusting, pledged,
and faithful women from antiquity.[40] All the others—the wifely
Penelope and Marcia, the beautiful Helen and Isolde, the fair
Lavinia and passionate Cleopatra, the suffering Thisbe and truthful
Hypsipyle—all are but dim and partial reflections of her light.

My lady cometh, that al this may dysteyne.

With her, too, comes her king and lord, Cupid, the emblem of the
best in natural love. He is clothed like the meadow in May, "in grene
al newe ageyn"; the "smale foules" that have escaped the fowler
(Death)—his traps, his nets, and winter's cold—greet their lord with
song (" 'The foulere we defye' ") and with observances to natural
love ("Ryht [longing] onto love and to nature"). This Cupid is not,
of course, the blind and foolish Bowboy of light love; nor is he a

Platonic symbol of spiritual or theological love. He is nature's loving force itself, sympathetic to old natural love and governed by the eyes of reason.

> And al be that men seyn that blynd is he,
> Algate me thoughte he myghte wel yse;
> For sternely on me he gan beholde,
> So that his lokynge doth myn herte colde.   (*LGW* G169–72)

We can scarcely reject him either!

Everything in the Prologue to the *Legend* is designed to make us believers. We are made ready to look for and accept what is good in faithful women and to reject any niggardly concern for women's weaknesses or follies; we see each Good Woman and all her followers—a tremendous crowd (*LGW* G186–94)—in terms of the virtue that they share, being "trewe of love." One may, of course, prefer to be a "worm" among flowers or a heretic against Cupid's "lawe" (*LGW* G244, 256), but those are not the roles for poet or believers. As Chaucer takes his tongue-lashing from lord Cupid, and then basks in the intervention of Alceste, "his erthly god," "his gide and lady sovereyne," we may also gradually sense the central mood of the *Legend*. For with all its later extremes of tragic pathos and comic satire it has, at heart, a cheerful, understanding gentleness which one can fairly judge to be "essential Chaucer." At our distance from the poem, we may also believe that the *Legend* was written for a pleasant occasion—or two different pleasant occasions—and that the contexts for its reading were love's "halydayes," "the firste morwe of May" or "whan passed was almost the month of May" (*LGW* F108, G89). True, we know too little about the medieval English observances of May to be assured "by preve"; but what we do know about the Queen of May, bedecked with flowers, and about her male counterpart, Jack-in-the-Green or the green Cupid whom Spenser mentions along with the goddess Flora, can persuade us that Chaucer's Queen Alceste and King Cupid are, among other things, kin to those chief functionaries of a seasonal celebration, the earthly "god and goddesse of the floury mede."[41]

> And thus thise foweles, voide of al malice,
> Acordeden to love, and laften vice
> Of hate, and songen alle of oon acord,

"Welcome, somer, oure governour and lord!"
And Zepherus and Flora gentilly
Yaf to the floures, softe and tenderly,
Hire swoote breth, and made hem for to sprede,
As god and goddesse of the floury mede;
In which me thoghte I myghte, day by day,
Duellen alwey, the joly month of May. . . .   (*LGW* F167–76)

Others had written for such festivals. In fact, Chaucer describes himself as following not in the footsteps of "Virgile, Ovide, Omer, Lucan, and Stace" on this occasion but in the footsteps of those who praised the Daisy, the Flower *and* the Leaf; he comes after them, "glenyng here and there," "ful glad" if he can find a "goodly word" to honor love and serve its flower (*LGW* F73–83).

One need not think of Chaucer as a pagan poet, honoring gods and goddesses, to accept this context. The little we know about observances to May suggests that they could just as often be religious as sensuous. And in the *Legend* Chaucer has defined an honest purpose clearly enough: to honor married love and truth in women. His poem will suit the season beautifully.[42] Moreover, without assurances, we can be secure in this: that we will be more in tune with Chaucer's Prologue and his legends if we put aside deadly fowlers and ironic worms and enter the poem with a good and loving heart—mirroring Alceste. In having set us up for this, Chaucer has done something with nature's classical background in the *Legend*—of Cupid, Alceste, and all her ladies—which seems the counterpart in heart's "compassioun" for what he had done, or would do, in intellect's "resoun" for the *Knight's Tale*. He has made the best that he can of a flawed and graceless past, one way and another. That classical past surely lacks the awesome and unequivocal grandeur that many later Renaissance and neoclassical artists would attach to it; but with reasoned affection Chaucer still treats it well.

With the *Legend of Good Women* Chaucer finished his work with one concept of classical time, and with it the contrast between heroes and heroines. In those of his later Canterbury stories where classical myth and legend play a part, the ancient past will seem closer to Chaucer's present, and distant places will seem nearer to home, as in a historical continuum. The rhetoric of contrasts in small units will expand to larger units—one story set against another, parody against piety, *Thopas* against *Melibee;* and the tales themselves will generally tend to develop through an intertwining of analogous, often incongruous details. Classical time will remain Nature's time, classical place past place, and the pagan deities physical, natural and real. The hint of what is to come can be found in the *House of Fame:* ancient times and peoples will share in the ironies of a perpetual human comedy. In the process Chaucer's classical world will grow increasingly familiar as it finds itself the quarry of parody, mock epic, and fabliau.

5 Classical Myth and Comic Radiance

Comedy touched everything that Chaucer wrote. No matter what the inexorable ruin of his tragedies, how sad their losses or pathetic their protagonists, his art consistently sought to move beyond the tears of the world to some kind of survival—either of nature or grace. One cannot speak with full assurance of those works that lack conclusions, but surely the *House of Fame* (like its narrator) grows in comedy; and the tragic legends of the Good Women are not only balanced by comic legends of bad men, but—if their Prologue anticipates the end—look forward to the joyous resurrection of the Daisy, the recovery of Alceste. In the *Book of the Duchess*, Alcyone's irretrievable loss of life and all that matters transforms, in her reporter's experience, to a means of sleeping and dreaming, and of waking up to life; and in the *Parliament*, where mythological allegory flows precipitously from love's desire to the deaths of "Eleyne, Cleopatre, and Troylus, / Silla, and ek the moder of Romulus," the comic intervenes and then overrides the scene of pathos in the confused, happy parliament where life and love go on, somehow unscathed. Taken in isolation, the story of Palamon and Arcite leads to tragedy.

> "What is this world? what asketh men to have?
> Now with his love, now in his colde grave
> Allone, withouten any compaignye."

But this view is lightened by the world around it—encompassed and made whole by Theseus's benevolence and nature's Jove. Indeed, even in the tale of Troilus's "losse of lyf and love yfeere," Chaucer cannot leave earthly woe alone: he begins with a gentle prayer for all lovers and himself, and he ends with another, from a perspective that looks beyond both sorrow and time. Like the stories which the Monk tells—Biblical and Christian, as well as classical—Chaucerian tragedy can be intensely ordered and single-minded; but its persistent, somber goal tells only part of what reality enfolds. The Knight must break the spell, for enough is enough, and perhaps too much: "for litel hevynesse / Is right ynough to muche folk, I gesse" (*NPT* 2769–70). The Nun's Priest must have his turn, since Chaucer will insist that there is more to life than dying.[1]

If the world that Chaucer makes has balance, above all else, that balance has a curious but understandable perversity which shows itself in classic myth. Like his tragic episodes, Chaucer's serious treatment of ancient materials tends to follow a logical process, clear to the point of destruction. In Books Four and Five Troilus truly suffers like Oedipus and Ixion; his torments *are* the ravages of Mars and the sorrows of the Furies; "Escaphilo" the owl cries for his death, the Fates spin out and cut his life, and his unfortunate trust in what Fortune gives and takes away leaves him betrayed like a hero at Thebes, like Nisus's daughter, and finally like Troy itself. For Chaucer, at least, meaningful and noble myth goes hand in hand with sorrow unto death. But, when Chaucerian comedy lays its hand on myth to give it life, it either mocks and debases the old deities and legends or it turns them into meaningless irrelevance. Mythology must pay for its survival with confusion. Like the other elements of Chaucer's comic chaos, it too will leave one wondering how (but for God's mercy and human luck) life can possibly continue as it does.

That great proponent of misrule,[2] the Wife of Bath, embodies a host of contradictions unresolved. As the defender and spokeswoman of her sect, she expounds the sharpest antifeminism in the Chaucer canon; even as she warns the Pardoner of the "tribulacion in mariage," she awaits her sixth husband and a peaceful wedlock of accord. She hates and she loves, pleases and devours—others and herself. Yet she goes on and somehow we rejoice. It should come as no surprise, then, that when the Wife turns to classical materials she handles them "all wrong": she makes a fool of them and shows them no respect. Instead of using myth to heighten her discourse with the grandeur of a reverent past, she drags it down to an incongruous, everyday reality where lovely Venus and the potentially dangerous pleasures of the senses turn into a birthmark ("the prente of seinte Venus seel") and then a pudendum ("the beste *quoniam* myghte be"): " 'my lust, my likerousnesse,' " " 'my chambre of Venus' " (*WBT* 604–18). The "sturdy hardynesse" of Mars, awesome and terrifying in a serious context, undergoes a comic metamorphosis to become " 'Martes mark upon my face, / And also in another privee place' " (619–20). And, as the Wife would have it, Mercury's "wysdam and science" bespeak the spiteful learning of the "children of Mercurie"—those senile, impotent bookmen!

> "The clerk, whan he is oold, and may noght do
> Of Venus werkes worth his olde sho,
> Thanne sit he doun, and writ in his dotage
> That wommen kan nat kepe hir mariage!"   (*WBT* 707–10)

The traditional "meanings" of the deities persist, of course: Mercury's learning, Venus's sensuous "feelynge" and Mars's battling "herte"; but the Wife has reduced mythology to its lowest, physical denominator. What we have seen before in the grand allegorical patterning of natural forces in the human soul, or in the personification of complex human instincts and actions, goes suddenly awry when Venus equals copulation and Mars flexes his muscles in a domestic brawl where a book is torn apart and a husband punched in the face.

With some tonal variations, the deities in several other comic tales suffer similar ·fates. In the Merchant's depiction of old January's wedding feast (*MerchT* 1709 ff.), "Bacus the wyn" overflows the cups as a traditional prelude to "Venus werkes"; and the banquet hall is filled with joyous melodies that outstrip the legendary music of Orpheus and "Thebes Amphioun," the trumpetings of Biblical Joab and Theban Theodomas, and lastly all the Muses' songs at the marriage of Mercury and Philology. Hymen, the "god of weddyng," never saw a happier "wedded man," nor Venus a hotter one as she leads the wild parade, torch in hand.

> And Venus laugheth upon every wight,
> For Januarie was bicome hir knyght,
> And wolde bothe assayen his corage
> In libertee, and eek in mariage;

> And with hire fyrbrond in hire hand aboute
> Daunceth biforn the bryde and al the route.   (*MerchT* 1723–
>   28)

But what company for Venus! A stupid, aged lecher who must hurry
to his aphrodisiacs—"Swiche as the cursed monk, daun Constantyn,
/ Hath writen in his book *De Coitu.*" And if the grisly details of
January's lovemaking were not enough, his goddess is degraded
further by her own promiscuous ways. Even as she burns "hir
knyght," she burns his youthful squire, Damian, and sends him
scurrying off to bed just like his lord.

> Almoost he swelte and swowned ther he stood,
> So soore hath Venus hurt hym with hire brond,
> As that she bar it daunsynge in hire hond;
> And to his bed he wente hym hastily.   (*MerchT* 1776–79; cf.
>   1727)

Venus's fire touches all around, and everywhere ridiculously. It
makes the "spices hoote" which January takes "t'encreessen his
corage" abed; it sets the "perilous fyr" of Damian's treacherous
passion, "that in the bedstraw bredeth!" And where it is physically
repulsive in the one case, it is absurd in the other. For Damian will
seek to quench his yearnings in the comfort of a pear tree, and his
traditional letter of love—inspired by "Venus fyr" (1875)—cools its
way down the Cloaca Maxima.

> And whan she [May] of this bille hath taken heede,
> She rente it al to cloutes atte laste,
> And in the pryvee softely it caste.   (*MerchT* 1952–54)

What has happened to the gentle ways of Venus, and her "messagerye," that they should come to this?

Another Chaucer hero, a noble rooster, suggests that Venus has
been reduced to nothing more than animal sex, laughable and self-
indulgent. Having forgotten an admonitory dream and all his
plodding learning, Chauntecleer turns to the beauty of lovely
Pertelote—"Ye been so scarlet reed aboute youre yen"—and asserts
his royal power.

    Real he was, he was namoore aferd.
    He fethered Pertelote twenty tyme,
    And trad hire eke as ofte, er it was pryme,   (*NPT* 3176–78)

All in a morning's work for this "servant" of Venus as he verges on a
tragic fall. Later, in the highest style, the Nun's Priest invokes the
same grand divinity only to put her down.

    O Venus, that art goddesse of plesaunce,
    Syn that thy servant was this Chauntecleer,
    And in thy servyce dide al his poweer,
    Moore for delit than world to multiplye,
    Why woldestow suffre hym on thy day to dye?   (*NPT* 3342–
        46)

As luck would have it, Venus's darling does escape his ruinous fate;
but his escape is posited, at least in part, on the mocking of his deity.
Venus is ridiculed, and Chauntecleer gets off scot free after having
learned only a small part of his folly. So, too, it is with January who
has learned practically nothing: with physical sight restored he exits
in his folly, Venus still in hand.

    This Januarie, who is glad but he?
    He kisseth [May], and clippeth hire ful ofte,
    And on hire wombe he stroketh hire ful softe,
    And to his palays hoom he hath hire lad.   (*MerchT* 2412–15)

And so, too, with the Wife who goes her merry way, marked by
Mars and Venus and still hoping to discover one of those rare
spouses who is "meeke, yonge, and fressh abedde"—and ready for
her.
    As opposed to the tormenting deities of history and their
suffering human kin, Chaucer's living gods and goddesses are really
funny people. They can be awesome, even destructive, as pictured
deities in the *Knight's Tale;* but when they speak or act as animate
"characters," they regularly make fools of themselves. Morpheus, in
the *Book of the Duchess*, takes his wake-up call like any "verray
sleper"; and for all his knowing ways and kind concern, Jove's eagle
is still the pompous windbag of the *House of Fame.* Priapus, in the
Parliament, embarrasses himself with his silly exhibition, and

Venus, guarded by money ("Richesse"), lies seductively on a golden bed to invite the voyeur's ogling. Like petty barons the deities squabble over their hegemonies in the *Knight's Tale*. Even "reasonable" Cupid in the Prologue to the legends of the Good Women turns out—like every other male—second best in comparison to a woman, for Queen Alceste will weigh the evidence with care and gently lecture Cupid, lord and god, on royal mercy and the proper conduct of a king. Given what Chaucer does elsewhere, it should come as no surprise that when Pluto and Proserpina (the king and queen of "Fayerye") enter the action of the *Merchant's Tale*, they sound like a husband-and-wife team from a fairyland invented by the Wife of Bath.[3] Pluto has nothing but the name of divinity as he sets himself down in January's garden ("upon a bench of turves, fressh and grene") to harangue his wife with a passel of antifeminist clichés that ready him for nothing more than ridicule. His human queen overwhelms him, for if he sounds like an "olde dotard shrewe," she retorts as though she had studied under the joint mastership of Alice of Bath and Christine of Pisa. She outdoes her husband's tired learning with reference to the "Romayn geestes" (2284); she transcends his literalistic reading of King Solomon with a useful spiritual interpretation; and she concludes with a delicious *ad hominem* attack which encompasses not only foolish Solomon from the Bible, but her stupid husband as well—that false god of pagan idolatry![4]

> "Ey! for verray God, that nys but oon,
> What make ye so muche of Salomon?
> What though he made a temple, Goddes hous?
> What though he were riche and glorious?
> So made he eek a temple of false goddis.
> How myghte he do a thyng that moore forbode is?
> Pardee, as faire as ye his name emplastre,
> He was a lecchour and an ydolastre,
> And in his elde he verray God forsook. . . ." (*MerchT* 2291–99)

In the face of such assaults against his humanity and divinity, Pluto wisely surrenders: " 'Dame,' quod this Pluto, 'be no lenger wrooth; / I yeve it up!' " And Proserpina responds with the familiar generosity which comes when husbands have learned their place:

" 'Lat us namoore wordes heerof make; / For sothe, I wol no lenger yow contrarie.' "

What holds for other deities holds especially true for Apollo in the *Manciple's Tale*. Poor Phoebus! Everything around him goes awry, and what remains of his world at story's end he wrecks like a spoiled child. From the first he is introduced as the Sir Thopas of the gods.[5]

> He was the mooste lusty bachiler
> In al this world, and eek the beste archer.
> He slow Phitoun, the serpent, as he lay
> Slepynge agayn the soone upon a day;
> And many another noble worthy dede
> He with his bowe wroghte, as men may rede.   (*MancT* 107–12)

It is one thing for a supposedly divine expert in archery to slay a serpent when it's down, but quite another to hit it "sleeping in the sun." One hardly needs "many another noble worthy" deed like that to sustain a reputation. But this is only the beginning of Phoebus's parodic transformation into a comic earthling. From the ancient god of music and chief of the Muses, he becomes a guitar-strumming singer. His kin are "hende" Nicholas with his "gay sautrie," Absolon with his "giterne" and "quynyble," and the Canterbury Squire, "syngynge . . . al the day."

> Pleyen he koude on every mynstralcie,
> And syngen, that it was a melodie
> To heeren of his cleere voys the sound. (*GenProl* 113–15)

Even the effort to heighten his divine skill bumps down to a human comparison when we read that Amphion, the King of Thebes, "koude nevere syngen half so wel as hee." But so it goes when gods fall into life: when the golden-haired deity of the sun becomes the handsomest of *men* ("the semelieste man / That is or was, sith that the world bigan"); when the god of wisdom and learning is reduced to teaching his pet crow how to talk, "as men teche a jay"; and when the god of prophecy has trouble learning from his crow the only thing worth knowing—or not knowing—in his story, that he has been cuckolded.

> And whan that hoom was come Phebus, the lord,
> This crowe sang "Cokkow! cokkow! cokkow!"
> "What, bryd!" quod Phebus, "what song syngestow?"
>   (*MancT* 242–44)

And in his own "hoom," on his own "bed" (256).

The Manciple is, of course, oblivious to what he has done to Phoebus. As nearly as *he* can tell the god is a complete gentleman—a well-featured bowman and minstrel, "fulfild of gentillesse, / Of honour, and of parfit worthynesse"; the "flour of bachilrie, / As wel in fredom as in chivalrie"; and utterly devoted to his lady—or rather to his wife.

> Now hadde this Phebus in his hous a wyf
> Which that he lovede moore than his lyf,
> And nyght and day dide evere his diligence
> Hir for to plese, and doon hire reverence. . . .   (*MancT* 139–
>   42)

A perfect fellow, this Phoebus, save for only one small fault. He is "jalous." And this, of course, is the motive of his actions. For having created a bourgeois, incongruous hero-god, the Manciple now proceeds to subject him to a series of violently ironic twists of fate. Thus the wife on whom Apollo dotes, to keep her faithful, beds down with a wretched lover "of litel reputacioun": one not worth (as crows would know) the value "of a gnat" compared to him. Then the crow, whom Phoebus taught to sing a "hondred thousand" times better than any nightingale, sings only "cokkow."[6] And the same crow, whom he had also taught to speak, plays dumb in the face of adultery ("Biheeld hire werk, and seyde never a word"); then reports to his master, with all the subtlety of a jackhammer, that "on thy bed thy wyf I saugh hym swyve"; and finally tells him "ofte" he saw it with his own eyes. Despite his "divine" virtues—which really amount to very little—Apollo has been badly paid. His world comes tumbling down, and as it does this gentle, worthy, honorable flower of "bachilrie," supposing that "his sorweful herte brast atwo," quickly slays his wife and wrecks his gear.

> His bowe he bente, and sette therinne a flo,
> And in his ire his wyf thanne hath he slayn.

This is th'effect, ther is namoore to sayn;
For sorwe of which he brak his mynstralcie,
Bothe harpe, and lute, and gyterne, and sautrie;
And eek he brak his arwes and his bowe. . . .   (*MancT* 264–
  69)

The crow alone remains, but not long: for "out at dore hym slong /
Unto the devel."

Chaucer's comic divinities live within an earthly range that
extends from body humor and bourgeois bathos to mock epic and
parody. They are reduced to everyday ordinariness or they are
inflated into grand grotesques. They are malleable. And this is so
not because pagan deities are words and signs which have meanings,
but because of their traditional association with the natural,
physical world. C. G. Osgood made this point some years ago when
he contrasted the artificial decorousness of mythology in the later
Renaissance with the earlier uses of myth which seemed to him
more striking and more real.[7] What Osgood sensed Chaucer proves,
for his gods and goddesses consistently depend on some kind of
clearly identifiable naturalness. They may be real people, like the
euhemeristic deities of a tradition too often belittled in literary
criticism: the Merchant's Pluto and Proserpina, the Manciple's
"Appollo." They may be human forces, like the gods and goddesses
of the old moral tradition from the Stoics: our own familiar, tangled
inclinations to sensual pleasure (Venus) or sleep (Morpheus), to
restraint (Diana), justice (Jove), or anger (Mars), and the like . Or
they may be the ancient physical divinities, the works and objects
of external nature: the sun, the moon, the sea, the winds, the
flowers in the field. There is nothing esoteric in the classical
mythology which Chaucer gives us, nothing foreign to the traditions which he knew, and nothing secret in the meanings of the
myths he used. Problems there certainly are, but they invariably
come from where we should expect them—from the manipulating
hands of a playful writer who liked to puzzle and surprise his
audience with his contrary ways and multiple effects.

The *Franklin's Tale* can be illustrative because its ancient
background and pagan deities are relatively clear and simple, and
yet they are governed by a rhetoric which aims to dazzle and
confound. The setting is *old* pagan times, of course, when those
"olde gentil Britouns in hir dayes" made poems of "diverse aven-

tures." In that ancient past a heroine prays to the Creator, the "Eterne God" of natural theology; a distraught lover prays to the sun, "Appollo, god and governour"; and a Clerk from Orleans practices a natural magic which the narrator thinks not worth a fly "in oure [Christian] dayes": "For hooly chirches feith in oure bileve / Ne suffreth noon illusioun us to greve" (*FranklT* 1132–34). But a curious situation develops. We should expect a pagan setting to disclose a natural world appropriate for natural actions; yet this story introduces and, indeed, hinges upon a work which the narrator thoroughly denounces as unnatural, or at least not super-natural. The Clerk of Orleans makes "his japes and his wrecched-nesse" of "supersticious cursednesse"; he takes his "tables Tolletanes," "his collect" and "his expans yeeris," "his rootes" and "his othere geeris"—and with these and more, he "subtilly" calcu-lates in such a way as to make it appear that the dangerous rocks on the Breton coast have gone. This, in turn, will mean that the lovely Dorigen must either betray her husband, Arveragus, because of her rash promise to Aurelius, or she must die to remain faithful. All because of "swiche illusiouns and swiche meschaunces / As hethen folk useden in thilke dayes" (1292–93). The effect of such ill practices would seem to be, as Dorigen exclaims, " 'agayns the proces of nature.' "

Still, not entirely so: in spite of the awe which the Franklin's language encourages, the Clerk of Orleans's skill at "japes" and at "jogelrye" is limited to those illusions which *any* artful "tregetour" might use to entertain a courtly crowd.[8]

> For ofte at feestes have I wel herd seye
> That tregetours, withinne an halle large,
> Have maad come in a water and a barge,
> And in the halle rowen up and doun.
> Somtyme hath semed come a grym leoun;
> And somtyme floures sprynge as in a mede . . .
> And whan hem lyked, voyded it anon.
> Thus semed it to every mannes sighte.   (*FranklT* 1142 ff.)

There is in fact nothing unnatural in the tale of the Franklin, only sights of strange seeming; nothing demonic, only "magyk natu-reel." Thus to seem to cover the rocks of Brittany near Penmarc'h, "thurgh his magik, for a wyke or tweye," requires no more from the Clerk of Orleans than some standard astronomical gear, plus paper and pen to calculate the proper "tyme" (1263, 1270, 1284). Nature does the rest. When the sun and moon are in the right position, and other conditions prevail, a great tide comes to the Breton coast, as such tides have been known to do ("from Gerounde to the mouth of Sayne").[9] And the Clerk's prediction of this remarkable event—like Pandare's prediction of a violent evening storm in Troy—involves no more than natural calculation: he gives the Coastal Waters Forecast.

The whole of the *Franklin's Tale* displays a similar "subtil" art, a seemingly cursed unnaturalness, but this has more to do with rhetoric than reality. Like the work of the magical Clerk, the tale's sophistical elaborations upon nature make us feel amazed. One such little trick, for example, describes the passing of time.

> But sodeynly bigonne revel newe
> Til that the brighte sonne loste his hewe;
> For th'orisonte hath reft the sonne his lyght,—
> This is as muche to seye as it was nyght!   (*FranklT* 1015-18)

And another functions as a grand *feu d'artifice*—Aurelius's plaintive prayer that " 'Appollo, god and governour,' " beseech his sister, "Lucina the sheene," to influence the sea of which "Neptunus" has deity, so as to cause a monstrous flood.

> "That fyve fadme at the leeste it oversprynge
> The hyeste rokke in Armorik Briteyne;
> And lat this flood endure yeres tweye.
> Thanne certes to my lady may I seye,
> 'Holdeth youre heste, the rokkes been aweye.' "   (*FranklT* 1060-64)

The great deities of this long and rotund prayer (1031-79) are really only figures of physical nature. Apollo is "the sonne" (1030); Neptune "the see" (1047); Lucina or Diana, the moon, "quyked and lighted" (1050) by the sun and followed "naturelly" (1052) by the sea; and Pluto is the area "under the ground" (1075) where Diana/Proserpina rules as sovereign lady. Except for the two years duration, everything about Aurelius's prayer is natural; that is, he pleads for nothing more nor less than a "spryng flood" (1070) of tremendous amplitude. Fortunately for western France, that flood does not come. Only after Aurelius has spent two more years pining for the love of Dorigen, and after he has promised to pay a large fortune ("a thousand pound") to the Clerk of Orleans, does nature bring a flood—and then a lesser one, and only for a week or two.

Although the *Franklin's Tale* should be read in terms of its ancient setting and pagan worship,[10] the only thing they tell us is that the noble ornaments of rhetoric and art—of mythological prayer and heathen illusion—must finally succumb to nature's own normality. It is doubtful that the Franklin himself recognizes this ultimate reality, but his story keeps insisting on the fact in each of its five major subjects: marriage, separation, courtly love, science, and gentle manners. Thus the Franklin portrays a lofty ideal of wedlock between Arveragus and Dorigen (738–803) but concludes with some perfectly familiar behavior: after more than a year of "blisful lyf" in marriage, the knightly husband goes off to England for a few years to "seke in armes worshipe and honour"; he leaves his tearful wife at home and goes about his business. But the Franklin is insistent. Such an ordinary outcome only stimulates him to further art so that, as art adjusts to facts, an idealized marriage gives way to idealized sorrow. Dorigen "wepeth" and "siketh" in her husband's absence, "as doon thise noble wyves whan hem liketh."

> She moorneth, waketh, wayleth, fasteth, pleyneth;
> Desir of his presence hire so destreyneth
> That al this wyde world she sette at noght.   (*FranklT* 819–21)

Inconsolable, she fears for Arveragus's safety and prays at length (865–93) that "Eterne God" should remedy his creation by removing from the Breton coast its deadly rocks. That prayer, which seems to be answered later in an ironic way, is never really answered. Naturally, it cannot be. Arveragus will arrive safely home, as husbands are wont to do, without incident or even a word about black rocks (1087–89).

Dorigen's completely perfect wifely sorrow next gives way to another ideal—Aurelius's flawless passion for a lonely, lovely wife. The garden of Courtly Love is set out like a "verray paradys," and the young squire who inhabits it is the epitome of a "servant to Venus" (901 ff.). He embodies all the old clichés: "fressher" and "jolyer . . . than is the month of May."

He syngeth, daunceth, passynge any man
That is, or was, sith that the world bigan.
Therwith he was, if men sholde hym discryve,
Oon of the beste farynge man on lyve;
Yong, strong, right vertuous, and riche, and wys,
And wel biloved, and holden in greet prys.   (*FranklT* 929–34)

The attributes keep piling up: he has secretly yearned for Dorigen for more than two years; he composes anonymous love poems for his beloved—"manye layes, / Songes, compleintes, roundels, virelayes"; and he dotes on her sorrowfully and desperately, languishing "as a furye dooth in helle."

And dye he moste, he seyde, as dide Ekko
For Narcisus, that dorste nat telle hir wo.   (*FranklT* 951–52)

So he says. But what happens from this abundant description, its tragic expectations, and the gentle, subtle phrasing of Aurelius's proposition? Only that Dorigen says "no."[11] She will, of course, complicate the future by decorating her refusal with a "rash promise," but her meaning is really simple. Moreover, like Arveragus's departure after his honeymoon, Dorigen's plain response also sets off a tide of magic rhetoric—Aurelius's prayer to Apollo, which comes to naught—and after that the "magic" science of the Clerk of Orleans.

In spite of their rhetorical guises, the classical divinities in the *Franklin's Tale* are reassuringly natural. Apollo and his companion deities are nothing but physical realities functioning as they must, in ways that are usual or unusual; and the human desires to rearrange realities, or to make them seem other than they are, are either wasted or illusory. And so it is with Venus, too. Her servant Aurelius enters the action through a garden of sensual delight, filled with the aroma of flowers and fresh sights, "of beautee with plesaunce"; but even with her decorous garb Aurelius's Venus is the same old (or young) thing. His love begins with two years "and moore" (940) of secret longing and looks forward to a languishing death; when it is disclosed to Dorigen and she declines, then Aurelius must quickly die "of sodeyn deth horrible" (1010). But, of course, he doesn't. Instead he again languishes "in torment furyus" for another two years "and moore" (1101–2) until his brother conceives of the scheme to satisfy him, at least "for a week or two" (1161, 1295). On the face of it, the tormenting and lovely Venus of the *Franklin's Tale* grows to look more and more like fancy sex laced with cynicism; for either Aurelius will trick Dorigen into suiting his wishes, "or elles he shal shame hire atte leeste" (1164). There is a smell of ungentle hypocrisy in this, as well as in Aurelius's later concern that Dorigen might want to keep her promise to him ("Madame, I speke it for the honour of yow"). Even in his final decision not to take Dorigen when she offers herself there is something less than noble. After all Venus's ways should be smooth and secretive, and what long-term gentleman would choose to be known as a short-term lecher?

There may well be philosophical and theological implications in the Franklin's narrative,[12] but Chaucer's handling of the deities suggests that a comic mode of rhetoric prevails, one which amuses with an elegant display. The obverse of its form can be found in the language of Bottom the Weaver, who insists on calling everything by its real name, even in make-believe.

> Nay, you must name his name, and half his face must be seen through the lion's neck; and he himself must speak through. . . . and there indeed let him name his name, and tell them plainly he is Snug the joiner.

For his part the Franklin works in just the opposite direction, through a "magyk natureel" of comic ornament so that after one imitates his handsome illusions and claps "his handes two," then "farewel! al oure revel [is] ago." At the last, the tale dissolves into aerial, sweet nothing, for its audience must finally judge between the "generosities" of a lover who abandons his intrigue, a husband who abets his own cuckoldry, and a clerk who refuses pay for what nature did.

Besides dressing (or exposing) the deities of mythology, Chaucer also used classical material for comical *exempla*. His most direct method follows the purpose and pattern of serious examples—as in the Pardoner's sermon and the *Monk's Tale*, where the stories of "Stilboun" and King Demetrius illustrate the disreputable nature of gambling, and those of Nero, Croesus and others help to show how "Fortune alwey wole assaille / With unwar strook the regnes that been proude." Normally *exempla* clarify a pattern of conduct for praise or blame; they give weight and authority to comments on human behavior.[13] Thus the deeds of ancient heroines may prove the treachery of love or the nobility of chastity; and the story of an individual may be a warning against one kind of conduct—like Orpheus's looking back at Eurydice (*Boece* III m. 12)—or an encouragement to another kind—like Hercules' fortitude in "harde travaile" (*Boece* IV m. 7). Usually, an example will reinforce and elaborate a point which is already clear; and in its simplest comic form it does just that. It magnifies and heightens something foolish or incongruous, and thereby extends the laughter far through time and space. The Wife of Bath, for example, seeks to defend her sex (or sect) against the antifeminism of husbands and clerks, and yet she oddly adopts some of their slanders and strengthens one of them with a long classical example.

In her tale, the "lusty bacheler" of Arthur's court will escape execution for having raped a maiden, provided he can learn the thing that "wommen loven moost." But everything the young man learns is pejorative of women: some have said that women most desire money; some have said honor or fun in bed; and others to be often widowed and often wed, to be as free as they please, or to be *considered* wise and chaste. The Wife seems to allow that each of these is a reasonable possibility; and one, she thinks, is very near the truth—"that oure hertes been moost esed / Whan that we been yflatered and yplesed" (*WBT* 929–30). Just before the correct answer is disclosed, however, in a rhetorically effective refutation prior to the affirmation of *the* truth, the Wife rejects out of hand the notion that "we" women want to be thought stable and secretive. That idea isn't worth "the handle of a rake"—and the Wife proves it from the story of Midas and his wife (952–82). With all the best intentions Midas's wife cannot be restrained. She has sworn herself to secrecy; she understands the danger to her husband's reputation; she is even sensitive to "hir owene shame" if the truth be known. Still, she goes off to the marshes and whispers to the water what no one knows but she: "My husband has two long ass's ears upon his head!" Thus Ovid's story shows, by example, that women "kan no conseil hyde." It is absolutely true—and from comedy's perspective, who cares?

When the Wife of Bath argues for something funny in itself, she uses the exemplary mode in a traditional way.[14] At such times ancient lore appears to be—like "glosynge" to a Friar—a "glorious

thyng, certeyn." And so, as Midas's story refutes the silly notion
that women are, or desire to be thought of as stable, other stories
(and authorities) can help affirm the fact that sovereign women
have magic powers for making perfect marriages: no matter how old
or poor they be, they are like poor or aged "gentils."

> Thenketh hou noble, as seith Valerius,
> Was thilke Tullius Hostillius,
> That out of poverte roos to heigh noblesse.
> Reedeth Senek, and redeth eek Boece . . .
>
> And certes, sire, thogh noon auctoritee
> Were in no book, ye gentils of honour
> Seyn that men sholde an oold wight doon favour,
> And clepe hym fader, for youre gentillesse;
> And auctours shal I fynden, as I gesse.   (*WBT* 1165–68; 1208–
>   12)

Authorities and examples are fine when they do what they should,
as in these cases, but when they restrict womanly authority and
freedom, or when they spread libels about wives, the Wife will
contradict and flout them. As a prelude to this sort of comedy,
which comes from wrecking traditional *exempla*, all authoritative
learning is first called into doubt.

And so the Wife begins her prologue by announcing that "experience . . . is right ynogh" for her; indeed, it would suit her fine if
"noon auctoritee / Were in this world." As soon as she establishes
this premise, she can put any kind of learning—classical or eccle-
siastical—right where it belongs, down and out. "The experience
woot wel it is noght so." Within this context she scorns the "olde
Romayn geestes" of Valerius Maximus which tell, for example, how
Metellius—"that foul churl, that swine"—beat his wife to death for
drinking wine (460–63). And just what does that show? It shows the
Wife that "he sholde nat han daunted me fro drynke!" No, sir.
Metellius had best watch out for himself. And so it goes with two
other examples which Jankyn had preached from Valerius's chapter
"On Severity" (641–49). Simplicius Gallus abandoned his wife
because she looked outdoors with her head uncovered; and another
Roman did the same when his wife, without his knowledge, went to
a "someres game." Well, if Roman wives succumbed to such

harshness they were badly treated; and the Wife implies that she could deal with husbands like theirs. Her classical examples, then, fit a recognizable pattern, for she has shaped them to sustain an extreme, severe morality which neither we nor Chaucer's audience would readily accept. These examples are straw men made for blasting, but what makes them peculiarly comical is that the Wife uses their severity to take a leap of logic. They become springboards to justify her own extreme behavior: she will drink as she pleases, dress as she likes, and go where she wants!

In his creation of the Wife of Bath Chaucer teaches no hidden moral. He does something far more devastating: he makes us laugh at an erratic, human pattern of logic and behavior. For the Wife keeps slipping by or skipping over the moral middle ground which comedy assumes. If her three old husbands want to spy on her for jealousy, they will discover soon enough that even Juno's watchdog, Argus, cannot help.

> Thogh thou preye Argus with his hundred yen
> To be my warde-cors, as he kan best,
> In feith, he shal nat kepe me but me lest. . . .   (*WBT* 358–60)

And she is correct on two counts: they *are* foolish and she *is* responsible. But then comes the comic jump—"Yet koude I make his berd, so moot I thee!"; she can dupe any Argus or cuckold any man. Several of the Wife's other examples work just like this. Thus she mentions King Darius's tomb—that model of an honor to the dead— but only to reject its wastefulness and explain her own response to the burial of husband number four.

> He deyde whan I cam fro Jerusalem,
> And lith ygrave under the roode beem,
> Al is his tombe noght so curyus
> As was the sepulcre of hym Daryus,
> Which that Appelles wroghte subtilly;
> It nys but wast to burye hym preciously.   (*WBT* 495–500)

We can imagine her restraint, and the "cheste" in which he lies.

Moreover, there is no doubt about her response to Jankyn's Book—that grand collection of *exempla* on the "wikkednesse" of wives and women. It tells of Eve, who was the "los of al mankynde," of Sampson's "lemman," and of ancient wives. It tells of "Dianyre," who slew her Hercules, of Socrates' scolding spouses, and Pasiphe— "Fy! spek namoore—it is a grisly thyng." It tells of lecherous Clytemnestra's murder of her husband-king; of Eriphyle's betrayal for the Brooch of Thebes, "an ouche of gold"; of Livia and Lucia, who poisoned their husbands; and of more, many more. This "cursed book" with all its cursed examples! If its fate were not written in the stars, it is surely written in the scheme of Chaucer's rhetoric. For in dismissing the richness of Darius's tomb, the spying of Argus, the stringency of Roman husbands, and so much more, the Wife has prepared the way for the ultimate destruction of male willfulness. She knocks Jankyn in the fire, and when he has been subdued his book is set ablaze. To make way for her own *imperium*, she must destroy the old examples. *Auctoritas delenda est.*

It is one thing for comedy to wreck classical examples—to beard the fabulous and beat the devil—but quite another to confound them with too many meanings and let them slip away forgotten. This latter mode governs nearly all the classical and other lore which fills the joyous story of the Nun's Priest. Chauntecleer, the epic hero, lords his learning over Pertelote's to prove that dreams should be believed and feared; to show that from his "avisioun" of a houndlike beast with glowing eyes, of reddish color tipped with black, will surely come "adversitee"! To prove his point Chauntecleer takes two brief *exempla* from Valerius Maximus ("oon of the gretteste auctour that men rede") and amplifies them. There is the tale of the two traveling companions lodged separately in town, one of whom is murdered when the other fails to heed a dream (*NPT* 2984–3063); the second tells of two young men who are warned in a dream against embarking on a ship which later sinks for no apparent cause (3064–3109). To these Chauntecleer adds seven more examples in rapid-fire fashion: one from a saint's life, three from the Old Testament, and three more from antiquity (3110–50). The extravagance of Chauntecleer's performance has multiple, comic effects. First, it illuminates his character—his ponderous learning and his overbearing patience with his wife. Then it strains the form itself, for too many examples are piled on; they seem to go on too long and they end by bursting in an orderly disorder.

> And forthermoore, I pray yow, looketh wel
> In the olde testament, of Daniel,

If he heeld dremes any vanitee.
Reed eek of Joseph, and ther shul ye see
Wher dremes be somtyme—I sey nat alle—
Warnynge of thynges that shul after falle.
Looke of Egipte the kyng, daun Pharao,
His bakere and his butiller also. . . .

Lo Cresus, which that was of Lyde kyng,
Mette he nat that he sat upon a tree,
Which signified he sholde anhanged bee?
Lo heere Andromacha, Ectores wyf. . . .   (*NPT* 3127 ff.)

As the form fragments,[15] its final cause and purpose break apart so
that the examples serve to prove not only what we should expect to
learn—"that many a dreem ful soore is for to drede"—but that
"mordre wol out" (3050-57); that Pertelote would benefit from
further study (3120-21); and that laxatives are ugly business.

Shortly I seye, as for conclusioun,
That I shal han of this avisioun
Adversitee; and I seye forthermoor,
That I ne telle of laxatyves no stoor,
For they been venymous, I woot it weel;
I hem diffye, I love hem never a deel!   (*NPT* 3151-56)

The final comic twist comes, of course, when Chauntecleer by-
passes *all* that he has said and shown. In a flash he casts his worries
and his dream, his learning and lessons to the wind and turns to
lovely Pertelote, his heart's desire: "Now let us speke of myrthe, and
stynte al this."

This last line sums up the consistent rhythm of the tale. For what
Chauntecleer does with magnificent obliviousness, the Nun's Priest
imitates by negligence and/or craft. At least twice he leads his
audience on aborted ventures into major problems. First he raises
the great scholastic question of necessity *versus* free will (3234-55),
and dismisses it in a line—"I wol nat han to do of swich mateere."
Next he raises the awesome question of women's counseling of men
(3256-66), from which he stumbles off ingloriously—"Thise been
the cokkes wordes, and nat myne; / I kan noon harm of no womman divyne." Then, collecting himself and returning to his fable,

he builds the loftiest of comic statements to describe "the Fall of Chauntecleer" (3338–3401). In a manner which resembles the description of the House of Fame,[16] he links the past and present in a grand continuum—like his earlier linking of Augustine and Boethius with England's Bishop Bradwardine. He invokes "destinee" on Chauntecleer's behalf, then Venus ("goddesse of plesaunce"), and last Geoffrey of Vinsauf, who had written tragically of England's first King Richard.

> O Gaufred, deere maister soverayn,
> That whan thy worthy kyng Richard was slayn
> With shot, compleynedest his deeth so soore,
> Why ne hadde I now thy sentence and thy loore. . . .   (*NPT* 3347–50)

In the midst of Chauntecleer's impending doom, he goes on to make a series of comparisons: the lamentations of the Trojan ladies—"whan Ylion / Was wonne" and Pyrrhus slew King Priam—resemble the cryings of "the hennes in the clos"; the shriekings of "Hasdrubales wyf"—her husband dead—as she leaps upon the pyre of burning Carthage are like the screams of Pertelote; and the cries of the Roman "senatoures wyves," when Nero fired Rome and slew their spouses, are like the sorrows of the "woful hennes" in the yard. The hysteria of history—from Troy to Carthage and to Rome—moves to the present when the barkings of the dogs and the noises of the barnyard are compared to the shrill yells of Jack Straw "and his meynee" in London, 1381. And the passage concludes almost apocalyptically, for "it semed as that hevene sholde falle."

With epic invocations and comparisons, the Nun's Priest announces through the sweep of history and tragedy: The Fox Has Got the Rooster! This is mock epic at its best and most absurd because, like the *exempla* in Chauntecleer's discourse, the Nun's Priest's invocations and comparisons ultimately come to nothing. They are incongruous, of course, as when great things are compared to small; but more than that, they are absolutely meaningless. Indeed, all that matters at the story's end is the stupid luck of Chauntecleer. "Sir Fox," he says, "if I were you I'd turn and curse them all." And when the fox does this, he also joins the comic world of happy chaos—a world about which one can only wonder: how or why do things happen as they do? However, if there is no satisfactory rational explanation for the conclusion of the *Nun's Priest's Tale*, its narrator still assures us of an underlying meaning: "Taketh the moralite, goode men"; "Taketh the fruyt, and lat the chaf be stille." His directive sounds encouraging, but when we begin to chase it down we soon discover (as with Chauntecleer and his *exempla*) that we are in a minefield of "moralite." Everything we touch "sets off" a lesson.

Thus pride and vanity go before a fall; and treacherous flattery—like that of Judas, Genelon, and "Greek Synon"—should be avoided.

> Allas! ye lordes, many a fals flatour
> Is in youre courtes, and many a losengeour. . . .
>
> Redeth Ecclesiaste of flaterye;
> Beth war, ye lordes, of hir trecherye.   (*NPT* 3325–30)

Women's counsel, too, has "been ful ofte colde," and it can lead to tragedy: "*In principio, / Mulier est hominis confusio.*" Moreover, male sensuality can be just as troublous, as when a servant of Venus expends "al his poweer, / Moore for delit than world to multiplye." Male obtuseness also plays its part, for Chauntecleer does not act freely and reasonably on the basis of what he knows. And if free will is somehow involved, so is "destinee," which "God forwoot moot nedes bee" and which is foreordained by "heigh ymaginacioun" (3217, 3234). All these, and perhaps more, fill the tale of Chauntecleer with an overflow of meanings for his fall. But then Chauntecleer really does not fall; or if he does, has it not been fortunate? In other words, from a comic perspective every serious moral in the *Nun's Priest's Tale* ends in evaporation or contradiction. Believe in dreams or not; take laxatives or don't; chase birds around and crow with regal pride, or avoid such foolish conduct. When things work out well, it really does not matter one bit. And if this is so, then the way by which Chauntecleer has multiplied examples, multiplied their meanings, and then forgotten them all turns out to be just a part of a large comic pattern whose real conclusion comes in a simple, submissive prayer that asks that God be good to us, and save us in the end.

> Now, goode God, if that it be thy wille,
> As seith my lord, so make us alle goode men,
> And brynge us to his heighe blisse! Amen.   (*NPT* 3444–46)

There is doubtless some truth in the claim that some of Chaucer's uses of exemplary materials suggest an effort to reduce a traditional rhetorical form to absurdity. But, as we have seen, modes of absurdity vary according to varying comic rhythms and tones. Of Chaucer's three major compilations of *exempla*—Jankyn's Book of wicked wives, Chauntecleer on dreams, and Dorigen's list of loyal women—the last, from the *Franklin's Tale*, seems least comical. Its mood is plaintive but distant, so that while feeling sympathy the reader may also be amused.[17] When Dorigen proposes that she has trapped herself by a "rash promise" to love Aurelius (should the black rocks of Brittany be removed), her options are not really funny. As an honest, noble wife she must be true to Arveragus; yet as a true and noble lady she must keep her word. The dilemma leads to her complaint: shameful life, or chastity and death. And the more than twenty old examples which Dorigen cites (1355–1456) point to the conclusion that an honorable death should be preferred or that, at the very least, a wife should be faithful. The daughters of "Phidon in Atthenes" and fifty maids from "Lacedomye" preferred death rather "than assente / To been oppressed of hir maydenhede." Stymphalis grasped Diana's statue until she was slain, and the wife of Hasdrubal "skipte adoun" into the fire rather than that any Roman "dide hire vileynye." Lucrece slew herself for shame when she had been "oppressed," and seven maids from Miletus killed themselves to avoid a similar fate. Their numbers grow. Indeed, "a thousand stories" and "ensamples" could be noted—and almost seem to be: "Demociones doghter deere," the daughters of Scedasus, and two unnamed Theban maids. As the list goes on, however, Dorigen becomes more distraught. She mentions chaste wives who had not been "oppressed" but who were faithful— Alceste and Penelope—and she concludes in a babble of distraction.

> "The parfit wyfhod of Arthemesie
> Honured is thurgh al the Barbarie.
> O Teuta, queene! thy wyfly chastitee
> To alle wyves may a mirour bee.
> The same thyng I seye of Bilyea,
> Of Rodogone, and eek Valeria."   (*FranklT* 1451–56)

In spite of the multiplication of *exempla* and a question about consistency,[18] Dorigen's complaint is not especially amusing in and of itself.

In its context, however, it becomes "comical" because nothing comes of it. Like the Franklin's account of Dorigen's perfect "wys accord" in marriage, like her sorrowing when her husband is away ("as doon thise noble wyves whan hem liketh"), like the perfect garden where Aurelius engages in his perfect, courtly courting—like so much in the Franklin's story—Dorigen's complaint is an extravagance in the gentle, noble style. And like the Franklin's and Dorigen's own previous idealizations, this one glides and gently bumps down to reality, for after she continues her complaining for "a day or tweye," and after she rehearses all her woe to Arveragus, we find that he dismisses it forthwith.

> This housbonde, with glad chiere, in freendly wyse
> Answerde and seyde as I shal yow devyse:
> "Is ther oght elles, Dorigen, but this?"   (*FranklT* 1467–69)

"This" may be too much for Dorigen, but to Arveragus it seems like nothing compared to his sense of "trouthe." Then, as soon as he has advised her to forget about the problem ("lat slepen that is stille")—which may recall Chauntecleer's forgetting what his *exempla* proved—Arveragus bursts into tears and recasts the old heroines' dilemma in curious masculine shape. Dorigen will keep *her* promise to love Aurelius and Arveragus will bear *his woe* as best he can (1484). Of course everything will work for the best, as it always does in comedy: Aurelius will be so impressed by Arveragus's gentle treatment of his wife ("sith I se his grete gentillesse / To yow")—preferring her "distresse" to his own "shame"!—that Aurelius will send her home again untouched. Thus, with a magical perversity that defies normal understanding, an action that runs counter to everything that ancient stories prove turns out to be a proof that Dorigen is the "treweste and the beste wyf" of all. There is gentle, quiet madness here, artful amusement.

In adapting classical *exempla* for various comic effects, Chaucer did not give up the customary directness of the traditional form. His examples do not become funny from a close reading of their source, or of glosses on the source, but rather from some contorted relationship between normal expectation (form) and fulfillment (context). As we have seen, Dorigen is "trewest" when she does *not* do what the "olde" examples teach her, Chauntecleer forgets what he has shown, and Jankyn's book goes to the fire. One way or another, these examples have no consequence, no relevance. Or they may prove something which is only comically true, like the Midas story. Or finally, they may be governed by some dramatic irony so that their obvious purpose goes obviously askew. Friar John cites three classical examples in the *Summoner's Tale* (2017–84), and each of them illustrates the way that pride engenders wrath, and wrath engenders sorrow. An "irous potestat" executes three guiltless knights; "irous Cambises" slays the son of a wise advisor; and "irous Cirus" (who even sounds funny) destroys the river where his horse had drowned. But instead of assuaging anger, the Friar's examples help to incite it. And in the end their characterization of anger applies better to Friar John himself, as he goes off raging to his lord, than to Thomas, the original audience.

The funny thing about Chaucerian *exempla* is not that they are longwinded or extravagantly decorous, but that they are cockeyed. The point is important, for we should not equate Chaucer's ornateness with irony or mockery. His extended lists of examples can be completely straight: the lovers in the *Parliament of Fowls* (288 ff.), the tragic victims noted in the *Troilus* (5. 1457–1519), and the Good Women in Alceste's "Balade" of praise. Even when examples clearly weigh heavy, as in the *Monk's Tale*, they do not lose their seriousness for that; as the Knight observes, they become oppressive and call for some relief.[19] Moreover, the peculiar kind of effectiveness which comes with *exempla* does not change radically in the shift from seriousness and logic to comedy and confusion. When comic examples multiply in number, in purpose, or in ironies, the laughter which they stimulate radiates through time and place and peoples, on and on; and like the "tears" which come with tragedy's *exempla*, the laughter seems always and everywhere, endlessly possible.

In two notable instances Chaucer took what might have been simple classical *exempla* and turned them into comic analogs. He changed the static form—designed to prove a point or illustrate a moral—into an active drama with its own identity, somewhat like but somewhat different from another drama close at hand. In the process he linked past with present, and extended the ramifications of his total narrative so as to make it seem perpetual and universal. Thus when King Pluto and Queen Proserpina enter the final scene of the *Merchant's Tale* only their names create an aura of antiquity. The setting is the medieval garden of old January, a Pavian-born knight of Lombardy; and the time is medieval springtime, once upon a time ("whilom . . ."), almost any time. Even with the accumulation of allusions to Orpheus and Amphion, to Bacchus, Venus, and Hymenaeus, to Paris, Helen, and others who add a mock-epic dimension to the action, everything in the tale—from courtly romance and debate to festival and "Fayerye"—comes together in a strange world of fabliau. And it works. Because he had "ravysshed" his young bride, and is the god of wealth and distrusts women, Pluto resembles January; and because she is young and lovely, craftier than her husband and able to outwit him in the end, Proserpina resembles May. The god and goddess, then, are not simply *ex machina*, dragged in to resolve an action otherwise insoluble; they intervene, not as divinities, but as a haggling couple from the petty nobility. And their primary role is clear from their own words: they broaden the scope, the rationale, and the significance of the primary action—and magnify its ironies. They serve as the representatives of all men and all women who think and act like January and May.[20]

> "Th'experience so preveth every day
> The tresons whiche that *wommen* doon to *man* . . .

> ". . . I shal yeven hire suffisant answere,
> And alle *wommen* after, for hir sake . . .

> "Yit shul we *wommen* visage it hardily,
> And wepe, and swere, and chyde subtilly,
> So that ye *men* shul been as lewed as gees."   (*MerchT* 2238 ff.)

Pluto and Proserpina are part of a total action which encompasses past and present, Lombardy and "Fayerye," and the ironic themes from one time and the other resonate to a continuous, omnipresent laughter. The stupid ravisher is ravished; the clever victim makes a victim of her assailant. Finally, too, we are given the impression, vague but still sure, that the entire ironic action extends on to the fictive present where the living Merchant-narrator finds himself "ycoupled" to a wife who can "overmacche" the devil himself, and where the pilgrims' Host will conclude with some reflection on "sely men," deceiving "wommen," and his own unhappy wedlock with a "trewe" but shrewish wife (1213 ff. and 2419 ff.).

The interweaving of classical myth, medieval fabliau, and Canterbury drama constitutes the whole performance of the Merchant. It
may also serve as a brief model for what Chaucer does in his most
mature work, and in what seems to be his final use of ancient lore.
As noted earlier, the Apollo of the *Manciple's Tale* is a nominal
divinity who dwelt "heere in this erthe adoun": not only a talented
and handsome cuckold and a petulant avenger, he is in the end a
dubious moralist. Indeed, "moralitee" becomes the high point of
Apollo's adventure.[21] Having rashly slain his wife for her reported
adultery, he begins to think (after a fashion) about what he has
done and reaches a series (*MancT* 271-308) of wrongheaded
conclusions. He eulogizes his "deere" adulterous "wyf" with a
curious epithet—"o gemme of lustiheed!"—and then affirms that
she was "giltelees," "sad," and "trewe." He errs, of course, on all
three counts. Next he blames his own rashness and warns all men
against it ("O every man, be war of rakelnesse!"). That judgment
seems fair enough, but his explanation of it raises a serious
question. Assuming that Apollo had acted on a suspicion which was
"fals"—and here he errs again—he solemnly implies that if he had
been certain of his wife's guilt, he would have killed her anyway.
"Don't slay too quickly, or at least not until you know what you're
doing."

> "Smyt nat to soone, er that ye witen why,
> And beeth avysed wel and sobrely
> Er ye doon any execucion
> Upon youre ire for suspecion."   (*MancT* 285-88)

Such an execution, soberly calculated by cool reason, like live burial
for incontinent Roman Vestals, sounds somehow worse than
murder in the heat of passion.

But there is more. For a fleeting moment Apollo considers
punishing himself—"Allas! for sorwe I wol myselven slee!" That
turns out to be a passing fancy, however, and in the end he blames
the crow for everything. He calls him a "false theef" twice over (292,
295), a teller of a "false tale." And again he errs. In fact, the crow
may be many things—stupid, insensitive, blabbering, short-sighted,
and voyeuristic; but ironically Apollo accuses him of one thing he is
not, namely, false. The god of truth not only talks like a fool, but he
proves it again with another rash punishment. He pulls out all the

white (and truthful) feathers of the crow, "everichon"; he makes the crow black for his falsehood; he takes away the crow's speech and "al his song"; "and out at dore hym slong / Unto the devel." Thus Phoebus amends his sudden violence against adulterous falsehood with further violence against the stupid truth. In the process he adds a new dimension to his deity by becoming the god of bird-pluckers.

Apollo is not the only one in his story who is morally inept. In his own way the crow is just as bad. He looks upon his mistress's adultery "and seyde never a word," but when his lord comes home he fills the house with blunt, stupid talk ("Cokkow! cokkow! cokkow!") and moral indignation.

> "Phebus," quod he, "for al thy worthynesse,
> For al thy beautee and thy gentilesse,
> For al thy song and al thy mynstralcye,
> For al thy waityng, blered is thyn ye
> With oon of litel reputacioun,
> Noght worth to thee, as in comparisoun,
> The montance of a gnat, so moote I thryve!
> For on thy bed thy wyf I saugh hym swyve."   (*MancT* 249–56)

Like the contrast in his language, which gently praises Phoebus only to offend him all the more (with "swyve"), the crow flies from discreet silence to callous moralizing. He does no one any good. He insults Phoebus, helps ruin his life, and incites him to murder because, basically, he is incapable of striking a balance between the perception and the communication of the truth. He responds aberrationally, so that his foolish report leads to a worse crime and then boomerangs on himself.

Unknown to the Manciple, there is a complex lesson in what he calls his "ensample," and its ironic truth reverberates and radiates through the rest of his performance. In the Prologue, for example, he foreshadows the role of the crow when he "openly" reproves the Cook for his drunkenness. He may mean well in "excusing" the Cook from telling a tale, but in needlessly detailing the Cook's offense, and offensiveness, he shows his own folly.

> "Of me, certeyn, thou shalt nat been yglosed.
> See how he ganeth, lo! this dronken wight,

As though he wolde swolwe us anonright.
Hoold cloos thy mouth, man, by thy fader kyn!
The devel of helle sette his foot therin!
Thy cursed breeth infecte wole us alle.
Fy, stynkyng swyn! fy, foule moote thee falle!"   (*MancT* 34–40)

Perhaps if he had "yglosed" a bit or kept his own foot out of his mouth ("cloos"), the Manciple might have done better; instead he fires the wrath of the Cook so that he is thrown from his horse in a catatonic stupor. With customary pragmatism, Harry Bailly sees the Manciple's folly: " 'thou art to nyce, / Thus openly repreve hym of his vice' "; he warns (as he might later have warned the crow): overly blunt speech does not work and it might even come back to haunt you sometime. " 'Another day he wole, peraventure, / Reclayme thee and brynge thee to lure.' " Then, as if preparing for the extremes of Apollo—i.e., slaying his wife and then exculpating her—the Manciple hastily backs off his nasty blaming and invites the drunken Cook to have a drink.

"That that I spak, I seyde it in my bourde.
And wite ye what? I have heer in a gourde
A draghte of wyn, ye, of a ripe grape. . . .   (*MancT* 81–83)

The Manciple's approach is at once thoughtlessly harsh and thoughtlessly indulgent, utterly confused. As in his prologue, so in his story. At times he insists on the naked truth. He is a rough, "boystous" man who calls things what they are. He is "noght textueel" (235). He cannot countenance that a dishonest woman of "heigh degree" should be called a "lady" when a "povre wenche" is called a "wenche" (207–22); and he sees no reason why a great "outlawe" should be called a "capitayn" when a little one is called a "theef" (223–34). Still, it is difficult to reconcile this staunch morality in language with the Manciple's earlier attitude toward wives. He could not agree with Apollo's jealous "keeping" of his wife for, on one hand, a "good wyf, that is clene of werk and thoght, / Sholde nat been kept in noon awayt, certayn"; and on the other, it is waste of time to "spille labour," to deal with wicked wives (148–54). "No man" can constrain a creature from acting according to its nature, he observes (160 ff.), so we must assume that wicked wives will act according to their natures—like the bird who flies from its golden cage, like the cat who prefers mice to milk or flesh, and like the "she-wolf" who gives her favor to "the lewedeste wolf that she may fynde" (163–86).

If we sense a rhythm of contradiction or inconsistency in the Manciple's moral stance, we are perceiving only what Chaucer has shown in various ways. For now, having ended with a feminine example to help illustrate how "no man," or no god, can restrain a naturally wicked woman, he concludes that he has (after all) been talking about lewd *men*, not lewd women.

> "Alle thise ensamples speke I by thise men
> That been untrewe, and nothyng by wommen.
> For men han evere a likerous appetit
> On lower thyng to parfourne hire delit
> Than on hire wyves, be they never so faire. . . ."   (*MancT*
>   187 ff.)

Moreover, the confusion goes on because we next learn that Apollo's wife (like the "she-wolf") prefers some little wretch to the handsomest of gods, or men. And after that, to keep the rhythm going, the Manciple apologizes for his coarse language, "lemman"— "Certes, this is knavyssh speche!"—only to defend his language and repeat the offensive word (207–39). Finally, after completing the tale of Apollo and the crow, which he had three times interrupted for the sake of moralizing comments, the Manciple ends with a lesson from his fable. It turns out to be the same lesson he had learned, or thought he had learned, from his encounter with the Cook: *don't say anything!*

Having jumped from a wide-mouthed candor which openly reproved the drunken Cook, all lecherous men, dishonest ladies, great thieves, and (from within his tale) Apollo's cuckoldry and the crow's blabbing, he now shows how he can give wine to a drunk, and why he should let nature take its course and faithless women have their ways. In one of Chaucer's finest passages of extended comic irony, the Manciple verbosely and insistently, repetitiously and earnestly, amorally and moralistically urges that the only right path of conduct—taught over and over by his mother—is to keep quiet!

> "Lordynges, by this ensample I yow preye,
> Beth war, and taketh kep what that ye seye:

Ne telleth nevere no man in youre lyf
How that another man hath dight his wyf. . . .

But nathelees, thus taughte me my dame:
'My sone, thenk on the crowe, a Goddes name!
My sone, keep wel thy tonge. . . .

My sone, thy tonge sholdestow restreyne. . . .

The firste vertu, sone, if thou wolt leere,
Is to restreyne and kepe wel thy tonge. . . .

My sone, speke nat. . . .

My sone, be war, and be noon auctour newe
Of tidynges, wheither they been false or trewe.
Whereso thou come, amonges hye or lowe,
Kepe wel thy tonge, and thenk upon the crowe."   (*MancT*
  309–62)

This preachment, like the classical story which gives rise to it and
like the whole of the Manciple's performance, tends to comic self-
destruction. It teaches its moral, belies its moral, and incidentally
suggests that not even a mother can restrain a thing that nature
seems to have "natureelly set in a creature." With assistance from
all over, the Manciple has disclosed a timeless message. Its truth
extends all the way from the pagan antiquity of Apollo and the crow,
"as olde bookes maken mencioun" (106), from the wisdom of
"Daun Salomon" (314) and "Senekke" (345), through the present
time of Flemish proverbs (349) and garrulous mothers, on to the
apparently "endeless" reaches of moral contradiction. But the
whole thing is not simply a bizarre parody of moralizing; it is really
moral in a sense which the Manciple and no other simpleminded
preacher could understand. It tells of man's silly, extreme reactions
to what is wrong: of tendencies to protest overmuch or inhumanly,
or not to protest at all, to be quiet and let things go. It is, at last, an
introduction to the final Canterbury tale, to the Parson's clear but
impersonal reproof of vice and to his call for penance, forgiveness,
and mercy.[22]
  Throughout Chaucer's comic uses of classical myth and legend
we may perceive the governing influence of a curious rhetoric

which appears, on the surface, to be fragmented or discontinuous.[23] In various ways these pages have argued for a recognition of Chaucer's inconsistencies and contradictions, but only to encourage some further understanding of the complex harmonies he created. Through analog on analog—classical, Biblical, medieval—his art sought to encompass all sorts of reality.

> All things counter, original, spare, strange;
> Whatever is fickle, freckled (who knows how?)
> With swift, slow; sweet, sour; adazzle, dim. . . .

From his comic height he tossed them down, like stones in water or sounds in air, so that their disruptions radiate and multiply in Gothic *rayonnant*—

> . . . fro roundel to compas,
> Ech [sercle] aboute other goynge
> Causeth of othres sterynge
> And multiplyinge ever moo,
> Til that hyt be so fer ygoo,
> That hyt at bothe brynkes bee.   (*HF* 798–803)

Episode generates episode, description description, example example, never the same but constantly suggesting a perpetuity of analogous forms like those of Nature herself. Of course, we in our day are familiar with rhetorics of fragmentation and discontinuity, rhetorics which seem designed to throw us into despair for their chaos or to encourage us to grasp for the security of apocalyptic visions of society or self. But Chaucer's broken forms have no such grand designs. They keep searching for resolutions and conclusions without stirring any anxious need to have them right in hand, fixed and set. In medieval fashion they may look forward (by implication) to a life without the anxieties of death, of fame, of love's contending claims, or the flux of joy and sorrow. But as comedic forms of human worry "in this world heere," they—and with them the classical lore which they embody—find their last fulfillment in gentle prayer, in patient acceptance of the world and one's own self.

6   Conjectures and Afterthoughts

Chaucer was a restless artist. From the beginning to the end of his poetic career he responded to what he read, developed new interests, and in the process found different ways for adapting the materials he absorbed. He used the story of Alcyone—along with its touches of comic contrast and relief—to establish a pathetic tone and state the traditional tragic theme, the "losse of lyf and love yfeere." From that start the Black Knight's story would grow toward a consolation on death and finally an awakening to life. In this Chaucer had a pattern, like the retrograde canon in music, and he would try it again with the more extended and complicated *House of Fame*. The mixed report from the *Aeneid* would tell of the glory of fame—the ill-fame of faithful love, the good fame of insensitive ambition—and lead the narrator to discover the whys and wherefores, and in the end reject all concern for fame's uncertainty.

The *Parliament of Fowls* shows African describing another set of contrasts: this "litel erthe" set against the "hevenes quantite"; the harmony of the spheres and "commune profit" set against the anguish of personal desire. But the resolution which comes from above at the beginning of the narrative fails to disclose a reasonable, earthly consequent. The search for the implications of authoritative truth goes on, even though it may conclude elsewhere (in "Palamon and Arcite") with the pursuit of moral virtue. Thus the pattern holds constant for Chaucer's early uses of classical stories; they set the mood, develop contrasts, and state a position which the ending turns around 180 degrees.

From the formula of the first three dream visions Chaucer went on to compose complete narratives of classical "aventure," the "love of Palamon and Arcite" and after that *Troilus and Criseyde*. He drew on Boccaccio for both, first reducing his source in a *commedia* and allegorizing the gods, then expanding his source in tragedy and historicizing the gods. Looking again for something new he returned to short narratives, but now in the form of a collection of exemplary tales like Boccaccio's *De Claris Mulieribus* and *De Casibus Virorum Illustrium*. He adapted one series to suit a dual theme concerning Good Women and bad men which apparently tended toward "comedy" once more; the other he adapted "in manere of a tragedie" (his *Monk's Tale*) so that among "the falls" of Biblical and contemporary personages he would deal with Hercules, Zenobia, Nero, Alexander, Caesar, and Croesus.

At the last stage of his "makynge" Chaucer reached out in many directions at once and adjusted everything to a complex drama of ordinary life. Harking back to the early dream visions he worked stories within a story within a story: the tale of the three young men, for example, within the story of a Pardoner, within the drama of a Canterbury journey. He appropriated and revised some previous work, including the "Palamon and Arcite," and he developed two classical narratives for two of his pilgrims—"Appius and Virginius" for the Physician, and "Apollo and the Crow" for the Manciple. He put some stories inside of stories as exemplary analogs—Midas for the Wife of Bath and a comic extension of *De Raptu Proserpinae* for the Merchant. And finally, as if taking his cue from Valerius Maximus or Saint Jerome's *Against Jovinian*, he created some fragmentary lists of *exempla* for comic use: the pompous lecture of Chauntecleer and the epical chase for the fox; the frenetic soliloquy of Dorigen and the *ad hominem* assaults by the Wife of Bath.

In all this we detect a pattern of development in Chaucer's use of classical story which may run parallel to the conjectures that others have made concerning the stages of his literary career.

1. Those stories that summarize a philosophical problem—death, fame, love—which larger narratives will explore for the benefit of the fictional Chaucer.
2. Those that embody a broad, noble statement about chivalric love, in comedy and tragedy.
3. Those that constitute parts of a compendium which evolves,

    (a) as a mechanical series in the same genre with a single theme, and then
    (b) as a dramatic series in different forms with various themes.

Such a development would not have been unique to Chaucer. There are analogs in the works of Boccaccio as well as in the legal, philosophical, and scientific writings of John of Legnano (*CIT* 34–35). After composing various tracts over a number of years, Legnano finally drew many of his pieces together (Vat. Lat. MS 2639) in a grand compendium.[1] Having isolated and studied a number of subjects—in a sense, having fragmented his thinking—he apparently felt the need to correlate a large part of what he had done.

But whatever might be hypothesized about Chaucer's changing approaches to classical stories and literary forms, he seems to have maintained a consistent attitude toward the people of antiquity. Within a broad range of human behavior these "olde" women and men lived in a naturalistic world, untouched by grace, where the best of persons "loved the lawe kinde." They kept their "trouthe" like the Good Women; and they pursued the ideals of moral virtue—acting justly like Hector, prudently like Egeus, bravely like Theseus, and temperately like Virginia.

> As wel in goost as body chast was she;
> For which she floured in virginitee
> With alle humylitee and abstinence,
> With alle attemperaunce and pacience,
> With mesure eek of beryng and array.   (*PhysT* 43–47)

In spite of gods and goddesses, they might also know from reason about nature's own Creator: "almyghty Jove" or "myghty God" (*Tr* 4. 1079, 1086); the "Firste Moevere" or "Juppiter, the kyng" (*KnT* 2987, 3035); or that "Eterne God, that thurgh [his] purveiaunce / Ledest the world by certein governaunce" (*FranklT* 865–66). Indeed, within a pagan context this Jove or God, "that auctour is of kynde," could be recognized as the one who "first made the faire cheyne of love": the harmony of nature which could be linked to the best aspects of Venus or Cupid (*Tr* 3. 1254–74).

Even allowing for the loftiest metaphoric use of mythical terminology, as well as a tendency to medievalize the classical scene from time to time, Chaucer was not inclined to confuse reason with revelation or heathen idolatry with Christian worship. His classical divinities were associated with nature too—historical, physical, or moral, whether allegorized or not. The prayers that they received might be in the affectionate medieval style.

> "A! mercy! swete lady dere!"
> Quod she to Juno, hir goddesse,
> "Helpe me out of thys distress. . . ." (BD 108-10)

or

> "Lord Phebus, se the teeris on my cheke,
> And of my peyne have som compassioun." (*FranklT* 1078-79)

They might even echo a familiar liturgical motif.

> "O chaste goddesse of the wodes grene,
> To whom bothe hevene and erthe and see is sene. . . ." (*KnT* 2297-98, cf. *SNT* 46)

Still, the intentions behind those prayers or the effects that flowed from them fell consistently short of the supernatural.

Alcyone's plea to Juno finds no consolation but death. Palamon wishes to die if his prayer for Emelye cannot be answered. And Troilus's prayer to love's joy—stable, concordant and "perpetuely durynge" (*Tr* 3. 1744-71)—turns from an impossible dream to death-wish and cursing (*Tr* 5. 204 ff.). This is, in fact, the pattern for many pagan prayers: my heart's desire or death! But where conditions vary so do the problems. Dorigen, for example, fails to understand the "purveiaunce" of nature's "eterne God"; Aurelius begs Phoebus for a miracle of nature that will shame Dorigen, "atte leeste," one way or another; and the best of pagans, Theseus, can wish for nothing beyond the ken of human wisdom—to accept the rhythm of nature, the sorrow of loss and death, and to rejoice in the continuance of life (*KnT* 3041-44; 3067-69).

In the final analysis, Chaucer was far more interested in people than in gods, in this world than in an airy mythology of antiquity. When we think of his deities and imagine backward and forward—to the statues of ancient Rome and Greece or to the reappearance of the gods in later Renaissance and baroque art—the differences can overwhelm us. What would Geoffrey have thought if he walked into the *Salon d'Apollon* at Versailles? How grand? Or simply, how ridiculous! Consider Apollo embodying an ideal or a symbol of kingship. Or on the other hand consider Chaucer's stupid and cuckolded Phoebus, his peremptory and testy Juno, his senile Pluto overmatched by a youthful wife, his amiable and stuffy messenger from Jupiter, his obscene Priapus, seductive Venus, menacing Mars, and mean-spirited Diana. When he read of Juno and Morpheus, he would think of the one God whom he knew, and he was skeptical of mythological miracles. He preferred his classical characters to the deities they worshiped, and given a choice of "erthly god" and "gide" he selected Alceste instead of Lord Cupid. In truth, when Geoffrey Chaucer strolled among the gods he walked with both feet on the ground.

Notes

Chapter 1

1. All references to Chaucer's writings are cited from F. N. Robinson, ed., *The Works of Geoffrey Chaucer*, 2d ed. (Boston, 1957).

2. Gilbert Highet, however, could not put this notion aside, showing more concern for Chaucer's "many shocking mistakes" in dealing with classical material than for his aims or the range of his accomplishments. *The Classical Tradition* (New York, 1949), pp. 93–103.

3. The most frequently repeated misconceptions have been (1) that all "interpretations" of pagan deities and legends can be lumped together as allegorical, whether they be etymological, historical (euhemeristic), physical (natural), moral, or Christian; and (2) that such interpretations of myth are somehow unpoetic or antiliterary. See, for example, J. S. P. Tatlock, "The Epilog of Chaucer's *Troilus*," *MP* 18 (1921): 637 n. 2 and 645 n. 3; C. H. Haskins, *The Renaissance of the Twelfth Century* (Cambridge, Mass., 1927), p. 108; and L. K. Born, "Ovid and Allegory," *Speculum* 9 (1934): 363–64. Some of the same attitudes appear occasionally in J. Seznec's excellent study, *The Survival of the Pagan Gods* (New York, 1953), pp. 173–74, 249–50 n. 110. It seems to me that Christian allegorical readings of pagan myth are rare in the Middle Ages, and that where they do appear (in the twelfth century, and then again largely in the fourteenth to the sixteenth centuries) they result either from the influence of Neoplatonic thought or from pietistic impositions upon classical material similar to those found in the *exemplum* literature of the fourteenth century. Generally, even the finest scholarship on the traditions of classical myth in the Middle Ages tends to lump these things together: to consider *all* "interpretations" of myth as allegorical, and nearly all moral interpretations of myth as Christian. Also, there are failures to distinguish the interpretation of myth as it appears in classical literature from the use of myth by Christian artists, and these from the consciously ahistorical imposition on myth of Christian meanings.

4. Any kind of idealized notion of the classical tradition or the "classical spirit" is bound to lead to misconceptions when it is imposed upon a writer. P. V. D. Shelly accepted a Pateresque concept of the classical ideal as involving "blitheness, repose, serenity, generality or breadth, and sensuousness" which led him to emphasize the "charm" and "sensitiveness to classical beauty" in Chaucer's treatment of myth. See *The Living Chaucer* (Philadelphia, 1940), pp. 185–87. It would be equally trouble-

some to apply Irving Babbit's idea of the "classical spirit," which he considered "consecrated to the service of a high, impersonal reason," and marked by "restraint and discipline, a sense of proportion and pervading law." *Literature and the American College* (Boston, 1908), pp. 168–69. We will see that neither of these views, nor anything like them, is relevant to Chaucer's approach to classical myth and legend.

5. *The Histories* II. 4 and 53.

6. C. H. Whitman, *Homer and the Heroic Tradition* (Cambridge, Mass., 1958), Ch. 10 and esp. pp. 223, 227–28, 241. See also M. P. Nilsson, *A History of Greek Religion* (Oxford, 1949), pp. 170 ff. and 182 ff. regarding the deities in Homer and Hesiod.

7. *Virgil: A Study in Civilized Poetry* (Oxford, 1963), p. 7. On Epicurus's conception, see J. Moreau, "Épicure et la Physique des Dieux," *Revue des Études Anciennes* 70 (1968): 286–94.

8. Otis, pp. 5, 12.

9. In his discussion of "The Gods" in *Plato's Thought* (London, 1935), Ch. 5, G. M. A. Grube observes that although anthropomorphism influenced the popular conceptions of divinity among the Greeks, and was employed by artists and poets, still the deities were "to the educated Greek, at least, definitely symbolic" (p. 151). Grube's discussion of Euripides' treatment of the divinities is also valuable: *The Drama of Euripides* (London, 1941), Ch. 4. Hercule Poirot's remarks are from Agatha Christie's *The Labours of Hercules.*

10. Xenophon's *Memorabilia* X. 1. 21–34 and Cicero's *De Officiis* I. 32. See also *Memorabilia* I. 3. 7 and 13 concerning Circe and Cupid. Despite its *moralitas* the story of Hercules' choice created problems for many Christian writers: see T. Mommsen's "Petrarch and the Story of the Choice of Hercules," *Journal of the Warburg and Courtauld Institutes* 16 (1953): 178–92.

11. On the Judgment of Paris, see L. G. Whitbread's *Fulgentius the Mythographer* (Columbus, O., 1971), pp. 21–24, which cites some examples of possible etymological borrowings from Cicero and discusses the tradition of this method of interpretation.

12. *Ovid as an Epic Poet*, 1st ed. (Cambridge, 1966), p. 325; also the same author's *Virgil*, pp. 227 ff.

13. Seznec gives a valuable account of these traditions in *The Survival of the Pagan Gods*, pp. 11–121.

14. In *The City of God*, Book VI, Augustine discusses Varro's learning (Ch. 2–3), his three categories of divinity—fabulous, natural, and political (Ch. 5), and Seneca's comments (Ch. 10). Varro's categories of myth are important for understanding the medieval traditions; they are also analogous to the later, fourteenth-century applications to myth of the Biblical four levels of meaning. See C. G. Osgood's introduction in *Boccaccio on Poetry* (Princeton, 1930), esp. pp. xviii–xix. Here and elsewhere I have used and cited the translation of *The City of God* by John Healey (1610), as revised in Everyman's Library.

15. *City of God* VII. 18–19.

16. H. Hagendahl, *Augustine and the Classics* (Göteborg, 1967), pp. 392–93, 437–41.

17. *De Ordine* I. 8. 24, cited by D. W. Robertson, Jr., in *A Preface to Chaucer* (Princeton, 1962), pp. 59–60, 337–38.

18. The reading of Virgil's fourth eclogue as a prophecy of Christ's advent may serve as a paradigm, for it is often wrongly assumed that that interpretation is typical of an early, pervasive Christian effort to allegorize classical literature. But there was a good deal of uncertainty even in this familiar instance. St. Jerome, for example, scorned the prophetic interpretation and others like it (*Epistle* 53. 7): "But all this is puerile, and resembles the sleight-of-hand of a mountebank." See P. Courcelle, "Les Exégèses Chrétiennes de la Quatrième Églogue," *Revue des Études Anciennes* 59 (1957): 294–319. In general, the early Christian writers accepted or adapted, to different degrees, certain aspects of pagan philosophy and theology, such as the Neoplatonic interpretations of Book VI of the *Aeneid*; but enthusiasm for syncretism or for special "secret knowledge" of Christianity by pagans (*priscia theologia*) was not prevalent. See below, n. 29 and P. Courcelle, "Les Pères de L'Église devant les Enfers Virgiliens," *Archives d'Histoire Doctrinale et Littéraire du Moyen Age* 22 (1955): 5–70.

19. *Mitologie* I. 17; II. 1. 70. My references are to Helm's edition, n. 22 below.

20. In a *pictura* the dress or details associated with a deity are listed—sometimes with their traditional meanings, and sometimes not. The format appears in a wide variety of places: in dictionaries such as Ridewall's *Fulgentius Metaforalis* and Boccaccio's *Genealogie Deorum*; in poetry such as Petrarch's *Africa*, in Boccaccio's *Teseida* (for which Boccaccio wrote a prose gloss), and in Chaucer's *Knight's Tale*, which borrows from Boccaccio for the pictures of Mars and Venus. (Chaucer's *pictura* of Diana in the same tale is his own.) Even if a *pictura* is unglossed it is still allegorical. Art historians (for example, Panofsky) have pointed this out for some time; and literary historians such as D. W. Robertson, Jr., have indicated the validity of the same assumption for literary works. In fact, *picturae* were associated with poetry specifically: Seznec, *Survival of the Pagan Gods*, pp. 171–72; and B. Smalley, *English Friars and Antiquity in the Early Fourteenth Century* (Oxford, 1960), pp. 165–83. Although there are some examples of mythological *picturae* in Fulgentius's *Mitologie*, the form is apparently much older. Augustine implies that it could be found in Varro (*City of God* VII. 5). See also Cicero's *De Natura Deorum* I. 29–30; II. 28; and T. B. L. Webster, "Personification as a Mode of Greek Thought," *Journal of the Warburg and Courtauld Institutes* 17 (1954): 13.

21. My translations are from the Latin texts of Servius, ed. G. Thilo and H. Hagen (Leipzig, 1881), I. 190; "Lactantius," ed. R. Jahnke (Leipzig, 1898), p. 262; and Isidore, ed. W. M. Lindsay (Oxford, 1911), Vol. 1. On the Lactantian glosses on Statius, see R. D. Sweeney, *Prolegomena to an Edition of the Scholia to Statius* (Leiden, 1969).

22. The *Virgiliana Continentia* in Fulgentius's *Opera*, ed. R. Helm (Leipzig, 1898), pp. 81–107, and in Whitbread's translation, pp. 119–35.

23. My translation and later references are from the Latin texts in G. Bode, *Scriptores Rerum Mythicarum Latini Tres* (Cellis, Belgium, 1834); here p. 74. On Fulgentius's reputation see M. L. W. Laistner's "Fulgentius in the Carolingian Age," in *The Intellectual Heritage of the Early Middle Ages*, ed. C. G. Starr (Ithaca, N.Y., 1957), pp. 202–15.

24. K. O. Elliot and J. P. Elder, "A Critical Edition of the Vatican Mythographers," *TAPA* 78 (1947): 189–207, esp. 204. On the authorship of the *Third Vatican Mythography*, see E. Rathbone, "Master Alberic of London, 'Mythographus Tertius Vaticanus,' " *Mediaeval and Renaissance Studies* 1 (1941): 35–38.

25. Elliot and Elder, p. 204.

26. F. Ghisalberti, "Arnolfo d'Orleans, un cultore di Ovidio nel secolo XII," *Memorie del R. Instituto Lombardo di Scienze e Lettere* 24 (1932): 201 and *passim*.

27. *Commentum Bernardi Silvestris super sex libros Eneidos Virgilii*, ed. G. Riedel (Greifswald, 1924), pp. 10–11. For Bernard's sources, and particularly for the Platonic and Neoplatonic influences on his commentary (by way of Macrobius), see J. R. O'Donnell, "The Sources and Meaning of Bernard Silvester's Commentary on the *Aeneid*," *Mediaeval Studies* 24 (1962): 233–49.

28. *Policraticus* VIII. 24–25. The translation is J. B. Pike's, *Frivolities of Courtiers and Footprints of Philosophers* (Minneapolis, 1938).

29. *Genealogie Deorum* XV. 8 in Osgood's translation (n. 14 above). John of Salisbury's reservations are implicit in his redaction of Bernard Silvester's commentary on the *Aeneid* (n. 28 above); they are explicit in *Policraticus* VII. 12. The tradition that divine truth could be found in pagan writings, and so in pagan myth, was not general or dominant in the Middle Ages. There is an outline of its history in D. P. Walker's "The *Priscia Theologia* in France," *Journal of the Warburg and Courtauld Institutes* 17 (1954): 204–59. Walker observes that the practice of the *priscia theologia* "increased greatly in the fifteenth and sixteenth centuries, partly because of the revival of Platonism and the desire to integrate it into Christianity, and partly because many more [Hermetic] texts became available" (204). See also Seznec's *Survival of the Pagan Gods*, pp. 96–101 and *passim*. The Platonic influence on Bernard Silvester, pointed out by O'Donnell (n. 27 above), apparently had a similar influence on his commentary on the *Aeneid*. The position which I took in my dissertation some years ago—that anagogical interpretations of pagan myth developed almost inexorably from the influence of the methods of patristic exegesis—no longer seems convincing to me ("Classical Myth in Chaucer's *Troilus and Criseyde*" [Princeton, 1955], pp. 62 ff.) because other influences can account for that development.

30. The notion that the classical deities became personifications during the Middle Ages is surely simplistic, for there is ample evidence that they were used as personifications in classical literature, for example, by Euripides and Virgil. See also T. B. L. Webster's article (n. 20 above).

31. P. Berchorius, *De Formis Figurisque Deorum*, ed. J. Engels (Utrecht, 1966), p. 2. "Quia ergo video quod Scriptura utitur fabulis ad alicuius veritatis tam naturalis quam historice designacionem, congruum michi visum est, post moralizacionem proprietatum rerum postque iam ad mores reducta nature opera, eciam ad moralizandum fabulas poetarum manum ponere, et sic per ipsas hominum ficciones possim morum & fidei misteria confirmare."

32. *Ibid.*, pp. 7–10. On the traditional interpretations of Saturn see the *Third Vatican Mythography* 1 and 2.

33. I. Lavin, "Cephalus and Procris," *Journal of the Warburg and Courtauld Institutes* 17 (1954): 263 n. 1 and 262 n. 4.

34. A parallel to the imposed, pious interpretations of classical myth can be found in fourteenth-century *exemplum* literature. Of their very nature medieval *exempla* were moral or moralistic, but in the fourteenth century two new currents appeared. There was a tendency to moralize nonexemplary material (e.g., the laws of physics and aspects of natural history), and to moralize (really, spiritualize) *on top of* what were already traditional moralizations. Thus religious interpretations were

imposed on material which was already moral. See J.-Th. Welter, *L'Exemplum dans la littérature religieuse et didactique du moyen age* (Paris, 1927), pp. 140 ff. and p. 335; also Robertson's *Preface to Chaucer*, pp. 355–56. I can only theorize that these tendencies were part of a general movement toward decoration and elaboration in fourteenth-century thought and art. Although works such as Bersuire's could later tie in with the increased concern for *priscia theologia* in the fifteenth and sixteenth centuries, they do not seem to have grown out of a Neoplatonic or Hermetic tradition. On imposed mythological allegory, see R. Tuve, *Allegorical Imagery: Some Medieval Books and their Posterity* (Princeton, 1966), Ch. 4, a learned and sane discussion.

35. See Christine de Pisan's *Epistle of Othea*, each part of which consists of "a Texte, a Glose and an Allegorie." The "Textes" serve " 'as a medium for instilling into the mind of the pupil . . . moral precepts or rules of behaviour, wrapped up in an allusion to some story from mythology, from the history of Troy or, very rarely, from other sources, without the least regard for chronological propriety.' " The Gloses amplify on the Textes and usually add material from ancient philosophers; and the Allegories provide further amplification, often including scriptural, patristic or other theological elaborations. The Allegorie on Venus, for example, deals understandably with vanity, but Mars "may wel be callid the sone of God" (with quotations from St. Ambrose and St. Paul); Midas is linked to Pilate; and by Cadmus, who conquered the serpent at the well, "we may vnderstande the blessid manhode of Jhesu Criste. . . ." See C. F. Buhler's edition of Scrope's translation, *EETS* 264 (London, 1970): xiii, 18, 22, 38, 40. Instances of the more traditional, historical, and moral (not "moralized" or spiritualized) uses of classical *exempla* are found throughout John of Salisbury's *Policraticus.*

36. See Seznec's *Survival of the Pagan Gods*, pp. 95–96, 274–75. Walsingham's work is edited by R. A. van Kluyve (Durham, N.C., 1968).

37. See, for example, E. F. Shannon, *Chaucer and the Roman Poets* (Cambridge, Mass., 1929); B. A. Wise, *The Influence of Statius upon Chaucer* (Baltimore, 1911); D. S. Fansler, *Chaucer and the Roman de la Rose* (New York, 1914); B. L. Jefferson, *Chaucer and the Consolation of Philosophy of Boethius* (Princeton, 1917).

38. See R. A. Pratt, "Chaucer's Use of the *Teseida*," *PMLA* 62 (1947): 598–621 and Robertson's *Preface to Chaucer*, pp. 90–91, 369–73 and *passim*. Traditional interpretations of mythical material not only appeared in standard dictionaries, but were carried over into scholia and commentaries on classical and medieval literary texts such as the *Thebaid*, the *Pharsalia*, the *De Nuptiis Mercurii et Philologiae*, the *De Consolatione Philosophiae*, and the *Divina Commedia* (e.g., Boccaccio's commentary). See, for example, C. Landi, "D'un commento medievale inedito della 'Tebaide' di Stazio," *Atti e memorie della R. accademia di scienze lettere ed arti in Padova*, n.s. 30 (1913–14): 328 and P. M. Clogan, "Chaucer and the *Thebaid* Scholia," *SP* 61 (1964): 599–615. Under the circumstances it is often impossible or fruitless to trace *a single specific* source for a medieval artist's understanding of mythological details.

39. References could be multiplied, but see, for example, Fulgentius's *Mitologie* I. 15 and I. 7 and *Iohannis Scotti Adnotationes in Marcianum*, ed. C. E. Lutz (Cambridge, Mass., 1939), p. 31.

40. The tradition of the Theban and Trojan tragedies is discussed in Chapter 4 of this book. See my "Trojan Scene in Chaucer's *Troilus*," *ELH* 29 (1962): 263–75;

and concerning Thebes, the *Vatican Mythographies* I. 151, II. 78, *Policraticus* I. 4, and Chaucer's own *Complaint of Mars*, lines 245 ff.

41. For some examples from the commentaries of Thomas Waleys and John Ridewall, see B. Smalley, *English Friars and Antiquity in the Early Fourteenth Century* (Oxford, 1960), pp. 99–100, 103–4, 130.

42. Although Chaucer was unusually alert to historical differences, he often turned things around and made his classical figures behave *as though* they were living in a medieval world; see M. W. Bloomfield's "Chaucer's Sense of History," *JEGP* 51 (1952): 301–13. Thus when Chaucer's ancient characters pray to Juno, Jove, or Apollo, their language often resembles Christian prayer.

43. Shelly, *The Living Chaucer*, p. 187 (quoting John Addington Symonds).

44. D. C. Fowler, "John Trevisa: Scholar and Translator," *Transactions of the Bristol and Gloucester Archeological Society* 89 (1970): 99–108 and esp. 103–4. Emphasis added.

45. There is still much to be learned about fourteenth-century French translations which Chaucer might have known, besides the translations of Boccaccio's *Filostrato* and Grieselda story, the *Ovide Moralisé*, and the *Livre de Melibé*. I am thinking of the translation of Ovid's *Heroides* (of which Professor Clem Williams of De Pauw University tells me); also of Golein's *L'Information des princes* and *Fleurs des chroniquers;* Simon de Hesdin's translation of Valerius Maximus; the translation of Boethius (ca. 1337) which postdates Jean de Meun's; Nicole Oresme's various translations from Aristotle and Bersuire's translation of Livy; Raoul de Presles's translation of the *City of God;* and Denis Foullechat's of the *Policraticus.*

Chapter 2

1. B. F. Huppé and D. W. Robertson, Jr., *Fruyt and Chaf: Studies in Chaucer's Allegories* (Princeton, 1963), p. 39. In their discussion of the Ceyx and Alcyone story Huppé and Robertson lean heavily on Alcyone's lack of a philosophical or Christian perspective on the death of her husband, as though that lack were blameworthy. But here and elsewhere I would suggest that Chaucer assumes that a Christian perspective is historically impossible for his classical heroines who lived under the law of nature. Because they cannot see with the eyes of faith, their actions, even if mistaken, are more understandable and occasion more sympathy than would otherwise be the case.

2. J. I. Wimsatt, "The Apotheosis of Blanche in *The Book of the Duchess,*" *JEGP* 66 (1967): 26–44. Although I agree with Wimsatt's notion, my view of the context differs from his.

3. G. L. Kittredge, "Chaucer's Lollius," *Harvard Studies in Classical Philology* 28 (1917): 50–55.

4. On the association of Mars with heat, furor, wrath, and finally the irascible appetite (the medieval "scholastic" adaptation), see C. E. Lutz, ed., *Iohannis Scotti Adnotationes in Marcianum* (Cambridge, Mass., 1939), pp. 20, 53; M. Manitius, "Zu Iohannes Scottus und Remigius," *Didaskaleion* 2 (1913): 72; *Third Vatican Mythography* 6. 8; *Genealogie Deorum* IX. 3, and Boccaccio's gloss on the *Teseida*, ed. A. Roncaglia (Bari, 1941), p. 413. On Mars and death, see above Ch. 1, n. 21; also *Second Vatican Mythography* 29, *Iohannis Scotti Adnotationes,* pp. 108, 159, and

the passage from Haly in W. C. Curry's *Chaucer and the Mediaeval Sciences* (New York, 1960), p. 123.

5. In two passages Chaucer refers to Minerva or Pallas as "wise" (*PhysT* 49 and *BD* 1072), and in one other she is the warrior goddess, Bellona (*Anel* 5). Various medieval sources develop the notion of the goddess's association with wisdom, learning, and the contemplative life: Fulgentius, *Mitologie* I. 21, II. 1, 6, and 11; *Third Vatican Mythography* 10, also 11, 20–23; *Genealogie Deorum* II. 3. Arnolph of Orleans notes that during the ancient feast of Pallas wise men gathered to hold disputations on learned matters (J. Holzworth, *An Unpublished Commentary on Ovid's Fasti by Arnulphus of Orleans* [Bryn Mawr, 1940] unpubl. diss., p. 134). Also, Richard de Bury is one of several who refer to classical studies in terms of Minerva, or Pallas: he says the Palladion of Troy, a sign of ancient learning, was passed (cf. "*translatio imperii*") from Troy, to Paris, and then to England (*Philobiblon* X).

6. For a medieval illumination of Criseyde in widow's garb, see F. Saxl and H. Meier's *Catalogue of Astrological and Mythological Illuminated Manuscripts of the Latin Middle Ages* III, *Manuscripts in English Libraries* II (London, 1953), pl. XXIV.

7. The *locus classicus* is St. Augustine's letter to the widow Juliana (*De Bono Viduitatis*) in which he especially commends to her the virtues of wisdom and chastity (c. 17), and urges that instead of enjoying carnal pleasures the widow should take delight in "reading, prayer, psalms, holy meditation, diligence in good works, hope of the world to come, and a heart uplifted" (c. 21). The translation is Sr. M. C. Eagan's in the *Fathers of the Church* XVI: *Saint Augustine: Treatises on Various Subjects* (New York, 1952). For a recent parallel, see "Christian Widowhood: An Address of Pope Pius XII to the World Union of Family Organizations," in *The Pope Speaks* 4 (1957–58): 287–92.

8. On the chastity as well as the wisdom of Pallas, see the references in n. 5 above, esp. *Mitologie* II. 1, *Third Vatican Mythography* 10. 2, and *Genealogie Deorum* II. 3, which point out that the goddess was a virgin, immortal and incorruptible. One of the passages cited from Chaucer in the same n. 5 also links Pallas with prudence ("for me purveye"), a familiar association because of her role as goddess of wisdom; see also Alanus's *Anticlaudian* II. 7, where Prudence is addressed as "Minerva," and P. Bersuire, *Metamorphosis Ouidiana Moraliter* (Paris, 1515), fol. xi^v (wrongly ascribed to Thomas Walleys).

9. Authorities could be multiplied, but see the *Sententiae* of Peter Lombard, ed. College of St. Bonaventura (Florence, 1916), I. Dist. V. c. 1; Dist. X. c. 1; Dist. XV. c. 8; Dist. XVII. c. 2; and the summary statement in I. Dist. XXXIV. c. 3: "Cumque unum et idem penitus sit in Deo potentia, sapientia, bonitas [elsewhere *amor, caritas,* or *dilectio*], in sacra Scriptura tamen frequenter solent haec nomina distincte ad personas referri, ut Patri potentia, Filio sapientia, Spiritui sancto bonitas tribuatur." The distinctions are also familiar in vernacular literature: see Dante's *Paradiso* VII. 30–33 and D. Zorzi, *Valori religiousi nella letteratura provenzale: la spiritualità trinitaria* (Milan, 1954), pp. 159–64. Chaucer uses another mythological "Trinity" (Jove, Apollo, and Cupid) in *Tr* 5. 207, where the context is serious.

10. Thus the mythical associations of Criseyde—as she sees herself (Pallas), as Troilus sees her (Venus), and as the narrative suggests toward its conclusion (with allusions to Cynthia, Lucina, Latona: the variable moon)—lend support to Mus-

catine's stylistic analysis, *Chaucer and the French Tradition* (Berkeley, 1957), pp. 153 ff. In a different context, Walter Map writes about false Minerva veiling Aphrodite: *De Nugis Curialium*, ed. M. R. James (Oxford, 1914), Book IV, c. xi.

11. Venus is usually a mythical figure or cliché for the voluptuous ("Epicurean") life, love, and the attractive pleasures of the senses—both in classical and medieval literature: Fulgentius's *Mitologie* II. 1 gives the traditional (Stoic) portrait of Venus: the foamy sea refers to the surge of passion (or the semen); Venus is naked because her adultery cannot be hidden, or because she comes together only with those who are naked; her roses are shamefulness, her doves are hot for copulation, etc. See also *Second Vatican Mythography* 30–33; *Third Vatican Mythography* 11. 1; *Genealogie Deorum* III. 22–23; and Boccaccio's gloss in Roncaglia's edition (n. 4 above), *Teseida*, pp. 417–18, 428–30. The representations of Venus in art and literature have been discussed by numerous scholars, including Panofsky, Seznec, and D. W. Robertson, Jr.; on the Boccaccio gloss, see D. S. Brewer, *Chaucer* (London, 1953), pp. 81–82, and B. M. McCoy's translation of Boccaccio, *The Book of Theseus* (New York, 1974), pp. 199 ff. The notion of twofold Venus, one "common" and the other "heavenly," can be traced from Plato (*Symposium* 180–81), Lucretius, Seneca, Ovid, and medieval glosses to the Renaissance. Although Chaucer occasionally alludes to a heavenly aspect of Venus and Cupid, he prefers dealing with heavenly love in nonmythological terms; he is inclined to use Venus and Cupid in more of an Aristotelian than a Platonic way: to refer to natural sensual pleasures which, uncontrolled, lead to aberrant behavior that may be comic and/or tragic.

12. The classical source is Terence's *Eunuchus* IV. 5: see Chaucer's *PF* 275 and Robinson's note; St. Jerome's *Against Jovinian* II. 7; and Boccaccio's gloss on the *Teseida*, ed. Roncaglia, pp. 418, 429. The association of Venus with feasting, dancing, singing, playing, and other *pleasant* activities is, of course, familiar: e.g., Curry, *Chaucer and the Mediaeval Sciences*, pp. 97–100; *Gen Prol* 89–98, *KnT* 2483–87, *MerchT* 1790 ff.

13. Chaucer nearly always refers to blind (irrational) Cupid. The traditional associations of the god can be seen in nearly all authorities, e.g., Isidore's *Etymologiae* VIII. xi (80); *Second Vatican Mythography* 35; *Third Vatican Mythography* XI. 18 ("Amor"); Map's *De Nugis Curialium* II. xii; *Genealogie Deorum* IX. 4. On the Petrarch reference which follows, see *The Triumph of Love* §1. Chaucer's Cupid who *can* see (*LGW* F226–40) is a lordly figure for reasonable natural love, not a Platonic representation of heavenly love; and he speaks more lordly than reasonably to Geoffrey. Again Chaucer seems to prefer Christian, nonmythological language when he deals with heavenly love: e.g., "Charite" in contrast to the God of Love (*Tr* 1. 15–49); and "Celestial" in contrast to natural love (*Tr* 1. 979).

14. On "Thesiphone" as the voice of the Furies which "bursts forth in words," see Fulgentius's *Mitologie* I. 7; also, for example, the Lactantian gloss on the *Thebaid*, ed. Jahnke, p. 54; *Third Vatican Mythography* VI. 23; *Genealogie Deorum*, the Prohemium and I. 14. There are other interpretations which especially focus on the discord of the Furies. Isidore of Seville, using Lactantius's *Divinae Institutiones* VI. 19, links the Furies with *ira*, *cupiditas*, and *libido* (*Etymologiae* VIII. xi [95]), and although that tradition of interpretation continues, with some variations, through the Middle Ages, it does not seem as clearly related to Chaucer's immediate context as the Fulgentian gloss. On the crying song and the bewailing of tragedy, see *MkT*

1991, 2762 and *Boece* II. pr. 2. 67–70. Isidore of Seville says that tragedies deal with the ancient deeds and crimes of wretched princes *in sorrowful song* ("luctuoso carmine").

15. The Niobe allusion needs no explanation, but Boccaccio (citing Cicero) makes it even plainer with his comment on her eternal sorrow in grief ("propter eius eternum in luctu silentium"): *Genealogie Deorum* XII. 2. The allusions to Tityus and Phlegethon, however, carried not-so-obvious connotations to sufferings that stem from lust and fiery passion. On Tityus, see Servius's commentary on *Aeneid* II. 82–83 with its reference to Lucretius (III. 978); also *Second Vatican Mythography* 105, *Third Vatican Mythography* VI. 5, and Map's *De Nugis Curialium* I. 6, IV. 3 and V. 7. Phlegethon, "the fery flood of helle," was generally associated with the burning heat of passion in anger, fury, and cupidity: Macrobius's *Commentary on the Dream of Scipio* I. 10, 10–12; *Third Vatican Mythography* VI. 4; and *Genealogie Deorum* I. 14 and III. 16.

16. Beyond suffering and sorrow, some of these allusions carry other relevant connotations: the blinding of Oedipus and the blindness of love; Orpheus's looking back to hell at Eurydice (and so losing her in the escape) and the notion that earthly attractions overwhelm man's reason and spirit (*Boece* III. m. 12); Myrrha's suffering for love; Ixion's torment on the wheel (of Fortune); and Athamas's punishment as a figure of treachery (n. 19 below).

17. For example, see the various references to blissful Venus (2. 680, 972–73; 3. 1 ff., 950–52, 1254 ff., 1807), to Calliope and the Muses (3. 45, 1809), the prayers to deities in love (3. 712 ff.), the denunciation of Crassus and Midas (3. 1387–93), and the apparent escape from Phlegethon (3. 1599–1600).

18. Servius on *Aeneid* VI. 603 and *Georgics* III. 7.

19. The marriage of "Argyves" (Argia) to Polyneices is ill-omened and characterized in Statius by the description of the cursed brooch she wears. After the wedding "Argyves" pleads with her father to support the war against Thebes ("da bella, pater") and then, later, bribes Eriphyle with the brooch so that she ("perfida coniunx") will disclose her husband, Amphiaraus, whose absence from the Argive forces threatens to prevent the expedition against Thebes. See *Thebaid* II. 244–305; III. 678–710; IV. 187–213. Also Chapter 1 (note 40) above.

20. *The Book of Troilus and Criseyde*, ed R. K. Root (Princeton, 1945), p. 525.

21. Ovid's *Metamorphoses* VIII. 6 ff.

22. "Troilus and Criseyde," in *Companion to Chaucer Studies*, ed. B. Rowland (Toronto, 1968), pp. 377–78.

23. The usual gloss on Clio as the Muse of history is appropriate, but it should be expanded to take into account the meaning of "history" and the long tradition that associated the Muses with different stages of knowledge and expression (philosophy's "noteful sciences" according to the gloss in *Boece* I. pr. 1). Clio was the first, the basic Muse, for she was connected with instruction (*doctrina*) and the most elementary modes of discourse. Chaucer's language at the beginning of Book Two implies that he has these notions in mind, for he invokes her simply to translate a report: "Me nedeth here noon other art to use" (2. 11); "But out of Latyn in my tonge it write" (2. 14); "For as myn auctour seyde, so sey I" (2. 18); and "Myn auctour shal I folwen, if I konne" (2. 49). See Fulgentius's *Mitologie* I. 15; *Third Vatican Mythography* VIII. 18; and *Genealogie Deorum* XI. 2. The traditional sense of

history associated with Clio has to do with "fame" or "report," in other words telling what one has previously heard or read. Lydgate links Clio specifically with rhetoric in *Troy Book* II. 173–79. The connection between Polyhymnia and "memory" ("vois memorial" in *Anel 15–20*) is in precisely the same etymological tradition as that which connects Clio with "report," and Calliope with the "best voice" (n. 24 below); it required none of the mental gymnastics described by J. L. Lowes in "Chaucer and Dante," *MP* 14 (1916–17): 154 and n. 1.

24. Encyclopedists and glossators consistently explain Calliope, the queen of the Muses, as meaning the best or beautiful voice (*optima vox* or *pulchra vox*), and sometimes the good sound (*bona sonoritas*). See the citations in n. 23 above; also, Macrobius's *Commentary on the Dream of Scipio* II. 3. 2; *Iohannis Scotti Adnotationes*, p. 31; *Didaskaleion* II. 67; and J. Holzworth, "Hugutio's *Derivationes* and Arnulfus' Commentary on Ovid's *Fasti*," *TAPA* 73 (1942): 271.

25. The double invocation to the Furies and Mars prepares for a series of analogous associations that run through Book Four: Furies = torment, sorrow, care, woe, complaint, weeping, etc.; and Mars = wrath, ire, rage, madness, death, etc. See, for example, "care" / "wood" and "wo" / "woodnesse" (4. 225–38); "furie and . . . rage" (253); "compleyne and crye" / "dye" and "slayn" (277–78); "sorwful lif" / "dyen in distresse" (301); "sorwen" / "mad" (393–94); "wepe and wailen / til I deye" (399) and *passim*. The dual motif appears obliquely in *Boece* I. pr. 5 and IV. m. 2 as "sorwe" and "ire"; and again in Benoit de St. Maur's *Roman de Troie* (lines 13235–38) as "ire et tristece" at the beginning of the section on the separation of Troilus and Briseida.

26. This is Troilus's and love tragedy's "double sorwe." See the *Complaint of Mars* 251–56. The notion that love doubles the sorrow of tragedy (death, loss, imprisonment) is found in *Boece* III. m. 12; see also KnT 1295–98.

27. "Five-Book Structure in Chaucer's *Troilus*," *MLQ* 23 (1962): 297–308.

28. *City of God* I. 1 and 30.

Chapter 3

1. For John the Scot's use of Fulgentius and Isidore, among others, see C. E. Lutz's introduction in *Iohannis Scotti Adnotationes in Marcianum* (Cambridge, Mass., 1939), pp. xxiv–xxv; and the same editor's remarks on the influence of Remigius's commentary on later handbooks and encyclopedias in *Remigii Autissiodorensis Commentum in Martianum Capellam* (Leiden, 1962–65), I. 41. See also Walsingham's *De Archana Deorum*, ed. R. A. van Kluyve (Durham, N.C., 1968), pp. xiv–xvi, F. Ghisalberti, "Paolo da Perugia Commentatore di Persio," *R. instituto Lombardo di scienze e lettere* 62, ser. 2 (1929), esp. 569–77; and *Arnulfi Aurelianensis Glosule Super Lucanum*, ed. B. M. Marti (American Academy in Rome, 1958), pp. XXIX–XXXIV, XLIX.

2. The studies by Fansler, Lowes, Meech, and others, need no elaboration here. Still, the variety of mythological allegorizations should be noted. For example, Alanus uses Jupiter, as he does Apollo, in both terrestrial and celestial senses (*Anticlaudian* IV. 7, V. 5 and 7): the terrestrial or planetary Jupiter represents a *natural* force of benevolence and accord, but Jupiter's epithet, "The Thunderer," is also applied to God the Father and Creator. The first is part of a mythical allegory of

natural philosophy and the second is a metaphoric transfer to Christian theology; the two are different and distinct. Consider also the figure of Venus as she represents sensual pleasure in both the *Anticlaudian* and the *Roman de la Rose: Anticlaudian* II. 3, VI. 8 and *Roman de la Rose* 15659 ff., 20683 ff., 21215 ff. Alanus's treatment is solemn, moralistic, and Neoplatonic, but Jean de Meun's is comically moral, flippant, and based on Aristotelian assumptions about the nature of earthly reality; these significances are related but not identical, and the tones are far apart. Or again, Boccaccio's Venus (like his Mars) in *Teseida* Book VII is part of a grand allegorization of the "sensitive soul"—of the powers of concupiscence and irascibility in human nature—which depends on commonplace notions in Aristotelian and scholastic philosophy that should not be *identified,* simply or directly, with the uses of Alanus or Jean de Meun.

3. As one illustration, that of a nonclassical *exemplum,* see R. P. Miller, "The *Wife of Bath's Tale* and Mediaeval Exempla," *ELH* 32 (1965): 442–56.

4. J. I. Wimsatt, *Chaucer and the French Love Poets* (Chapel Hill, N.C., 1968), pp. 28–29. Although I agree with Wimsatt that Chaucer replaces traditional allegory with realism and abstractions with "people," it seems to me that Chaucer still works within a frame of psychological allegory that is peculiarly his own. On his mixing of allegory and realism, see E. Salter, *Chaucer: The Knight's Tale and the Clerk's Tale* (London, 1962).

5. Although I assume more philosophical stability, and perhaps more comedy, in the poem than does Sheila Delany, my discussion is often close to hers in *Chaucer's "House of Fame": The Poetics of Skeptical Fideism* (Chicago, 1972). On the medieval traditions of much of the poem's classical material, see B. G. Koonce, *Chaucer and the Tradition of Fame* (Princeton, 1966), and J. A. W. Bennett, *Chaucer's Book of Fame* (Oxford, 1968).

6. J. M. Steadman, "Venus' *Citole* in Chaucer's *Knight's Tale* and Berchorius," *Speculum* 34 (1959): 620–24; and B. N. Quinn, "Venus, Chaucer, and Peter Bersuire," *Speculum* 38 (1963): 479–80.

7. L. B. Hall, "Chaucer and the Dido-and-Aeneas Story," *MS* 25 (1963): 148–59.

8. J. M. Steadman, "Chaucer's Eagle: A Contemplative Symbol," *PMLA* 75 (1960): 153–59; and B. G. Koonce, pp. 129–36, 142 ff.

9. See, for example, R. A. Pratt, "Chaucer's 'Natal Jove' and 'Seint Jerome . . . agayn Jovinian,'" *JEGP* 61 (1962): 244–48; J. A. W. Bennett, pp. 52–99; W. C. Curry, *Chaucer and the Mediaeval Sciences* (New York, 1960), p. 127. Among others, one tradition by way of Fulgentius says that Jupiter or Zeus is heat or life, the animating force in living things: *Mitologie* I. 3 and the *Third Vatican Mythography* 3. 1 and 4. But the notion is commonplace: in Salutati's words, ". . . natura sive agens naturale, quod Iovem volunt nostri poete" (*De Laboribus Herculis,* ed. B. L. Ullman [Zurich, 1951], II, 4); according to the pagans, by St. Augustine's report (*City of God* VII. 7–11 and 16), Jupiter "rules the causes of all effects in the world," is "nature's master," "giver of all good causes to nature," "Progenitor, genetrixque deum," and "the Nourisher."

C. G. Osgood's translation from Boccaccio's *Genealogie Deorum* XI. 1 (*Boccaccio on Poetry,* p. xx) gives a good summary: "But the really enlightened men of that time [antiquity], as often as they were aware of the true God, instead of this Jove, though they inaccurately use the name Jove, actually mean the natural process or operation of the forces of nature (naturae naturatae), which is, of course, the work of

God." Regarding "Jove's" assocation with natural justice, benevolence, and order, see *Anticlaudian* IV. 7; *Genealogie Deorum* XI. 1 and the passages from Haly and Alchabitius cited by W. C. Curry.

10. "The rumblynge of a fart, and every soun, / Nis but of eir reverberacioun, / And evere it wasteth litel and litel awey" (*SumT* 2233-35). See J. Leyerle, "Chaucer's Windy Eagle," *UTQ* 40 (1971): 247-65; on the wind of fame and glory, see *City of God* V. 20 and 26, and B. G. Koonce, pp. 23, 229-31.

11. Whether Hercules and Alexander represent good and bad fames respectively (Delany, pp. 92-94) or a mixture of fames (Koonce, pp. 214-15) is not as clear a matter as the overall picture of the greatest human glory depending on a shrewish, ugly, fickle lady.

12. Like many other small details, the "wynd-melle" repeats a dominant motif which links fame to wind, air, blowing, flying, or fleeing; and the bathos found here persists throughout the poem—from the opening lines which pour out all sorts of learning about the names and causes of dreams, only to end peremptorily with two "I-don't-knows" (*HF* 7 ff., 52 ff.) to Geoffrey's silly responses to the eagle's long discourses ("Yis"; "Wel"; "No fors"). These bathetic patterns suggest that if there was once a conclusion to the *House of Fame* it must have been in some way a comic "letdown," a gorgeous anticlimax. See P. T. Overbeck, "The 'Man of Gret Auctorite' in Chaucer's *House of Fame*," *MP* 73 (1975-76): 157-61 for an interesting hypothesis that "Chaucer's rollicking poem" might be a "prelude to a *trionfo d'amore* and the appearance of Lord Cupid."

13. With appropriate changes, R. W. Frank, Jr.'s comments on the variety and unity of the *Parliament of Fowls* could apply equally to the *House of Fame:* "Each part differs from the others in its sources, content, mode of treatment and tone. . . . Each part has its own method. In the moral prelude the method is expository; in the garden scene it is descriptive; in the parliament scene it is dramatic. Each part also possesses its own recognizable diction, syntax, rhythm and tone." See "Structure and Meaning in the Parlement of Foules," *PMLA* 71 (1956): 530.

14. There are valuable comments on particular allegorical details in J. A. W. Bennett, *The Parlement of Foules: An Interpretation* (Oxford, 1957), and B. F. Huppé and D. W. Robertson, Jr., *Fruyt and Chaf: Studies in Chaucer's Allegories* (Princeton, 1962), esp. pp. 115-22.

15. "The Harmony of Chaucer's *Parliament*," *ChauR* 5 (1970): 22-31. The discussion is especially indebted to R. W. Frank, Jr.'s article (cited in n. 13, above) and C. O. McDonald's "An Interpretation of Chaucer's *Parlement of Foules*," *Speculum* 30 (1955): 444-57.

16. See F. N. Robinson's note to *PF* 117 in his edition of Chaucer; the reading is J. M. Manly's.

17. My discussion is indebted to two different, and in some ways opposing kinds of criticism: one which emphasizes the balance and order of the tale—its dignity (e.g., C. Muscatine, "Form, Texture and Meaning in Chaucer's *Knight's Tale*," *PMLA* 65 [1950]: 911-29); and another which stresses the destructive forces in the tale and the uneasy response which they invite (e.g., E. Salter, *Chaucer: The Knight's Tale and The Clerk's Tale* [London, 1962], pp. 9-36 and D. Underwood, "The First of *The Canterbury Tales*," *ELH* 26 [1959]: 455-69).

18. The red of Mars, associated among other things with the blood of battle and

the "rede colera" (*NPT* 2926–32) of a fiery disposition—as well as with the color of the planet—needs little explanation. Although it might be glossed in other ways, whiteness, by contrast, has connotations (like "goode faire White," in the *Book of the Duchess*) of loveliness, temperance ("atempre governaunce"), and the softer, more attractive aspects of gentle behavior (*BD* 817 ff.). See also the red banner of Mars and the white banner of Venus in *KnT* 2583, 2586. The gold of wisdom is, of course, traditional (Rabanus Maurus, *De Universo* XVII. xii in *PL* 111: 475); and for the significance of the killing of the Minotaur—the prudent man's victory over *bestialitas*—see Boccaccio's *Genealogie Deorum* IV. 10.

19. See n. 6 above for the articles by J. M. Steadman and B. N. Quinn.

20. Other references aside, the best gloss on the allegories of Venus's and Mars's oratories will be found in Boccaccio's own comments on the passages which Chaucer borrowed (*Teseida*, ed. A. Roncaglia [Bari, 1941], p. 417): "Ad evidenza della quale cosa è da sapere che come di sopra, dicendo Marte consistere nello appetito irascibile, cosi Venere nel concupiscibile." As R. A. Pratt has noted in his important study ("Chaucer's Use of the *Teseida*," *PMLA* 62 [1947]: 598–621), Boccaccio's glossing is thoroughly conventional. Still it is important to note that its flavor and vocabulary are Aristotelian and scholastic rather than Neoplatonic. The figural significance of the deities, in other words, should be limited to the two principal aspects of the sensitive soul, the natural appetites of concupiscence (Venus, with Cupid) and irascibility (Mars). Note the following passage (ed. Roncaglia, p. 412), for example: "Ad intelligenzia della qual cosa è da sapere che in ciascuno uomo sono due principali appetiti, de' quali l'uno si chiama appetito concupiscibile, per lo quale l'uomo desidera e si rallegra d'avere le cose che, secundo il suo guidico, o ragionevole o corrotto ch' egli sia, sono dilettevoli e piacevoli; l'altro si chiama appetito irascibile, per lo quale si turba o che gli sieno tolte o impedite le cose dilettevoli, o perché quelle avere non si possano."

The point seems crucial because readers sometimes assume that the pagan divinities in the *Knight's Tale* represent either (1) divine forces beyond human control—and then treat the text with deterministic arguments; or (2) "evil forces" (*in malo*) which require spiritual counterbalance—and then treat the text with Christian theological arguments. Actually the allegory rests on a human middle ground. R. Neuse has fairly observed—at least in the case of Venus and Mars—that "despite appearances, it may be argued that the real causality of events [in the *Knight's Tale*] lies in the human will or appetite. As we have seen, the gods ultimately function as metaphors of man's will, which (we conclude), instead of being powerless over against Fate, is his fate" ("The Knight: The First Mover in Chaucer's Human Comedy," *UTQ* 31 [1962]: 307). In "The *Knight's Tale* as an Impetus for Pilgrimage," *PQ* 43 (1964): 527, J. Westlund remarks that the poem's "world view is largely a pagan one," and that its nobility is built upon a naturalistic rather than a supernatural ideal. The point is well taken.

21. The image of "devouring" which appears here (*KnT* 2048) and in the sow eating the child (*KnT* 2019) and the hounds eating the battledead (*KnT* 947) stems from the old etymological explanation of Mars's name: from the word Mavors < *mares vorans*, devouring men. See *Totius Latinitatis Lexicon . . . Aegidii Forcellini* (Prati, 1887), IV. 369.

22. Although Chaucer did not find Diana's oratory in his source, the temples of

Teseida still gave him the basis for his more extended allegory. The *Teseida*, for example, had told him of the cruelty of the Amazons and their Scythian homeland— "crude e dispietate"; and it mentioned the Amazons' unnatural flight from pleasure, for which, as Hippolyta says, they are justly punished by Venus (Book One, stanzas 6, 13, 24, and 117). In addition, the moral allegories of Venus and Mars would have encouraged Chaucer to associate Diana with the related scholastic notion of *insensibilitas.* See Giles of Rome's *Rule of Princes* (*Aegidii Columnae Romani . . . De Regimine Principium Libri III* [Rome, 1607], I. ii. c. 15); "Sic Temperantia, media est inter delectationes et insensibilitates. Vocamus autem insensibilem et agrestem, qui omnes delectationes corporales fugit." Giles is reworking an Aristotelian commonplace, found, for example, in St. Thomas's *Summa Theologiae* II–II, Q. 142, a. 1: "Et ideo naturalis ordo requirit ut homo intentum huiusmodi delectationibus utatur, quantum necessarium est saluti humanae, vel quantum ad conservationem specei. Si quis ergo intantum delectationem refugeret quod praetermitteret ea quae sunt necessaria ad conservationem naturae, peccaret, quasi ordini naturali repugnans. Et hoc pertinet ad vitium insensibilitatis." See *Summa Theologiae* II–II, Q. 150, a. 1 and Q. 153, a. 3; also E. Gilson, *The Christian Philosophy of St. Thomas Aquinas* (New York, 1956), pp. 263–64, 295 ff. A lay audience and a courtly crowd might be expected to have even stronger notions about *insensibilitas* than their clerical contemporaries; and this may account in part for the light touches which characterize the Knight's treatment of Emelye's restraint.

23. The ultimate source for this concept of justice is Aristotle's *Ethics:* e.g., "Justice sums up all the virtues in itself" (V. i. 15); "Justice . . . is not a part of virtue, but the whole of it" (V. i. 19). See Giles of Rome, *De Regimine Principium* I. ii. c. 10–12; also n. 9, above, concerning Jupiter and justice.

24. Although Chaucer humanizes and complicates his characters, and avoids turning them into allegorical figures (as the "gods" are allegorical figures), I would still suggest that many of the changes he has made in their makeup—in comparison to the characters in his source—can be traced to his mythological allegory of the theatre and to his desire to associate his characters with it. Thus he enhances Palamon's role and he reduces Arcite's so as to balance them in the same way that he balances the instincts of concupiscence and irascibility; he also gives to each of them a vocabulary appropriate to these instincts, to Venus and to Mars. Emelye, who is so much more interesting and thoughtful in the *Teseida*, becomes in Chaucer's hands a relative "lightweight," probably to compensate for Theseus's more weighty role, and to keep the balance which Chaucer evidently wanted to maintain between joy and sorrow, lightness and heaviness, comedy and pathos.

25. See A. Gaylord, "The Role of Saturn in the *Knight's Tale*," *ChauR* 8 (1974): 172–90.

26. Although Chaucer's allegorization of Saturn is self-explanatory (*KnT* 2443–78), its traditional roots can be found in such works as Fulgentius's *Mitologie* I. 2; *Second Vatican Mythography* 1; and *Third Vatican Mythography* IX. 10. The connection between Saturn and Prudence apparently goes back to passages in Fulgentius (Saturn: "divinum sensum creantem omnia") and the *Third Vatican Mythography* II. 2: "Nonnulli Saturnum *sacrum sensum*, id est divinam providentiam omnia procreantem, sive satorem omnium interpretatur." The fourteenth-century English friar John Ridewall gives the most elaborate explanation for the connection: *Fulgentius Metaforalis*, ed. H. Liebeschütz (Leipzig, 1926), pp. 71–78.

Through reference to Ovid's *Metamorphoses* Ridewall links Saturn with the Golden Age when wise men ruled (p. 72); he then explores a variety of relationships between aspects of Saturn and Prudence, e.g., age, time, great experience, authoritative advice and counsel.

> Virtus enim prudencie in senibus et non in iuvenibus dicente Aristotele in suis topicis: Nemo iuvenes eligit duces, eo quod constet eos non esse prudentes. Et nota, quomodo poete isti dixerunt Saturnum deum temporis; unde vocabatur ab aliquibus Cronos. Et enim Cronos in Greco idem quod tempus in Latino et hoc, quia prudencia per Saturnum designata requirit tempus. Prudencia enim requirit magnam experienciam que non habetur nisi in spacio magni temporis. Notari eciam possunt hic, que dicit Tullius in suo libro de senectute de prudencia senum. Non viribus, dicit Tullius, aut velocitate aut celeritate corporis res magne geruntur sed consilio, auctoritate et sentencia; quibus non modo non orbari, sed eciam augeri senectus solet. . . . Si ergo plus habeat senectus de consiliativa, sequitur quod plus habeat de prudencia, sicut patet ex 6 ethicorum (p. 74).

Aristotle's discussion of prudence is relevant, directly or indirectly, to Chaucer's allegorization of Saturn and, indeed, his characterization of Egeus. For example, Aristotle observes that prudence enables one "to deliberate well . . . not with a view to some particular end, but with a view to well-being or living well" (VI. 5. 1); and in his general summary he points out how Prudence must go hand in hand with the other moral virtues (VI. 13. 1–8).

27. Theseus's speech has often been overread, being glossed more often from its source in Boethius than from its own context. As Chaucer adapted his material from the *De Consolatione*, he focused primarily on the rhythmic, natural order of creation and on the role of death within that order. In other words, his Theseus shows less concern for "the faire cheyne of love" as a motif than for the facts of mortality, misfortune, and the sorrow which they bring. Theseus looks at what has recently happened—the debacle of the tournament, the death of Arcite, the funeral—and he seeks to place these events in an orderly perspective within the nature of things.

> "Loo the ook, that hath so long a norisshynge
> From tyme that it first bigynneth to sprynge,
> And hath so long a lif, as we may see,
> Yet at the laste wasted is the tree.
> Considereth eek how that the harde stoon
> Under oure feet, on which we trede and goon,
> Yet wasteth it as it lyth by the weye.
> The brode ryver somtyme wexeth dreye;
> The grete tounes se we wane and wende.
> Thanne may ye se that al this thyng hath ende.
> Of man and womman seen we wel also
> That nedes, in oon of thise termes two,
> This is to seyn, in youthe or elles age,
> He moot be deed, the kyng as shal a page. . . .   (*KnT* 3017 ff.)

28. The most authoritative basis for these vocabularies appears in the *Knight's Tale* itself: not only in the oratories of Venus and Mars and in the prayers of Palamon and Arcite to their deities, but also in the language used to describe Theseus's balanced actions at the beginning of the story. The source for these double (*duplex*) arrangements, however, ultimately rests in medieval moral philosophy. See, for example, Giles of Rome's discussion in *De Regimine Principium* II, ii, c. 2, quoted here in part. "Propter quod sicut in nobis duplex est cognitio, sensitiva, et intellectiva: sic etiam est in nobis duplex appetitus videlicet, sensitivus, qui sequitur formam apprehensam per sensum: et intellectivus, qui sequitur formam apprehensam per intellectum. Appetitus autem sensitivus duplex est. . . . unum per quem prosequuntur propriam quietem, et propriam delectationem, ut concupiscibilem: et alium per quem resistunt, et aggrediuntur prohibitiva, ut contraria, ut irascibilem."

29. "Accipiendo ergo virtutem moralem large prout ipsa prudentia dicitur quaedam virtus moralis, dicere possumus quod secundum has quattuor potentias animae in quibus habet esse virtus, sumptae sunt quattuor Virtutes Cardinales; videlicet, Prudentia, Iustitia, Fortitudo et Temperantia. Nam Prudentia est in intellectu, Iustitia in voluntate, Fortitudo in irascibile, Temperantia in concupiscibile." Giles of Rome, ibid.

30. "Five Book Structure in Chaucer's *Troilus*," *MLQ* 23 (1962): 297–308.

31. *Gothic Architecture and Scholasticism* (New York, 1957).

Chapter 4

1. *Chaucer: A Critical Appreciation* (Durham, N.C., 1958), Ch. 1.

2. G. B. Parks, "The Route of Chaucer's First Journey to Italy," *ELH* 16 (1949): 174–87.

3. C. P. Segal, *Landscape in Ovid's Metamorphoses*, *Hermes* No. 23 (Wiesbaden, 1969). There are some important reminders of the differing ways in which a traditional setting may be used in P. Damon's "Modes of Analogy in Ancient and Medieval Verse," *Univ. of California Publ. in Classical Philology* 15, No. 6 (1961): 261–334.

4. For some discussions of Chaucerian settings, see D. W. Robertson, Jr., "The Doctrine of Charity in Mediaeval Literary Gardens: A Topical Approach through Symbolism and Allegory," *Speculum* 26 (1951): 24–49; C. A. Owen, Jr., "The Crucial Passages in Five of the *Canterbury Tales*: A Study in Irony and Symbol," *JEGP* 52 (1953): 294–311; G. Joseph, "Chaucerian 'Game'–'Ernest' and the 'Argument of Herbergage' in *The Canterbury Tales*," *ChauR* 5 (1970): 83–96. Chaucer's approach to idealized natural settings almost reverses what Leo Marx finds among American writers in *The Machine in the Garden* (New York, 1964). The harmony of Chaucer's "natural world" is based on a loving balance between conflicting forces; when he portrays an idyllic scene *in the world*—one without any hardships, death, evil, and sorrow—it invariably turns out to be artificial, manmade trouble, like the gardens in the Franklin's and Merchant's tales.

5. *Against Marcion* I. 1 (*Pl* 2. 270–72) and *Apologeticus* c. 9 (*PL* 1. 372–73); the reference to Herodotus is from *The Histories*, Book Four. Herodotus distinguishes the Scythians from nearby tribes, but others blur the distinctions.

6. F. P. Magoun, Jr., links the Amazons with the northern region of Asia Minor exclusively, and implies that Chaucer was ignorant or confused about their proper

locale: *A Chaucer Gazetteer* (Chicago, 1961), pp. 18 and 140. But Herodotus explains how some of the Amazonians reached Scythia; see also Ovid, *Tristia* I. viii. 40 and I. xi. 31–34; Statius, *Thebaid* V. 144–46, 203–07, and XII. 519 ff.; Orosius I. 15; and *Ekkehardi Uraugiensis Chronica*, *PL* 154. 729 ff.

    7. See W. Smith's *Dictionary of Greek and Roman Geography* (London, 1857), II. 1150, and Tertullian's *De Anima* c. 20 (*PL* 2. 683).

    8. Ovid's *Metamorphoses* III. 1 to IV. 603 begins and ends with Cadmus's story and includes several of the legends from early Thebes. Statius's *Thebaid* begins with Oedipus's cursing of the city and his sons, Etheocles and Polyneices, to fury and strife; it also incorporates other events from the Theban legend, as does Boccaccio's *Teseida*. Drawing on both Ovid and Statius, Boccaccio conveniently summarizes the whole disastrous business in *Genealogie Deorum* II. 62–75.

    There is a brief, pseudo-Fulgentian allegorization of the *Thebaid* which R. Helm published in his edition of Fulgentius's *Opera* (Leipzig, 1898), pp. 180–86. In its method this work more closely resembles Bernard Silvester's allegorization of the *Aeneid* than Fulgentius's. Thebes is *dei be (nignitas)* and represents the human soul; Laius is *lux sancta*, Jocasta *iocunditas casta*, Oedipus *lascivia*, Etheocles *avaritia*, Polyneices *luxuria*, Adrastus *philosophia*, Argia *providentia*, Theseus *deus*, Creon *superbia*, and Clementia plays herself. The allegorization had no apparent influence on Boccaccio or Chaucer; their handlings of the Theban story, metaphorically or symbolically, depend entirely on "the facts" of legendary history.

    9. On the Brooch of Thebes, see Chapter 2 (note 19) above.

    10. Isidore of Seville, *Etymologiae* XV. 1. 44 (*PL* 82. 532).

    11. *City of God* 18. 9, which draws on *Pro Flacco* XXVI (62).

    12. *Boece* I. pr. 1, 64–67; pr. 3, 21 ff.; pr. 4, 27–39; and V. pr. 1, 63–66; m. 4, 1–3.

    13. See Magoun's *Chaucer Gazetteer*, pp. 24–27 and R. A. Pratt, "Chaucer's Use of the *Teseida*," *PMLA* 62 (1947): 616–17. Mythological allusions are practially the only means that Chaucer uses to indicate the antiquity of the setting in the *Knight's Tale*, and they are balanced by other materials which tend to make the narrative appear contemporaneous—Hippolyta's arrival in Athens, the tournament, and the portraits of Theseus and Demetreus. See J. Strutt, *The Sports and Pastimes of the People of England* (London, 1834), Book III, Ch. 1, esp. Sects. 20–29; and the articles by Lowes, S. Robertson, and Cook cited in Robinson's notes on the *Knight's Tale* in his edition of Chaucer's *Works*.

    14. Magoun's observation in *Chaucer Gazetteer*, p. 160.

    15. G. L. Kittredge, *Chaucer and His Poetry* (Cambridge, Mass., 1915), pp. 117–21. There are useful criticisms of Kittredge's position in H. R. Patch, "Troilus on Determinism," *Speculum* 6 (1931): 225–43 and R. D. Mayo, "The Trojan Background of the *Troilus*," *ELH* 9 (1942): 245–56. My discussion is substantially the same as its original, "The Trojan Scene in Chaucer's *Troilus*," *ELH* 29 (1962): 263–75.

    16. In general, see Horace's *Epistles* I. ii. 1 ff., which Chaucer may have known: R. A. Pratt, "A Note on Chaucer's Lollius," *MLN* 65 (1950): 183–87. The pride of Troy was commonplace: the "superbum / Ilium" of *Aeneid* III. 2–3. The criminal lust of Troy developed from the city's complicity in Paris's crime. Thus, in *Against Jovinian*, I. 48 (*PL* 23. 280) Jerome blames the Trojan War on the rape of a single *respecteuse* ("muliercula"); and the popular medieval *Pergama flere volo* . . . puts the blame more bluntly on "the fatal whore": Carmina 101, 43–45 in *Carmina Burana*, ed. W. Meyers, A. Hilka, and O. Schumann (Heidelberg, 1930–41), 2 vols.

17. On Troy as a familiar civic example of Fortune's infidelity, see H. R. Patch, *The Goddess Fortuna in Mediaeval Literature* (Cambridge, Mass., 1927), p. 114; as an exemplar of tragic lust, wantonness, and foolish love, see A. Neckam, *De Naturis Rerum*, ed. T. Wright (London, 1863), p. 350; Brunetto Latini, *Li Livres dou Tresor*, ed. F. J. Carmody (Berkeley, 1948), p. 290; and C. Salutati, *De Laboribus Herculis*, ed. B. L. Ullman (Zurich, 1951), I. 252. The traditional explanation of the judgment of Paris—preferring Venus's fleshly pleasures to either Juno's riches or Pallas's wisdom—was carried over to the city; see Fulgentius, *Mitologie* II. 1; Boccaccio, *Genealogie Deorum* VI. 21; and J. Seznec, *The Survival of the Pagan Gods* (New York, 1953), pp. 107 ff. Thus, in one of Godefroid de Reims's poems, Achilles harangues the Trojans for being effeminate and sluggish devotees of Venus: A. Boutemy, "Trois oeuvres inédites de Godefroid de Reims," *Revue du Moyen Age Latin* 3 (1947): 364.

18. On the Latin diminutive in -lus, -la, -lum, see W. M. Lindsay, *The Latin Language* (Oxford, 1894), pp. 331–33. On Chaucer's awareness of name-play—e.g., Thopas, Cecilia, January—as well as anonymity, see N. E. Eliason, "Personal Names in the *Canterbury Tales*," *Names* 21 (1973): 137–52. In *Filostrato* VII. st. 86 Cassandra tells Troilo that he has "suffered from the accursed love by which we all must be undone, as we can see if we but wish."

19. Mayo, *ELH* 9: 250. One passage (*Tr* 2. 1111–13) suggests that Sinon has arrived in Troy. When Pandare visits Criseyde for the second stage of his "paynted proces," he takes her aside to deliver Troilus's letter; as an excuse for speaking alone with her, he says he has just heard new tidings from the Greek spy who is a guest in the city: " 'Ther is right now come into town a gest, / A Greek espie, and telleth newe thinges, / For which I come to telle yow tydynges.' " Although the presence of Sinon, or any spy, provides an analogy for Pandare's deceptions (e.g., *Tr* 2. 409–20; 3. 267–80, 1564–68), the news is still announced as another sign of Troy's good fortune.

20. It is difficult to be sure who is deceiving whom in this scene; Deiphebus and Helen may be having their own quiet liaison. See E. H. Kelly, "Myth as Paradigm in *Troilus and Criseyde*, *PLL* (1967): 28–30.

21. *Tr* 3. 1313–36, 1527–47, 1618–38.

22. John of Salisbury, *Policraticus* VI. 23.

23. When Chaucer's characters moralize on their own conditions, as they often do (e.g., *Tr* 4. 270–73, 379–92, 834–47), there seems to be no problem; and when the narrator moralizes lightly (*Tr* 1. 211–17), or silently ("Ne me ne list this sely womman chyde / Forther than the storye wol devyse"), or in general terms (*Tr.* 5. 1744–50), there seems to be no problem. But the combination of a serious, personal, and direct moral from the narrator comes only at the conclusion, to be softened by nothing more than Troilus's own similar perception from the heavens. In a manner familiar to tragedy, moral import grows together with the stature of the protagonist; see S. Wenzel, "Chaucer's Troilus of Book IV," *PMLA* 79 (1964): 542–47.

24. *Mimesis*, trans. W. Trask (Princeton, 1953), pp. 28–29.

25. The notion that London was "New Troy" was much alive in Chaucer's day; see G. Rudisill, Jr., and J. P. McCall, "The Parliament of 1386 and Chaucer's Trojan Parliament," *JEGP* 58 (1959): 276–88.

26. The ideas of *imperium* and *gloria* appear at the beginning of the legend of Cleopatra where Anthony's assignment as a Roman "senatour" is described: "For to conqueren regnes and honour / Unto the toun of Rome, as was usuance, / To han the world at hire obeÿsaunce . . ." (*LGW* 585–87).

On the associations of ancient Rome, see D. Earl, *The Moral and Political Tradition of Rome* (Ithaca, N.Y., 1967); and L. S. Mazzolani, *The Idea of the City in Roman Thought*, trans. S. O'Donnell (Bloomington, Ind., 1970).

The Rome which Saint Augustine describes in the *City of God* likes to think itself the perfect state. It has a deep-seated ambition to rule, and prides itself on its justice and honor, its modesty and good name. In some of his best rhetoric, Augustine points ironically to the gulf between self-image and historical facts: Romans are proud and arrogant, but their lust for sovereignty has made them slaves of a desire to rule (I. 29); they are depraved by prosperity and unreformed by adversity (I. 32); they assert their staidness and modesty, but their public ceremonies are full of licentious embarrassments (II. 14 and 27; VII. 21 and 24). Augustine particularly derides the city's justice and modesty (II. 17; III. 16) with reminders of Romulus's fratricide, the Sabine rape, its attendant parricides, and so forth.

27. With the outbreak of the Western Schism in 1378, England supported Urban VI, the *Roman* Pope, as opposed to a continuing Avignon papacy. The popular tradition concerning the corruption of the papal court may be hinted at in the description of the Pardoner (*Gen Prol* 671), but Chaucer nowhere emphasizes it. On the Rome of Church and Empire, see C. T. Davis, *Dante and the Idea of Rome* (Oxford, 1957), Introduction and Chapter One.

28. See Augustine's discussion in *City of God* I. 17–29. There have been several good discussions of the rhetorical conflict in the Physician's story, but see especially B. Rowland, "The Physician's 'Historial Thyng Notable' and the Man of Law," *ELH* 40 (1973): 165–78. The critique on law and lawyers which Rowland finds in the tale may be ironically complemented by the Physician's failure to recognize that his story also inadvertently undermines the nature which he serves and the "good" natural governance which he admires.

29. J. E. Grennen, "Saint Cecilia's 'Chemical Wedding': The Unity of the *Canterbury Tales*, Fragment VIII," *JEGP* 65 (1966): 466–81; B. A. Rosenberg, "The Contrary Tales of the Second Nun and the Canon's Yeoman," *ChauR* 2 (1968): 278–91. Because the change from pagan to Christian Rome also carries the story into contemporary time ("into this day"), it is possible that Chaucer expected that his references to the first Pope Urban—"Seint Urban," "the goode Urban the olde," etc.— would remind his audience of Urban VI (d. 1389), also of "recent" time.

30. The recurring emphasis on Custance's work in propagation of the Christian faith may be underlined by the traditional image of the ship, *ecclesia*.

31. Six references to Rome are clustered in *MLT* 953–1001; at the beginning there are three (*MLT* 141–56).

32. The dramatic sense of history, which Christianity borrowed from Judaism, encompasses this notion. The increasing awareness of the pastness of the past in the later Middle Ages was accompanied, as Morton Bloomfield has observed ("Chaucer's Sense of History," *JEGP* 51 [1952]: 301–13), by a clarifying distinction between God's dispensations with Jews and Christians in contrast to nature's dispensation with other peoples.

33. One might be tempted to include Nature's rule in the *Parliament* in the same category with the natural philosophy of the *Knight's Tale* and Nature's rule in the case of Virginia. I would hesitate, however, because the context in the *Parliament* may be avian-Christian: Nature's being "ful of grace" (*PF* 319) may be more than a courteous rhyme-tag.

34. My reading of the *Legend* is particularly indebted to Pat T. Overbeck, "Chaucer's Good Woman," *ChauR* 2 (1968): 75–94, and R. W. Frank, Jr., *Chaucer and the Legend of Good Women* (Cambridge, Mass., 1972).

35. Although Chaucer may have known the *City of God* in Latin or in the French translation of Raoul de Presles (1371–75), his specific reference to Augustine on Lucrece appears indebted to Simon of Hesdin's translation of Valerius Maximus's *Memorabilia* (ca. 1376). Simon sometimes includes copious glosses; for example, in his translation of *Memorabilia* VI. 1 ("de chastete") he expands what Valerius has to say about Lucrece ("le premier exemple") by including the complete account of Livy and a summary of Augustine's comment. See Paris, Bibliothèque Nationale MS fr. 41, fols. 276v–278. Chaucer's knowledge of Valerius has been recognized (e.g., *WBT* 460, 642, 647; *NPT* 2984 ff.), but his knowledge by way of the French translation (of which I am preparing a study) helps explain several things beside *LGW* 1689–91. It will account, as well, for his brief use of Livy in the Lucrece legend (1847–49), for his acquaintance with Livy's account of the Virginia story (*PhysT* 1), and for the accuracy of Chauntecleer's comment on the order of his *exempla* in *NPT* 3064–66. See also n. 40 below.

36. Just as he turns Augustine around at the beginning of the Lucrece legend, so Chaucer turns a Biblical passage around at the end (*LGW* 1879–82). There is really no reason to assume that Chaucer had to treat his sources in precisely the ways that they came to him—in content or tone.

37. R. M. Lumiansky, "Chaucer and the Idea of Unfaithful Men," *MLN* 62 (1947): 560–62.

38. See this writer's "Chaucer and the Pseudo Origen *De Maria Magdalena*: A Preliminary Study," *Speculum* 46 (1971): 491–509, esp. 498. Although it runs against the grain of most criticism on the *Book of the Duchess*, I suspect that Alcyone's helpless plight is meant to stand over against the less understandable and, to some extent, comical complaints and plights of men—Christian men at that! But if the narrator does not understand the tragic message of Alcyone from the dark past (except for learning how to go to sleep), it may be that he and his surrogate, the Black Knight, will have learned something about life from another woman, "goode faire White," by the end of the poem. In any event, I would suggest that Chaucer seems to benefit from a reading slanted in favor of women, despite the traditions of medieval antifeminism.

39. The word "old" is one way Chaucer reminds his reader of the classical or natural setting. Even his Good Women are "olde" (*LGW* G301).

40. The closest parallel that I have been able to find for Chaucer's use of Alceste (= the best example of good wifehood and truth in love) is Simon of Hesdin's translation of Valerius Maximus's *Memorabilia* IV. 6 ("de lamour de mariage"): Paris, Bibliothèque Nationale MS fr. 41, fols. 225v–227. In the customary style of this work, chapters are linked to those that immediately precede: "Married Love" is therefore linked to "Modesty" (IV. 5 "de vergongne"). Then the brief prologue to IV. 6 focuses on "the stability or great firmness of faith" in "Married Love" ("les oeuvres faictes entre les maries par la stabilite et grant fermete de foy"). Valerius's first example in IV. 6 is Tiberius Gracchus, who gave up his life for his wife's life; as a contrast with Gracchus, Valerius mentions King Admetus, whose wife surrendered her life for his. In Simon's translation Valerius's contrast becomes the second *exemplum* of the Chapter; Alceste becomes, therefore, the feminine equivalent of

Gracchus, and the prime womanly example of "lamour de mariage." Simon glosses his translation with Fulgentius, *Mitologie* I. 19. In addition, John Ridewall also drew on Fulgentius to make Alceste the *figura* of "continent wedlock": see *Fulgentius Metaforalis* (Leipzig, 1926), pp. 56–57.

41. May celebrations could take place on almost any day of the month. For some interesting, effervescent comments, see Strutt, *Sports and Pastimes*, Introd. (pp. lvii–lviii), and Book IV, ch. 3, sects. 15–20; R. Chambers, *The Book of Days: A Miscellany of Popular Antiquities* (London, 1864), 2 vols., I. 569–82; and J. Bédier, "Les Fêtes de Mai et les commencements de la poésie lyrique au moyen age," *Revue des Deux Mondes* 4°, 135 (1896): 146–72.

42. The early prize-winning works at the Jeux Floraux, established at Toulouse in 1324, were religious poems; different categories of prizes were later created. See Dom. C. Devic and Dom. J. Vaissete, *Histoire Générale du Languedoc* (Toulouse, 1885), X. 177 ff.; F. de Gélis, *Histoire Critique des Jeux Floraux*, Bibliothèque Méridionale, 2d Ser., XV (Toulouse, 1912). We do not really know how extensive the "Floral Games" became. Thomas Warton thought that they grew to be "common through the whole kingdom of France": *A History of English Poetry* (London, 1840) 3 vols., II. 24 (Sect. XVIII); but as G. L. Marsh observed some years ago, there is no evidence for Warton's claim: "Sources and Analogues of 'The Flower and the Leaf,' " *MP* 4 (1906): 139, 322–23. The fact that the Jeux Floraux were held on May 1 and prizes awarded on May 3 may suggest (in the light of Chaucer's frequent and familiar use of the May 3 date) that Warton may have known more than we do. In "Chaucer's May 3," *MLN* 76 (1961), 201–5, I discussed the appropriateness of Chaucer's three uses of the date in the light of the classical Feast of the Floralia; but it may be that that bookish explanation, by way of Ovid's *Fasti*, can be supplemented by the existence of a popular celebration in Chaucer's England—familiar to him and his courtly audience, but unknown to us.

Chapter 5

1. See Paul G. Ruggiers, "Notes Towards a Theory of Tragedy in Chaucer," *ChauR* 8 (1973): 89–99.

2. David S. Reid, "Crocodilian Humor: A Discussion of Chaucer's Wife of Bath," *ChauR* 4 (1969–70): 73–89.

3. For the farcical, medieval character of Pluto and Proserpina, see Bertrand H. Bronson's "Afterthoughts on the *Merchant's Tale*," *SP* 58 (1961), esp. 593–95; also, Mortimer J. Donovan, "The Image of Pluto and Proserpine in the *Merchant's Tale*," *PQ* 36 (1957): 57–58.

4. Bruce A. Rosenberg, " 'The Cherry-Tree Carol' and the *Merchant's Tale*," *ChauR* 5 (1971): 270.

5. On the characterization or caricature of Apollo, see Richard Hazelton, "The *Manciple's Tale*: Parody and Critique," *JEGP* 62 (1963), esp. 7–17; also, Earle Birney, "Chaucer's 'Gentil' Manciple and His 'Gentil' Tale," *NM* 61 (1960): 264, and Jackson J. Campbell, "Polonius Among the Pilgrims," *ChauR* 7 (1972): 141.

6. Birney, p. 267, n. 2.

7. *Boccaccio on Poetry* (Princeton, 1930), pp. xxii–xxiii.

8. See Laura Hibbard Loomis, "Secular Dramatics in the Royal Palace, Paris, 1378, 1389, and Chaucer's 'Tregetoures,' " *Speculum* 33 (1958): 242–44.

9. We should not be too precise about the illusion or the natural reality of the high tides at Penmarc'h, for Chaucer (or the Franklin) has obviously taken liberties with the setting while adding some technical exactness. For example, there are no high points along the Penmarc'h shore from which one can look down at the black rocks, as Dorigen does (849, 858–59); and there were no castles "faste by the see" (847): J. S. P. Tatlock, *The Scene of the Franklin's Tale Visited*, Chaucer Society, 2d Ser., No. 51 (London, 1914), pp. 7–9. In addition, if the Penmarc'h rocks *were* to be covered by the sea—particularly if they were to be covered by the thirty feet of water for which Aurelius prayed (1059–61)—there would be no need to go down to the low-lying shore to see what had happened, because large areas of Brittany and western France would be under water or covered with illusion.

In light of lines 1142 ff., I would suggest that the *Franklin's Tale* simply gives an extravagant, exaggerated picture of the remarkable sort of tide which is familiar on the Breton coast and which is abnormally high at certain times: a tide which covers large offshore rocks in an apparently amazing way.

The temporal setting of the tale, given in astronomical terms (1244 ff.), invites this interpretation because the Clerk creates his illusion on or about January 3, a date which coincides with the normal highest tides. See J. S. P. Tatlock, "Astrology and Magic in Chaucer's *Franklin's Tale*," *Kittredge Anniversary Papers* (Boston, 1913), pp. 343 ff. (which adds some unwanted assumptions about black magic); and H. H. Lamb, *Climate: Present, Past and Future* (London, 1972), I, 218–19 (which observes that the normal highest tides occur "in the middle of the northern winter about 3 January").

There is a scientific pattern here because Aurelius's earlier, extravagant prayer was also linked to a natural phenomenon. He had asked that the rocks be covered during one of the normal summer high tides, but actually the tides are higher in winter. For those who are curious about natural reality, H. H. Lamb points out (I, 220–21) that rather than being the same as it is now, the "tidal maximum of the late Middle Ages was clearly the greatest for many thousands of years." For help on this matter I am indebted to Chauncey Wood, *Chaucer and the Country of the Stars* (Princeton, 1970), pp. 245 ff. I also thank P. R. Giot of the Université de Rennes, who has written to me about some of the unusual floods at Penmarc'h—the two most recent being in December 1896 and January 8–9, 1924. During the tempest and inundation of 1896 the waters must have reached three or four meters above mean sea level; at nearby St. Guénolé, "(altitude of the lower part 4m) people had to get up in their attics or on their roofs."

Finally, the Franklin's ornamented description of the Clerk's activities—in a style of "magical mumbo-jumbo"—does not encourage us to take his work too seriously: Harry Berger, Jr., "The F-Fragment of the *Canterbury Tales*," *ChauR* 1 (1966–67): 145, and Stephen Knight, "Rhetoric and Poetry in the *Franklin's Tale*," *ChauR* 4 (1969–70): 25. The Clerk is, after all, only reading the sky, checking charts, and making calculations.

10. Kathryn Hume, "The Pagan Setting of the *Franklin's Tale* and the Sources of Dorigen's Cosmology," *SN* 44 (1972): 289–94.

11. Here and elsewhere my reading is variously indebted to Alan T. Gaylord, "The Promises in *The Franklin's Tale*," *ELH* 31 (1964): 331–65; and Harry Berger, Jr. (cited above, n. 9), 88–102 and 135–56. See especially Berger's comments on the control and rhythm of the tale—e.g., between play and work, lyric and narrative (p. 151); also the movement between the fantastical and businesslike in Russell A. Peck,

"Sovereignty and the Two Worlds of the *Franklin's Tale*," *ChauR* 1 (1966–67): 253–71; and between appearance and reality in Charles A. Owen, Jr., "The Crucial Passages in Five of the *Canterbury Tales*: A Study in Irony and Symbol," *JEGP* 52 (1953): 295–97.

12. Gerhard Joseph, "The *Franklin's Tale*: Chaucer's Theodicy," *ChauR* 1 (1966–67): 20–32.

13. The standard authority is J. Th. Welter, *L'Exemplum dans la littérature religieuse et didactique du moyen age* (Paris, 1927), citing numerous references to the use of classical materials—historical, legendary, and mythological—from Ambrose and Jerome (pp. 23–24) to John Bromyard in fourteenth-century England (pp. 328–34).

14. It seems wrongheaded to argue that the Wife's version of the Midas story is inaccurate or that she misses the story's moral tone: Judson Boyce Allen and Patrick Gallacher, "Alisoun Through the Looking Glass: or Every Man His Own Midas," *ChauR* 4 (1969–70): 99–105. Humor and irony may develop from the way someone adapts exemplary material to a certain moral and in a certain tone, but there is no such thing as a *requisite* version, lesson, or tone for an *exemplum*. See, for example, John of Salisbury's playful adaptation of the Acteon-Diana story in *Policraticus* I. 4.

15. For some recent comments on Chaucer's tendency to fragment moralizations and entwine them in inconsistencies, see Jill Mann, "The *Speculum Stultorum* and the *Nun's Priest's Tale*," *ChauR* 9 (1975): 271 ff., and Anne Middleton, "The *Physician's Tale* and Love's Martyrs: 'Ensamples Mo Than Ten' as a Method in the *Canterbury Tales*," *ChauR* 8 (1973): esp. 15 and 26.

16. James F. Royster, "Chaucer's 'Colle Tregetour' " *SP* 23 (1926): 382.

17. James Sledd, "Dorigen's Complaint," *MP* 45 (1947–48): 36–45; Germaine Dempster, "Chaucer at Work on the Complaint in the *Franklin's Tale*," *MLN* 52 (1937): 16–23; and Donald C. Baker, "A Crux in Chaucer's *Franklin's Tale*: Dorigen's Complaint," *JEGP* 60 (1961): 58–64.

18. It does not help much to learn (Dempster, n. 17) that "Bilyea," from the next to the last line in the complaint, was faithful to her husband despite his halitosis. Dorigen does not tell us this and we are not likely to know it on our own.

19. William C. Strange, "The *Monk's Tale*: A Generous View," *ChauR* 1 (1966–67): 167–80.

20. My discussion follows those of Charles A. Owen, Jr. (n. 11 above), Mortimer J. Donovan (n. 3 above), and especially Karl Wentersdorf, "Theme and Structure in *The Merchant's Tale*: The Function of the Pluto Episode," *PMLA* 80 (1965): 522–27. On the connection between Proserpina (as "a deliverer" of her people) and the Biblical women mentioned in the tale, see Charlotte F. Otten, "Proserpine: *Liberatrix Suae Gentis*," *ChauR* 5 (1970–71): 277–87.

21. My discussion is indebted to Birney, Hazelton, and Campbell (n. 5 above); also, J. Burke Severs, "Is the *Manciple's Tale* a Success?" *JEGP* 51 (1952): 1–16; Morton Donner, "The Unity of Chaucer's Manciple Fragment," *MLN* 70 (1955): 245–49; and Lee C. Ramsey, " 'The Sentence of it sooth is': Chaucer's *Physician's Tale*," *ChauR* 6 (1971–72): 185–97.

22. For some comments on connections between the Manciple's and Parson's fragments, see Wayne Shumaker, "Chaucer's *Manciple's Tale* as Part of a Canterbury Group," *UTQ* 22 (1952–53): 147–56 and Britton J. Harwood, "Language and the Real: Chaucer's Manciple," *ChauR* 6 (1971–72): 279.

23. The major statement is Robert M. Jordan's *Chaucer and the Shape of*

Creation: The Aesthetic Possibilities of Inorganic Structure (Cambridge, Mass., 1967).

Chapter 6

1. J. P. McCall, "The Writings of John of Legnano with a List of Manuscripts," *Traditio* 23 (1967): 417–18.

Index